# Why Can't I Change?

## How to Conquer Your Self-Destructive Patterns

# Why Can't I Change?

## How to Conquer Your Self-Destructive Patterns

Shirley Impellizzeri
Foreword by Gary Small

SUNRISE
River Press

SUNRISE
River Press

Sunrise River Press
39966 Grand Avenue
North Branch, MN 55056
Phone: 651-277-1400 or 800-895-4585
Fax: 651-277-1203
www.sunriseriverpress.com

Edit by Debby Young
Layout by Connie DeFlorin

ISBN 978-1-934716-37-3
Item No. SRP637

Library of Congress Cataloging-in-Publication Data

Impellizzeri, Shirley, 1966-
Why can't I change? : how to conquer your self-destructive patterns / by Shirley Impellizzeri.
   p. cm.
Includes bibliographical references and index.
ISBN 978-1-934716-37-3
1. Behavior therapy. 2. Habit breaking.  I. Title.
RC489.B4I47 2012
616.89'142--dc23
                                              2012000614

Printed in USA
10 9 8 7 6 5 4 3 2 1

To my sweet little Sydney.
Thank you for choosing me as your mom in this lifetime.

# Contents

# Foreword

*W*hy can't I change? This is one of the most fundamental questions people ask themselves at some point in their lives, and it can also be one of the hardest to answer. Dysfunctional behavior patterns can become so entrenched that changing them seems like an insurmountable feat. Many people give up, resigning themselves to a life that isn't what they truly want.

In this important work, Dr. Shirley eloquently explains how the foundation of our earliest emotional attachments gives rise to dysfunctional patterns of behavior. She teaches us that as far back as infancy, these attachments influence how our brains develop and what thoughts and beliefs get set into place and often remain throughout our lives.

From the moment we are born, the attachment process begins and by our third month of life, the person we are primarily attached to is already imprinted in our brains. This individual is most often a parent or primary caregiver, who has the opportunity to either nurture us and build our self-esteem or to remain emotionally distant and erode our sense of self-worth. How this attachment figure treats us during these early formative years has a profound effect on how our brains develop and how we perceive ourselves and others in the future.

In our culture, we are taught to believe that after a certain age, we should stop blaming our parents for the problems in our lives. Dr. Shirley helps us realize that blaming our parents is not the road to change. Instead, gaining an understanding of how our parents influenced and shaped our development is the most effective means for letting go of our self-destructive behaviors.

*Why Can't I Change?* explains this process and clarifies how it can provide the building blocks we need to become who we truly want to be, as well as offer us the emotional and practical tools to change and move beyond our self-destructive patterns. When we understand the patterns behind our self-doubts, those patterns lose their power over us, and we can adopt new, healthy ways to understand ourselves and the people who are important to us. That is the key to how we can truly change and live healthier, more fulfilling lives.

Gary Small, MD
Professor of Psychiatry
David Geffen School of Medicine
UCLA

# Preface

Why do people make the same mistakes over and over again? Why do we choose the wrong partners, stay in dead-end jobs, or fall into bad habits or addictions? Why are some people perpetual victims? Why can't we just change whatever isn't working and get on with it?

These questions about the human condition fascinated me and led me to a career in psychology. During my early years in private practice, I noticed that many of my patients had a distinct pattern of self-destructive behavior that seemed to repeat over and over again. I found this pattern pervasive in almost all areas of their lives, although it was most apparent in their intimate relationships.

When I pointed this out to my patients, many had no idea there was a pattern at all. Those who admitted being aware of their patterns became aware of them only after the patterns were established. They were not conscious of what had created these patterns and what had gotten them to this place. They seemed to be sleepwalking through life. I began to research this phenomenon. I knew from my studies that childhood experiences affect our behaviors and the way we think about life. During a fateful trip to Tahiti, I was introduced to attachment theory, which specifically correlates our feelings, thoughts, beliefs, and what we expect in life as adults to the way we attach to our primary caregivers as infants. The latest studies in attachment and brain development indicate that the effects of these early experiences shape the way our brain develops, causing us to behave in ways that we may not be aware of. As I learned more and more about attachment in early life, it all began to make sense. The programming that begins in infancy is stored in the unconscious. When it is triggered, it ignites a pattern of behavior that is simply a reaction to that early programming. Thanks, Mom and Dad!

With this knowledge, I began to better understand the psychological defenses, emotional reactions, beliefs, and behaviors my patients were displaying. It was not simply a matter of blaming our parents; their part in the process is in the past and often unintentional, and we can't change that. However, understanding *why* the behavior exists is the first step in changing it. It became clear that helping my patients gain insight into their patterns led to awareness and that awareness presented a choice for them: either stick with their old behaviors and continue to sleepwalk through life or try new behaviors and release themselves from their unconscious patterns, ultimately living the lives they wanted. Insight and awareness alone do not produce change, but new experiences do. And new experiences create new neural pathways in the brain and literally change it. The adage "You can't teach an old dog new tricks" is a lie.

I wrote this book to share my insights and strategies beyond the scope of my practice. When we become aware and let go of old patterns that no longer work in our lives, we can change our behaviors and stop sleepwalking through life, free from the effects of the past. How exhilarating and grand!

# Acknowledgments

I'd like to thank everyone who serendipitously came together to make me who I am today, beginning with Judith Pillsbury, RIP, whose understanding and kind words I will never forget, and continuing with my first two mentors, Dr. Paul Abramson, who believed in me when I didn't and Dr. Lawanda Katzman-Staenberg who taught me everything I know. Matt Jackson introduced me to my wonderful manager, Marilyn Atlas, who found Mike Farris at Farris Literary Agency who decided to take a risk and took me on as a client. He, in turn, found Sunrise River Press, and I was lucky to have them take a chance on me and publish my words. Karen Chernyaev is a kind, patient, and intelligent editorial director who had the wherewithal to put me together with Debby Young. I have never had the experience to work with an editor and feel blessed to have worked with such a talented one from the get go. Debby immediately got me, heard my voice, and understood the message I wanted to convey and made me sound eloquent doing so!

To my friends who supported me and understood when I went MIA to write and meet my deadlines. And to my family: my mother who I know would have been very proud of her gordita, Frankie-boy, and especially my sister Jackie, who I have always looked up to and with whom I am extremely proud to share a wonderfully close relationship. You were instrumental in helping me, always inspiring me with kind words and giving me great feedback while writing this book.

Gigi and Gary Small have always been a wonderful support ever since that fateful day when we met on the first day of our kids' nursery school.

Dr. Drew Pinsky, thank you for supporting me in this effort.

A special thanks to the scientists, many of whom I reference throughout the book, who have dedicated their lives to studying the effects of trauma. A very special thanks to Dr. Perter Levine, whose brilliance has given us a beautiful and profound way to heal our wounds.

To all of the people I have had the privilege of working with, I do not take lightly the trust you have placed in me and feel honored and humbled by it. Thank you to those who read parts of the manuscript and gave me such rich and wonderful feedback.

Last but certainly not least, my dear Sydney. I learn from you every day and strive to be the best parent I can be. I am privileged and honored to be your mom.

Song lyrics reprinted with permission:

**Page 127**
**That's The Way I've Always Heard It Should Be**
Words and Music by Carly Simon and Jacob Brackman
Copyright (c) 1970 Quackenbush Music Ltd. and Maya Productions Ltd.
Copyright Renewed
All Rights Administered by Quackenbush Music Ltd.
All Rights Reserved  Used by Permission
*Reprinted by Permission of Hal Leonard Corporation*

**Page 96–97**
**The Look of Love**
Words by Hal David
Music by Burt Bacharach
(c) 1967 (Renewed 1995) COLGEMS-EMI MUSIC INC.
All Rights Reserved  International Copyright Secured  Used by Permission
*Reprinted by Permission of Hal Leonard Corporation*

**Page 121**
**ALREADY GONE**
Words and Music by JACK TEMPCHIN and ROBB STRANDLUND
© 1973 (Renewed) WB MUSIC CORP. and JAZZ BIRD MUSIC
All Rights Administered by WB MUSIC CORP.
All Rights Reserved

# Introduction

*We cannot change what has been done to us,*
*but we can refuse to be reduced by it.*
—Maya Angelou

We all operate in very personal and particular ways. From the minute we are born, we begin to develop skills to survive childhood. We come into this world with the innate expectation that someone will meet our basic needs. That *someone* is the people who created us. We expect that our mother and father will care for our needs and love us unconditionally. In some cases, our primary caregivers will not be our biological parents, howerver this expectation still applies.

My daughter's expectation of unconditional love from me was clear when she was four years old. I noticed her picking up all her toys and putting them away at the request of my sister. Exasperatedly, I asked her, "Why do you listen to Aunt Jackie so nicely and you don't listen to me when I ask you to do something?" She automatically responded, "Because you're my mom. You're supposed to love me. But Aunt Jackie doesn't have to." In other words, she minded my sister to ensure my sister's love, innately assuming that she didn't need to ensure my love for her. Because I'm her mom, I just *do*.

As newborns, we understand, at some level, that we depend on our parents or primary caregivers for absolute survival. If they don't feed us, we die. Consequently, the process of attachment begins immediately after birth. Our brains are hardwired to attach to ensure our physical survival. The number one goal of attachment is to feel safe in the world. How we attach to our primary caregivers directly affects how our brains develop. Thus our earliest experiences guide our feelings, thoughts, beliefs, and experiences in later relationships.

As toddlers and children, we look to our parents for comfort and approval. When we get hurt, we run to them to be soothed. When we do something well, we look to them for praise. These are automatic behaviors within the process of attachment. When parents are sensitive to their children's needs, secure attachments are formed. When parents' attention is sporadic, nonexistent, or abusive, insecure attachments are formed.

Children have only one way to interpret insecure attachments: "What is wrong with me?" When a parent is not present or is neglectful or abusive, the child interprets the parent's behavior not as a deficiency in the parent, but as a deficiency in him- or herself: "If I were only more lovable, my parent would have stuck around or wouldn't have treated me that way."

Parental absence, neglect, or abuse always results in a child feeling unlovable, defective, and not worth the parent's time or effort. It would be too threatening and scary to think something was wrong with the parent; after all, the child literally depends on the parent for physical survival. The parent needs to be perfect in a child's mind because the opposite is much too frightening. Consequently, what becomes programmed at an unconscious level is that something is wrong with these children. When they become adults, they behave in ways that confirm what they were programmed to believe—that they are defective, unlovable, and not valuable—by choosing friends or partners who treat them as they were treated at home or by not achieving their potential. These beliefs turn into automatic patterns of behavior because they are repeated over and over again and become well-traveled pathways in the brain. As with any well-traveled path, we often get to our destination without an awareness of how we got there. Many of us may not like the destination, but because we don't know how we got there, we don't know how to travel down a different path and change our end results. We are sleepwalking through life.

I, too, was sleepwalking through life. I remember the exact moment when I woke up, and I want to share this information with you. This book is not about labeling yourself or feeling somehow inadequate or shamed because you didn't have an ideal childhood. It is about developing the awareness to notice which thoughts, beliefs, and behavior patterns are not working for you, and learning techniques for change. Join me on this journey as I show you how to put an end to dysfunctional patterns of behavior. I'll help you discover what your attachment style is, learn how that attachment style affected the development of your brain, and learn to recognize your unconscious patterns. I will then give you tools to help you let go of old patterns, so you can try out new behaviors. Insight leads to awareness, and awareness offers choices that can bring about change.

# 1

# Planting the Seeds That Lead to Your Patterns

*What you are aware of you are in control of;*
*what you are not aware of is in control of you.*
—Anthony de Mello

I will never forget the day my "adult self," the person I had become, began to make sense to me. I was on a cruise to Tahiti with my daughter. I was on this cruise because it was a way to earn twenty continuing education hours. (Psychologists need thirty-six hours of continuing education every two years to renew their licenses.) As an added bonus, it was a tax write-off and a vacation with my daughter. What could be better? The topic and speaker? *Who cares!* I thought. If it wasn't interesting, I'd suffer through it and enjoy all the wonderful benefits.

There I was sitting in the ship's ballroom, which turned into a disco at night, listening to a child psychiatrist talk about attachment theory and deciding whether to go kayaking or Jet Skiing right after the lecture. I started to pay attention because he was kind of cute, and I thought I might have to take a test at the end to get credit for my hours. Suddenly, something he said caught my attention. As he began to describe a particular attachment style and the general behavior of adults with this attachment style, I realized he was describing me.

## Attachment Theory and the Infant

We are all influenced by our past. The relationships we had with the first people who were supposed to take care of us and love us unconditionally influence the beliefs we develop about ourselves as adults. These first people might be our parents or other caregivers, including adoptive parents, nannies, grandparents, aunts, and uncles. Our parents' or caregivers' sensitivity to our needs directly affects our behavior patterns and the perception we develop about ourselves and others. To keep it simple, I refer to "parents" throughout the book as the primary caregivers, but keep in mind that the people who serve as a child's primary caregivers, regardless of biological relationship, will be the people who most profoundly influence that child's view of himself and the world.

To understand how we develop a sense of self and how we relate to others, we need to learn how we build a sense of safety in the world. As I stated in the introduction, we are born with an innate expectation that our parents or caregivers will meet our basic needs for protection, food, and unconditional love. We depend on them for approval, comfort, and praise. But if our parents don't provide food when we are hungry, aren't there to soothe us when we wake at night, don't give us comfort when we need it, or give no praise or proud and loving glances, over the years we develop the belief that we don't deserve their love. Sadly, this belief controls how we perceive the world and our place in it. The strength of the belief is determined in part by how consistently our parents didn't meet our needs. The continuum is long, from our parents never meeting our needs to occasionally not meeting them. Consequently, it is important to understand how we attached, or bonded, to our primary caregivers.

In his groundbreaking book *Attachment and Loss*, psychologist John Bowlby, credited as the father of attachment theory, defined attachment as "a lasting psychological connectedness between human beings." He found that we have an innate need to connect and that the process of forming an emotional bond with attachment figures is universal. A child needs to develop a trusting relationship with at least one caregiver for social and emotional development to occur normally. The most secure situation for an infant is to have both mother and father available for attachment. Usually an infant attaches to his mother within the first year of life and she becomes his primary attachment figure. The attachment with the father is strengthened in the second year, however, and both become just as strong and impact the development of the infant's brain. If the mother and father aren't available, infants will attach to any person they spend a lot of time with—a nanny or a grandparent, for example. An infant who has *someone* to attach to will show fewer signs of emotional damage as an adult than an infant who has not attached to anyone, such as an infant with unavailable parents and a series of different, short-term nannies.

For an infant who has only one sensitive parent, the damage is less, but not being nurtured and acknowledged by the other parent may still negatively affect her self-esteem later on in life. The healthiest adults develop from a situation in which both parents are sensitive to the infant's needs, and the infant is given the opportunity to attach to both. Bowlby shared the psychoanalytic view that early experiences in childhood have an important influence on development and behavior later in life.

For all of us single parents out there, do not fret! Being consistent and available will mitigate the effects of having only one available parent and your infant can still develop into a well-adjusted adult.

For many years, scientists believed that infants attached to the mother because the mother fed them. However, when Bowlby began to study this phenomenon, he noticed that when an infant was separated from her mother, she would cry and show an enormous amount of distress even when other caretakers were feeding and caring for her. This led him to wonder what caused an infant to attach to her mother. (The primary attachment figure can be anyone with whom the child becomes bonded. Usually it's the mother, but not always. For the purposes of simplification, I will use *mother* to refer to the primary attachment figure throughout this book.)

Bowlby found that there was a biological function to attachment behavior. In other words, infants attach to their primary caregivers for protection. This makes sense when we think about our ancestors who lived millions of years ago. Infants who strayed from their mothers might be eaten by wild animals; those who stayed close were protected. Staying safe by bonding to the people around us is an innate behavior of humans and all mammals. Our brains are biologically hardwired to stay alive.

While studying attachment, Bowlby noticed that infants looked to their mothers not only for safety but also to regulate their nervous systems; in other words, to calm down. For instance, when an infant was scared or felt stress, he looked to his mother for comfort. If the mother was responsive, the infant calmed down and felt safe again. Stress could be brought on by hunger, pain, fatigue, illness, or fear. Think back to the last time your infant crawled toward you. Did the neighbor's dog scare her? Was she hungry? What memories do you have of seeking out your own mother when you were little? Did you skin your knee playing outside? Were you sick?

Bowlby also noticed that infants learn about themselves and the world through their mothers' responses to them. He found that through interactions with the mother, an infant made mental images of her (or another attachment figure), the self, and the environment. Later, children use such images as templates to anticipate what to expect from others, themselves, and their environments. If, for the most part, your needs are met, your mental template of other people becomes: "I can trust people to be there when I need them." Your mental template of yourself becomes: "I am worthy of love and support, and the world is a safe place."

If you were abused as a child, whether the abuse was severe, mild, or someplace in between, your mental template of other people becomes: "People are dangerous and not to be trusted." Your mental template of yourself becomes: "I am defective, and the world is a very dangerous and scary place." If you were left alone a lot, not played with, or neglected, your mental template of other people becomes: "People are not to be trusted to meet my needs; I am the only person I can depend on." Your mental template of yourself becomes: "My needs are not important because I am an unworthy person. The world is a disappointing place that I cannot trust." It is important to understand that the mental templates or beliefs you develop as a result of your attachment to your primary caregiver(s) can fall anywhere on a broad continuum, from extreme rigid traits to mild characteristics.

Dr. Dan Siegel, a child psychiatrist who has extensively studied how attachment affects brain development, describes how we develop a mental template of ourselves. He believes that if parents are abusive, scary, neglectful, or insensitive to a child's needs, there are only two ways the child can react to the parents' behavior: to go insane or to go into blame. If a child interprets a parent's neglectful or abusive behavior as a deficiency in the parent, the child will *go insane*. It is much too scary and threatening for a child to think that the person who is responsible for keeping him alive and safe is flawed or imperfect. Alternatively, children who are neglected or abused see themselves as deficient, feel shame, and *go into blame*. This is a much more tolerable explanation. Infants are born with an innate capacity to love others and to let others love them. If someone experiences a lot of disappointment throughout childhood due to abuse or neglect, without repair, the belief that he is "a flawed and defective human being" is planted. The ability to love and let someone love him becomes too scary and leaves him feeling too vulnerable. Consequently, his innate capacity for love shuts down.

The seeds of shame can get planted every time a parent is not sensitive to a child's needs. Sally runs home because she cannot wait to tell her mom that she got the lead role in the school play. Her mom is on the phone. Sally bursts through the door yelling, "Mom, Mom, guess what?" Her mom looks up with a scowl on her face and shoos Sally away with her hand. Sally immediately stops in her tracks. An overwhelming feeling of hurt and disappointment comes over her, and she runs to her room. A seed of shame has been planted. If Sally's mom goes into Sally's room, apologizes, validates how hurt Sally must have felt, and gives Sally her undivided attention, she has repaired the damage. Repair is just as important as doing it right in the first place. However, if Sally's mom angrily storms into the room and yells at her for being inconsiderate by not noticing that she was on the phone, humiliation is added to the experience, which deepens the sense of shame. Children do not have the capacity to see themselves as good people in bad situations. If a situation is bad or hurtful, the child blames herself.

Everything Bowlby observed and proposed was considered theory until Giacomo Rizzolatti came along. Rizzolatti is a neurophysiologist who discovered mirror neurons, cells in our brain that enable us to form mental representations or images. This discovery substantiated what Bowlby had observed. Mirror neurons cause our brains to light up when we see someone doing an activity, as if we were actually doing the activity ourselves.

For example, when you watch a tennis match, the area of your brain that would be active if you were actually playing tennis lights up. Similarly, if a baby watches his mother play with a toy, the part of the brain that would be active if the baby were actually playing with the toy is stimulated. Did you ever wonder why you cry while watching a sad scene in a movie? Mirror neurons! The "sad" area of your brain is stimulated when you see another person in distress. Ever wonder why we get turned on when we watch pornography? You guessed it! Mirror neurons. So the next time your partner says that he didn't feel a thing after watching that sex scene, you can say, "Don't lie to me. I know all about your mirror neurons!" Your subsequent conversation about mirror neurons will no doubt extinguish any prior brain activation.

Rizzolatti was able to show that mirror neurons, or mirror brain cells, are stimulated and subsequently affected by the actions of others. Mirror neurons help explain why we grow up and repeat what we witnessed our parents doing. Let's look at domestic violence. Children see themselves in the same-sex parent, so the "hitting" part of the brain is stimulated every time a boy watches his father beat his mother. As we will learn in chapter 2, when certain areas of the brain are stimulated together, associations are formed and patterns that create specific brain circuitry develop. Thus the boy who has a violent father is likely to be more reactive in general or hit and become violent as a way of dealing with stress. If a girl watches her mother get hit and become terrified, the pain and fear circuitry in *her* brain will light up, possibly increasing the girl's overall feelings of fear and intimidation, decreasing a sense of empowerment and strength.

Even more fascinating and groundbreaking were subsequent studies demonstrating that if we watch someone simply grasp a cup, without knowing what the person is going to do next, the "drinking" area of our brain lights up, as if *we* were about to take a drink. This was a completely different and very significant discovery in terms of attachment theory. It implied that our mirror neurons learn to anticipate another person's intention. If we had never seen a person drink out of a cup, the "drinking" part of our brain would not light up, because we would have no idea what the person was about to do with the cup. Consequently, Bowlby's theory that parents' sensitivity, or lack of sensitivity, affects an infant was no longer just speculation.

We now know that a parent's actions directly affect what an infant learns to *anticipate* about others and therefore about his own self-worth.

In his book *Mirroring People,* psychiatrist Marco Iacoboni further describes how mirror neurons work. Iacoboni explains that through our interactions with others, our mirror neurons form a template or image about others' intentions, and we begin to anticipate their behavior based on this image. Eventually, this anticipated behavior gets programmed into our brain and causes us to believe that everyone will behave toward us in this way, even people we have never met. Bowlby was right on with his theory of mental images. As adults, the way we expect others to behave is a direct consequence of interactions with our attachment figures from childhood.

Imagine you are walking on a sidewalk with a friend when she suddenly raises her arm. If you had grown up in New York City and watched your mother do this over and over, chances are the "hailing a taxicab" part of your brain would light up. If your mother owned a gym and you had been raised among people who worked out, the "exercise" or "stretching" part of your brain would light up. However, if you had been physically abused as a child, the "danger/pain" part of your brain would light up. You might notice your heart beginning to race and a feeling of panic coming over you—and most likely you would have absolutely no idea why this was happening.

### How We Attach

During the first year of life, infants select one primary attachment figure. It's usually the mother, since the baby has been hearing her heartbeat and muffled voice in the womb for nine months. It can also be the person the infant spends most of his time with. Once selected, this person is set apart from all other adults in the infant's mind. This special bond continues throughout life, which explains why, regardless of age, some people continuously seek the approval of their mother or father. By the end of the first year, this person is the center of the infant's world. The infant will closely monitor this person's whereabouts and will display four characteristic behaviors to make sure the person stays in close range:

1.  Proximity Maintenance: The infant will make physical adjustments to stay close enough to the primary attachment figure to feel safe.

2. Safe Haven: The infant will return to the attachment figure for comfort and safety in the face of fear or a threat.
3. Secure Base: The infant will use the attachment figure as a base of security from which to explore the surrounding environment.
4. Separation Distress: The infant will react with anxiety or distress when separated from the attachment figure.

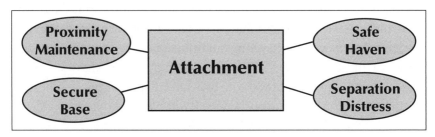

Infants display these four characteristic behaviors with the person to whom they have formed a primary attachment.

Dr. Mary Ainsworth, a developmental psychologist and student of Bowlby's, expanded his work on attachment and labeled four phases an infant goes through to form an attachment to a particular caregiver. First is the preattachment phase. Infants are in this phase from birth to about two months of age. During this phase, an infant is open and responsive to interaction from almost anyone, although recent studies show that an infant as young as one month of age recognizes her mother's voice. At about two to six months, the infant begins to discriminate among caregivers by responding differently to certain individuals. She will smile and be more vocal to the person to whom she is becoming attached. Additionally, the infant will greet this person in a more animated way and show more distress when separated from this person. This is the attachment-in-the-making phase. By six or seven months, the person who is the primary attachment figure is abundantly clear. In this clear-cut attachment phase, the four characteristic behaviors are present, but only toward the attachment figure. The infant will make active attempts to stay close to this person, use the person as a secure base and a safe haven, and become very distressed if separated from the person. The last phase, called goal-corrected partnership, happens at around thirty-six months. It is represented by a less urgent need to be close to the attachment figure, as toddlers begin to explore their environment and gain autonomy.

Infants need to feel a connection with their primary attachment figures and will do certain things to try to get their attention. These behaviors can include smiling, clinging, calling, following, and crying. These bids for connection stop if the infant consistently does not get a response from the attachment figure. This is not to say that infants and children do not attach to other adults in their world; they do, and in fact they can become attached to many people. However, only one person occupies the *primary* attachment position.

## Four Distinct Attachment Styles

Dr. Ainsworth conducted a seminal study on attachment, the Strange Situation Experiment, that shed new light on this critical area of child development. She observed attachment behaviors in infants twelve to eighteen months old to see how they reacted with their mothers in different situations. In the first scenario, the mother and infant were together in a room filled with toys. After a few minutes, the infant would typically begin to explore and play with the toys. Three minutes later, a stranger would enter the room and talk to the mother. Three minutes after that, the mother would exit the room, leaving the infant and the stranger alone. The stranger would try to engage the infant. Three minutes later, the mother would reenter the room. She would greet and/or comfort the baby. Then she and the stranger would exit the room, leaving the infant alone. Three minutes later, the stranger would enter the room again. Three minutes after that, the mother would come back for a second reunion with the infant.

Dr. Ainsworth noticed that all the infants became agitated when their mothers left the room, as one would expect. However, upon the mothers' return, the infants reacted very differently from one another, based on their attachment styles. The experiment led Dr. Ainsworth to identify three distinct attachment styles: secure attachment, insecure-ambivalent attachment, and insecure-avoidant attachment. Later, Dr. Mary B. Main, a researcher at the University of California–Berkeley, identified a fourth attachment style by observing infants who did not fit into the other three categories. She named this fourth attachment style insecure-disorganized/ disoriented attachment. The Strange Situation Experiment has been replicated many times, and these attachment styles have proven to be universal, although a very small percentage of infants do not fit any of the categories and fall under a "cannot classify" group.

Children with secure attachment sought comfort directly from their mothers when the mothers returned to the room. The children were easily soothed and went back to their play activities confidently. Children with insecure-ambivalent attachment had inconsistent reactions when their mothers returned, sometimes approaching their mothers and sometimes avoiding them. Their agitation persisted, they were not easily soothed, and they could not readily go back to what they had been doing. Children with insecure-avoidant attachment disregarded and ignored their mothers when the mothers returned to the room. They kept playing with toys, barely noticing that the mothers had returned. They distracted themselves from their distress rather than having the natural developmental reaction of running to the mother for comfort when she returned. Children with insecure-disorganized/disoriented attachment displayed conflicted behaviors with their mothers when the mothers returned to the room. They approached their mothers for comfort but also reacted with anger toward them.

These different attachment styles were directly related to how sensitive and responsive overall the mothers had been to their infants' signals for attention since birth. Secure infants have mothers who are sensitive to their needs and respond in loving ways to their bids for attention. The mothers are dependable and consistent in their availability and provide comfort when their infants show distress. These mothers are able to understand their infants' needs and respond in a synchronized way. Daniel Stern, a psychiatrist who specializes in infant development, calls this process attunement, which he defines as a parent's ability to be sensitive to the verbal and nonverbal cues of a child and to put herself into the mind of the child as a way to synchronize with him. This parental capability plays a central role in the child's ability to regulate his emotions later in life. Imagine feeling so deeply understood by another person that you feel "felt" by her, or completely connected. Infants in this situation feel secure in exploring their environment because they are sure that if something or someone scares them, they can return to their mothers and be protected and comforted.

This is not to say that these mothers are perfect and always respond to their infants in a sensitive manner. In fact, studies show that to build a secure attachment with your infant you need to be sensitive to your infant just 40 percent of the time. What these mothers are able to do, however, is repair when a rupture in attunement has occurred. In other words, these mothers are able to notice when what they are doing is not comforting their infants or they have inadvertertly scared or frustrated them, and they then "repair" the damage by doing something that reestablishes the connection. Attachment theorists believe that to develop a secure attachment with our children, we don't have to be perfect; we just have to be "good enough." What a relief!

Insecure-ambivalent infants have mothers who are inconsistent in their availability and inconsistent in providing comfort when their infants are distressed. The mothers are significantly less sensitive to their infants' needs and do not always respond to their signals for attention. However, they are also intrusive at times and interfere with their children's behavior. For example, these mothers might abruptly interrupt or switch activities their infants are engaged in, or overstimulate their infants, not picking up on an infant's cues that he needs a break, such as looking away or crying. Because of the inconsistency in having their needs met, insecure-ambivalent children become more clingy and unsure of themselves and their decisions. At times, they may exaggerate their needs in an effort to keep their mother close. They fear separating and becoming autonomous because they fear losing the attachment bond. They don't yet have the stability to face the world if the secure base (the mother) is not there. Since the mother's ability to respond to her infant's needs has been inconsistent and there has been no repair, the infant stays close to the mother in an anxious way, fearing complete abandonment.

Mothers of insecure-avoidant infants may be mostly absent, as in the case of latchkey kids, or may be physically present but do not interact much with their infants and thus do not connect with them. These mothers express little emotion when they are with their infants and are insensitive to their bids for attention. They also do not appear to enjoy holding their infants and actually demonstrate a dislike for close physical contact. Children of these mothers learn to suppress their need for connection. They engage in behaviors that keep them distracted from the distress they are feeling, ultimately detaching from all feeling. They isolate and avoid contact with their mothers to avoid rejection. Such infants and toddlers can appear very independent and self-sufficient. However, when the degree of independence and self-sufficiency is not within what is considered developmentally age appropriate, that behavior can signify a problem with attachment.

The mothers of insecure-disorganized/disoriented infants respond to their bids for attention in ways that frighten the infants. This could be due to overt physical or sexual abuse, but can also be due to aggressive play. For example, aggressive play could be engaging in chasing games using low verbal tones (see chapter 3) or using threatening facial expressions that scare the infant or toddler. By not picking up on the fact that the infant is scared and is not enjoying the interaction, the parent will continue the scary play or play too aggressively. This situation is contradictory and confusing for the infant. The safe haven is also a source of fear. Insecure-disorganized/disoriented infants become very confused and act in contradictory ways. Under the extreme stress, they can dissociate (tune out and detach themselves) from their emotions, bodies, and immediate surroundings and will later act in disruptive and aggressive ways.

To assess the attachment style of adults based on their childhood experiences, Main and two of her colleagues developed the Adult Attachment Interview (AAI). Research shows that based on your attachment style, the AAI can determine with 85 percent accuracy the attachment style of your child. I guess the expression "the apple doesn't fall far from the tree" fits pretty well here. Interestingly, when a mother is not aware of her own attachment style, she will most likely parent her child in the same manner in which she was parented. Of course, if a parent is securely attached, there is no problem. But if the parent is insecurely attached, a problematic cycle repeats. We cannot change that which we are unaware of.

# Child and Caregiver Behavior Patterns

| Attachment Pattern | Child | Caregiver |
|---|---|---|
| Secure | Uses caregiver as a secure base for exploration. When frightened will go to the caregiver, is comforted by them and feels safe with them. | Is dependable and sensitive to the infant's needs. Responds appropriately and promptly. |
| Ambivalent | Shows some anxiety even when caregiver is present. When distressed becomes clingy and cannot be easily soothed. | Inconsistent and vacillates between appropriate and neglectful responses. Can also be intrusive and insensitive to the infant's needs. |
| Avoidant | Too independent for their developmental age. May appear to not notice or ignore the caregiver. | Does not interact or engage much with the infant. |
| Disorganized | Shows contradictory behaviors. Wants to get close to the caregiver but is also frightened by her. | Abusive or displays aggressive and frightening actions toward the infant while engaging with him. |

## Emotions and Arousal Regulation

As we attach in our early years, the seeds are planted for the ways in which we will view our place in the world and how we will interact with others. Our attachment style determines how we deal with many areas of our lives, including how sensitive we are to our own feelings and to the feelings of others. Do you remember how your parents responded when you expressed a feeling? If you cried, did they comfort you or tell you to get over it? Did they try to find out what was wrong or did they yell at you: "Stop crying or I'll give you something to cry about"? When you were angry, did they allow you to have those feelings and help you navigate through them, or did they send you to your room for acting inappropriately?

The way your parent responded to you when you expressed a feeling taught you everything you know about emotions. As you will learn in chapter 2, emotions are simply a sign that our nervous system is out of a homeostasis state, or out of balance, and we have become aroused or dysregulated. If your caregiver was sensitive to your feelings, whether you were scared, or felt angry because your friend Julie ignored you all day, or disappointed when you didn't get the lead in the school play, you learned that an emotion can simply be something you feel, acknowledge, and get past. If your caregiver was insensitive to your feelings, perhaps because she was never taught how to deal with her own feelings, you got the message that emotions are somehow wrong, scary, and bad. At the sign of any emotions, you become anxious, or you will unknowingly push them down and throw them into your "internal basement" by minimizing them, ignoring them, or completely dissociating yourself from them. Emotions, then, become these looming scary things that you have no idea what to do with. But because emotions automatically come with being human, they come out anyway, and, at times, in the most inappropriate ways. Have you ever felt rage when the store ran out of your favorite flavor of ice cream? Did you ever become teary at a Hallmark card commercial?

When children are able to identify their feelings and work through them, they don't have to overreact or suppress them and can deal with them in healthy ways. One of the best and most useful gifts parents can give children is showing them how to identify their feelings, which is done simply by validating what a child is feeling. This process helps the child identify and name his emotions. Saying to a child, "Did that scare you?" "That must have been so frustrating," or "I bet that made you sad" validates the experience the child is having. On the other hand, saying, "That's not scary," "Don't let that bother you," or "He didn't mean it" causes a child to become confused and not trust what he is in fact feeling.

Feelings are very specific, so if you are a parent, don't be afraid of putting words into your child's mouth. If you guess wrong, your child will let you know: "No, that's not how I'm feeling." Making a wrong guess initiates a great opportunity to explore different emotions as you help your child identify exactly what she is feeling. If you have a difficult time recognizing emotions, have no fear. You can buy charts with all the major emotions and their corresponding facial expressions on cartoon faces. You and your child can point to the facial expression that best describes what you or your child may be feeling. Validating someone's feelings, whether a child or an adult, allows the person to feel understood and connected, which more often than not calms the person down. The calmness comes from that feeling of connection and being fully understood by another human being—what Daniel Stern calls attunement.

When children learn to identify their feelings through a parent's validation and feel their emotions calm down, they eventually learn to regulate their aroused states. With repeated experiences of this type, children develop the necessary skills and learn to anticipate calm after emotional dysregulation. Under these circumstances, secure attachment is formed. Many people who were not taught to identify their emotions can feel taken over by them or conversely become numb to them. In either case, they are not in control of their emotions; their emotions control them.

Feelings should be a source of information, not a source of danger or something that overwhelms. For example, if I notice myself feeling angry, that tells me that something has angered me. If it happened during a conversation with my friend, it could be that something he said hurt my feelings or upset me. When you experience any emotions—sadness, happiness, anger, or fear—you have gone out of a state of emotional homeostasis into an aroused or dysregulated state. When the aroused or dysregulated state is happiness or excitement, it feels good and we are not in a rush to calm down and go back to a homeostasis state. However, regardless of whether the dysregulation feels good or bad, eventually we all need to go back to our baseline or emotional resting state, as our nervous systems can't handle too much on either extreme to function properly.

We all have an emotional baseline that is set by our past experiences. If we experienced an unsafe childhood with a lot of trauma, our emotional baseline may be more on the sad, shut down, or numb side of the continuum, or, conversely, on the angry or anxiety-ridden side of the continuum. I'm sure you have met people who appear depressed or sad all the time and others who look like they are about to lose it at any moment.

On the other side, you may have come across people with a Susie Sunshine disposition, who don't get upset very easily, if ever. As with most things, achieving balance is the healthiest way to be. In chapter 5, you will learn how to expand your capacity for positive emotions and how to change your depressive or anger-prone baseline. Those who cannot identify their emotions, even when they're extreme or intense, will learn how to become familiar with them so they don't erupt at inopportune times.

Neuroscientist Jaak Panksepp has studied emotions extensively. He defines them as our ability to subjectively experience different states of our nervous system. Since emotions are a part of being human, if we have not developed the ability to recognize them, we have instead developed the ability to push them deep inside and ignore them. There is no such thing as *not* having feelings, which is easy to understand if you look at feelings or emotions as simply your nervous system being out of balance. The question then becomes, "How do I get back to baseline without freaking out or having to ignore my emotions?" This is a great question that chapter 5 will help answer!

As parents, many of us feel compelled to fix things or make it all better for our children. One day, when my daughter was three years old, I took her to the park to play on the swings. As we were walking toward the swings, a huge Great Dane walking past us decided to stop and smell her dress. The big dog scared her, and she started to cry. I immediately went into fix-it mode and said, "No, look Syd, he's a friendly dog. You don't need to be afraid of him." I proceeded to pet the dog to show her she was safe and didn't have to be scared. Gee, what a great mom!

I can now imagine the unconscious monologue that must have gone on in her mind: "That huge dog is so big and scary. It's going to eat me up with one bite! But wait, my mom is petting the dog. Oh no! What if the dog eats her too! I'm so scared. My mom says the dog isn't scary, but I feel scared. My feelings must be wrong. I feel scared, but I'm not supposed to. I can't trust what I feel."

Sydney proceeded to cry in a confused and inconsolable way and refused to go on the swings. After a few attempts to get her to forget the dog and play on the swings, my brilliant parenting skills just knew no bounds and we left the park.

As I run over this incident in my mind now, I realize that all I had to do was simply validate her feelings with, "Wow, that big dog was really scary. Mommy will protect you." And off we could have gone, Syd feeling understood and protected by me, and I with the satisfaction of knowing that I had just taught my daughter to identify her feelings, not be afraid of them, and realize they would pass. This would have taught her how to regulate her own arousal in the future, because she would have had the experience of being in an emotional homeostasis state (walking to the park), becoming dysregulated or out of baseline (frightened by the dog), and reestablishing an emotionally regulated state (my validation of and sensitivity to her fear). If I had simply validated her feelings, she would have begun to develop an expectation that relief comes after stressful events, which in turn would have helped increase her ability to tolerate future stressors. Incidentally, validating a child's emotions enables her to move on from the emotions more quickly, because feeling understood is very soothing. Try it the next time your child, adolescent, partner, or friend has an emotional reaction. Just validate what you think he is feeling—anger, sadness, hurt, disappointment—and notice how he reacts. If your words cause another human being to feel "felt," you are creating a bond, which is at the core of attachment.

After learning what emotions were, I stopped being scared of them. I understand that emotions, my own and those of others, are simply sources

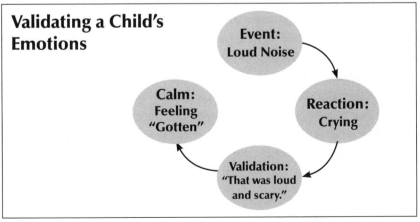

Validating a child's feelings builds essential skills for tolerating future stress.

of information. I no longer freeze or don't know what to say when friends experience a death in the family. I simply acknowledge their sad feelings, because sad is what they are supposed to be feeling. I no longer feel uncomfortable or that I have to do something to make my friends feel better. Similarly, if a friend tells me that something I said angered or hurt her, I am better able to acknowledge her feelings, letting her know that I hear and understand her. Although at times I am tempted to become defensive, I no longer feel the need to immediately jump into defend mode. I am able to let her have her feelings, whether I agree with them or not. Then, and only then, can I either own a misstep or explain the intention behind my behavior.

### Self-Regulation

Adults with secure attachment learned to regulate their emotions as infants and children because their primary caregivers were there to teach them. When they cried, they were soothed and comforted. When they skinned their knees, they knew their primary caregivers would "kiss it and make it all better." Children treated this way develop a template of themselves as loved and valued and a template of others as loving and dependable. They internalize how they are treated and responded to by their attachment figures, developing the necessary internal skills, so when no one else is around, they are able to soothe themselves without their world coming undone. Secure children learn how to soothe themselves by the way adults respond to them when they are stressed or frightened. They also learn to anticipate relief after upset. This template is what secure adults use to calm themselves. As adults, they are better able to tolerate frustration by knowing that it will pass and by also knowing that they have options to help themselves. For example, they can choose to take a deep breath, wait, and calm themselves before responding or even walk away and not engage in that moment. They are comfortable using their support systems to cope, because in a securely attached adult's world, other people are dependable and responsive.

### Auto-Regulation

Those with insecure attachment may have been neglected or ignored when they cried as infants or may even have been yelled at when they fell and skinned their knees. They weren't taught how to calm down when they were scared or hurt. No one shared in their joy when they accomplished a difficult task. They developed a template of themselves as unloved and rejected, and they developed a template of others as distrustful and undependable. These children learned that they could not depend on anyone to soothe them, so they learned to do it on their own. Since they weren't taught how to soothe themselves, they tried to regulate themselves in ways that, in the long run, proved disruptive and not very helpful.

For the most part, someone with an ambivalent attachment style may use others to help regulate them by consistently calling friends or partners and "needing to talk," but never really finding comfort in others' words for very long. They might act out and blame others for their feelings because these feelings are too intense and scary to confront directly. People with an avoidant attachment style tend to dissociate, cutting themselves off from their feelings completely. One of my patients used to say that when emotions became too intense, he would "shut 'em down," which meant he was cutting himself off from the neck down. He was so good at it that I remember he actually looked like a head walking in with his body trailing behind the first time I saw him. These kinds of coping mechanisms work when we are children because we do not have any other choices. However, they do not allow us to live our lives to the fullest as adults. Now we do have a choice.

## Attachment in Adulthood

The attachment style we develop in childhood, based on the sensitivity of our primary caregiver and the other adults in our lives, greatly influences our beliefs, thoughts, and behaviors as adults. Although there are critical developmental periods during which attachment is formed, a nurturing and sensitive adult can, at any time in infancy, childhood, or adolescence, significantly shape our attachment style. As I previously pointed out, we can fall anywhere on the continuum of attachment styles, from extreme rigid traits to mild characteristics, so when reading the styles below, note which style you think best describes you.

### Secure Attachment

As adults, people with secure attachment feel valued by others and worthy of affection. They assume that the people in their lives will be responsive, caring, and reliable because their caregivers were responsive, caring, and reliable. In fact, they recognize and invite people who have these characteristics into their lives as their partners and friends.

Adults with secure attachment can easily ask for help or support and are comfortable developing close relationships without feeling threatened. Forming bonds and developing close connections doesn't cause them to feel vulnerable or exposed. In relationships, they are able to deal with their partners' negative behavior with constructive anger that asserts their needs and discourages the negative behavior. This kind of anger is not intended to hurt, destroy, or promote a hateful attitude. It is about sharing and exchanging information to reestablish a safe and warm relationship. This is possible because people with secure attachments have an overall belief that their partners have generally good intentions and that a negative behavior is temporary and transitory. They also believe that they will be able to work through the incident without extreme hostility and maintain the overall quality of the relationship.

Securely attached individuals have an inner resource that allows them to come toward a partner or a friend in distress and feel empathy because they have confidence that they can help them. Conversely, they feel what is called "empathic happiness" when something good happens to their partners, family members, or friends, such as a promotion, a marriage proposal, or a lucrative business venture.

The attuned attention of their caregivers taught them how to self-regulate, so their interpersonal stress is low. Consequently, they can go from being stressed to feeling calm in short periods of time. Shifting from being alone to engaging with people and vice versa are easy transitions that do not cause any undue anxiety. People with secure attachment can tolerate disagreements and know they won't be abandoned. They know that someone can be angry with them but still love them at the same time, and they have the capacity to do the same. They can handle ambiguity and ambivalence. Although they might miss a loved one when separated, they have the ability to hold that person in their mind's eye and feel secure that the loved one is doing the same. This is not to say that people with secure attachment feel less pain, fear, anger, or sadness. But these emotions don't pose a threat for them, and they don't feel completely consumed by emotions.

I do not want to paint people with secure attachment as zen-like creatures who do not get knocked off balance at times. They do, as we all do, because life happens. People with secure attachment, however, seem to know that they will be able to handle whatever life throws their way. This may not be a conscious knowing, but it may manifest itself in a deep calm within. They generally don't panic or feel the need to deny their emotions. Even if, at times, they regress to these modes of coping, once this is pointed out to them, they will take a step back and reevaluate. People with secure attachment are also able to own when they make mistakes, something people with insecure attachments have a difficult time doing.

Dr. Peter Fonagy, a psychology professor at University College London, describes the essence of secure attachment as a person's ability to be aware of and to contemplate what he is feeling—internal experience—and to make sense of it. At the same time, he is also aware of the other's internal experience. This capacity is instilled in an infant when a caregiver responds to her verbal or nonverbal messages in a sensitive and caring way. The infant sees herself through her parent's eyes. Her sense of self is shaped by how attentive and sensitive the parent is to her needs. This allows the infant to feel deeply understood and deserving of care, comfort, and love, planting the seeds of self-worth. These seeds then lead to an emotionally healthy adult.

## *Ambivalent Attachment*

Children who develop an ambivalent attachment style tend to become preoccupied adults. The adult with ambivalent attachment is on the other end of the continuum from the adult with avoidant attachment. The most important thing for someone with ambivalent attachment is to feel connected. This boundless need to connect can at times be exhausting to others, and for people on the severe end of the spectrum, that connected feelings can never be quite satisfied or quenched by anyone. This person has high levels of anxiety and can be suspicious, controlling, or clingy.

He needs a lot of interaction with people and has a tendency to talk a lot. Many times he has difficulty editing what he says and includes too much detail in his storytelling or goes off on tangents. He can also express himself with exaggerated emotions or facial expressions. Such adults regulate their nervous systems externally. In other words, they need someone to help them calm down, having a very difficult time relaxing on their own. This is the friend who calls you in a panic, certain that her boyfriend has met someone else because it is seven fifteen, and he said he would call at seven. Unfortunately, your reassuring words never calm the panic for any extended period of time, because your friend seems to have a bottomless barrel of need. Your words slide through her, never sticking long enough to calm her before the panic sets in again.

Adults with ambivalent attachment have an exaggerated desire to be close to others but do not believe that others will be available or responsive to their needs. Their sense of self-worth depends upon the approval of others, and they live in fear of being rejected or abandoned. For the ambivalent, the feeling of connection and safety comes from being in close proximity to others. They have a very difficult time transitioning from being with people to being alone. Communicating via text or e-mail can cause them to feel disconnected, ignored, and not important enough for someone to pick up the phone and call them.

Because they assume and expect to be rejected or abandoned, people with ambivalent attachment can be thought of as the "word police." They pay attention to every word that is being said and the tone in which it is communicated. Every word is taken literally. If you say, "I'll call you later," this may mean fifteen minutes to one person and an hour to another. It is important to be very specific when communicating with an ambivalently attached person because calling back in an hour when the person was expecting a call back in fifteen minutes may be cause for alarm and enough to start an argument as she may believe you were being purposely inconsiderate. Similarly, ambivalently attached people can be hypervigilant and have a tendency to scrutinize everything—a look, a facial expression, a tone of voice—and often misinterpret another person's feelings, thoughts, or intentions, assuming the worst. Unfortunately, in order to try to stay a step ahead of the abandonment, this hypervigilance and scrutiny tends to exist only for the perceived negative or hurtful things a partner does whether real or imagined. The positive and caring behaviors are not usually retained for long periods of time. Writing down these positive behaviors often helps to remind the ambivalently attached person of the caring things their partners do and to balance out the negative bias.

In relationships, when a partner leaves for work or to run an errand, the adult with ambivalent attachment might feel abandoned and yearn for her, but when she returns, feel angry as a reaction to the feelings of abandonment. To someone with ambivalent attachment, a partner going out with friends is internalized as, "My partner prefers being with them more than being with me." A partner sitting in another room working or sending e-mails is internalized as, "My partner doesn't want to spend time with me and would rather do things without me." Someone with ambivalent attachment views any activity a partner is engaged in without him as bumping him off the level-of-importance totem pole. Panic sets in when he feels he is nearing the bottom of the totem pole. To the ambivalent, out of sight means out of mind, causing a cascade of fear as he becomes convinced that his partner doesn't love him anymore. (A person with secure attachment knows that even if his partner is engaging in an activity that doesn't include him, he retains top priority on the partner's level-of-importance totem pole.) Any arguments or disagreements can cause an increase in anxiety that his partner will leave and abandon him. Lacking the capacity to know that his partner can love him even when there is a disagreement causes him to become clingy and needy, which incidentally might cause the partner to leave. This is what is known as a self-fulfilling prophecy.

Another dynamic that can often occur with a person who falls on the ambivalent continuum is the partner's fear that what he says to her may cause anger or hurt feelings. The ambivalent wants to know the truth, as most people do, and will plead with him to "just be honest" with her. However, because she tends to view the world through eyeglasses of rejection, his *honest* response of, "My friends and I ended up staying out till two in the morning," may be met with the panic of, "He met somebody else and is going to leave me," or "If he really loved me he wouldn't stay out so late with his friends," causing an argument to ensue. This, in turn, may tempt the partner to hold some details back or not be completely honest, not necessarily because there is something to hide, but to try and avoid an argument. More often than not, these half-truths are found out and legitimate mistrust becomes an issue.

### Avoidant Attachment

In avoidant attachment, the caregiver is either not physically present, as in the case of "latchkey kids," or is around but is not available, so the child spends a lot of time alone, in her own little world. She learns to ignore her needs and to pretend she doesn't have any. This situation can trick an adult into believing that she was well parented, because "mom was always around." However, if your mother never played with you or rarely interacted with you, you were neglected, even if she cooked dinner every night, washed your clothes, and said "I love you" once in a while.

Research shows that neglect can have a worse effect than physical or sexual abuse on a person's psychological well-being because of the lack of interaction. As we learned from Bowlby, we have an innate need to connect. Our nervous system needs connection with others to develop in a healthy way. In fact, scientific studies have proven that interacting and connecting with others can improve the immune system, causing people to live longer and more fulfilled lives. Touch has been shown to stimulate the part of the brain that helps us deal with stress.

Adults with avoidant attachment expect to be rejected and distrust others, so they avoid close relationships and feel uncomfortable with intimacy. For the avoidant, eye contact can cause shame, based on the notion that "if someone sees me, they will realize how defective I really am." He might turn away to avert your gaze or look at other parts of your face during a conversation. You may find that the favorite sexual position of someone with avoidant attachment is intercourse from behind, therefore ensuring no eye contact during this very vulnerable and intimate act. He may also tend to be better able at having one-night stands, without any emotional attachment, and sometimes even prefer them to long-term relationships. Marriage can feel like ownership to him. Often you may hear people who are avoidantly attached say that they "don't need to sign a piece of paper to prove their level of commitment."

People with avoidant attachment place a high value on privacy in relationships, including friendships. At times they can appear secretive. They often don't want to share their problems because they don't want to burden people for fear of abandonment. Additionally, the idea of needing support causes a feeling of shame. However, this behavior does not allow people to feel close to them. It keeps others from reaching out to them and to consequently abandon them because the relationship does not feel reciprocal. This is yet another example of a self-fulfilling prophecy.

Avoidants are do-it-yourself people. They don't need help and don't want help. In fact, someone helping them causes anxiety, because it makes them feel shame. They feel defective for needing the help. They are so used to detaching and being in their own worlds that they go there without even noticing. Many people with avoidant attachment startle easily when someone walks in a room, because it causes them to pop out of their private worlds. In fact, even if an avoidant doesn't startle easy, coming up behind them while they are cooking or washing the dishes and giving them a big hug may feel really good to you, but to them it can feel intrusive and you may notice them stiffening up. Imagine how rejected someone would feel if they noticed their partner's body stiffen up at a gesture that is supposed to create connection and intimacy. Many times, this reaction alone can cause an argument to ensue. The rejected partner, feeling hurt, will question or accuse the avoidant of not loving them anymore. The avoidant has a sense that the problem has nothing to do with their partner, but because they don't understand why the hug makes them recoil, they may mistakenly start to question their feelings toward their partner. In reality, what's occurring is that when avoidants are not interacting with another person, even in a room full of people, they go into their own little worlds. They are so used to doing this that it can happen at the drop of a hat. Unlike the ambivalents, avoidants don't transition well from *not* interacting to interacting. A hug from behind them can interrupt the vacation they were on in their minds, causing the body to react and stiffen. Announcing your arrival, even if from the next room, or letting them know you are coming up behind them for a hug allows them to prepare for the interaction and enjoy it. Wouldn't this be valuable and necessary information to know about your partner?

In relationships, avoidants need alone time or they may begin to feel trapped. They so enjoy their alone time that they almost prefer it when their partners go off to work or to run errands. People on the extreme end of avoidant attachment would feel very comfortable with partners who traveled for work, and would prefer to live next door to their partners or, at the very least, have separate bedrooms. This makes sense if you have a core belief, which is usually unconscious, that you are defective and that people are not to be trusted. For the avoidant, being around people causes anxiety, because at any time, someone will figure out how defective they really are. These seeds were planted long ago and have nothing to do with how much they love their partner. However, when a partner doesn't have this information, they can't help but take it personally.

This lack of connection that occurs with children who do not have frequent interaction with a caregiver very often shows up in an adult who is less animated, is more detached, and appears more serious than most people. Often you will hear women who have an avoidant attachment complain that they are never approached by men when they are out with their friends, while their friends get hit on often. This has to do with the overall facial expression of the avoidant, which is more flat and guarded, and hence, not very approachable. People with an avoidant attachment style tend not to have many memories of their childhood, because the lack of interaction didn't stimulate the brain to form memories. The memories they do have are often very brief, without much detail. Neglectful situations are rationalized and minimized and the avoidant adult often claims that those experiences made them who they are today—independent, strong, and resilient. While texting and e-mail are the ambivalent's nightmare, they are the avoidant's dream, allowing them to communicate in a less intimate or vulnerable fashion.

Who do you think people with ambivalent attachment usually get into relationships with? You guessed it, the avoidant. Why, you ask? Great question! At some level, we strive toward healing our past wounds. The person with ambivalent attachment has a deep-rooted fear of abandonment, which will be discussed in chapter 3. The person with avoidant attachment has a deep-rooted fear of engulfment, or being swallowed, and completely losing his or her identity (also discussed in chapter 3). The fear of abandonment in the former triggers the fear of engulfment in the latter every time, because people who believe they are going to be left become clingy, which causes people who believe they are going to be swallowed to run away, perpetuating a hamster wheel type of cycle. However, by working together and creating a safe space for their vulnerabilities, these two types can help each other through their fears and insecurities, and the relationship can become securely attached.

It is important to remember that, given all of our experiences in infancy, childhood, and adolescence, we can fall anywhere on the attachment continuum. You might find a person who appears securely attached displaying ambivalent or avoidant traits at times. What may produce extreme anxiety to someone at one end of the ambivalent continuum may show up as just a heightened awareness to a person with minor ambivalent traits. Someone with extreme avoidant traits *needs* time alone, whereas someone who displays only some avoidant characteristics may simply *prefer* time alone.

### Disorganized Attachment

Adults with disorganized attachment tend to be the most damaged and often display pathological behaviors such as extreme aggressiveness or defiance. Because they usually come from abusive parents, they expect abuse at every turn. They are stuck in a "ready to fight back" mode and very often misinterpret others' intentions. Research shows that neutral facial expressions are interpreted by them as negative and hostile. Chaos seems to follow them wherever they go. They have a desperate need to get close to people, but because closeness terrifies them (remember that as an infant the caregiver was scary), they end up rejecting any intimacy by accusing those close to them of doing something hurtful. They can view themselves as victims, and they certainly were in childhood, but as adults they tend to be unaware of how their own behavior contributes to their unhappiness.

They have a really difficult time in any kind of relationship, whether it involves work, friendship, family, or love. The manner in which they tell stories of their childhoods can reflect their chaotic reasoning, and at times they have flashbacks and tell the stories as if they were actually reliving them.

For the purposes of this book, I will describe and refer to secure, avoidant, and ambivalent attachment in the following chapters. Disorganized attachment characteristics are much more complex and require a more in-depth discussion, which is beyond the scope and purpose of the information presented in this book.

### Earned Secure Attachment

There is good news! Neurobiologists have discovered that we can change our brains, create new neural pathways, and learn to treat ourselves with love and compassion. We can learn to trust others, the world, and ourselves. We can make sense of what happened to us as children and know that the way we were treated stems from our caregivers' shortcomings and is not an indication of our worth. We can learn how to regulate our emotions and go from a dysregulated state to a regulated state without our world coming undone. We can learn to respond and not react and to form healthy relationships that are supportive and reciprocal. This is referred to as *earned secure attachment*. In later chapters, I will teach you techniques to help you attain earned secure attachment and become the human being you want to be.

## What Is Your Attachment Style?

It is important to identify your own attachment style because it profoundly affects your life, whether you are consciously aware of it or not. It also provides a deeper level of understanding into your beliefs, thoughts, and reactions and those of the people around you. If you are interested in getting a formal attachment style assessment, you'll need to contact a therapist trained in giving and scoring the AAI. Refer to the "Resources" section in the back of this book for contact information.

The following questions will help you ascertain generally whether you have secure attachment, are more on the avoidant side, or are more on the ambivalent side. You may have characteristics of two or all three attachment styles, but notice if one is predominant. Keep in mind that this is just a simple guide to give you an idea of your attachment style. It is not meant to unequivocally determine which category you fall into.

In response to the following questions, circle Y for yes or N for no.

## Part 1

1. Do you turn to your partner for relief from distress?     Y  N
2. Is your partner the first person you go to when something good or bad happens?     Y  N
3. Are you able to go from a calm state to a distressed state and back to a calm state without much interpersonal stress?     Y  N
4. Are you able to move easily from being alone to interacting with other people?     Y  N
5. Do you believe people are generally dependable?     Y  N
6. Is it easy for you to ask for help?     Y  N
7. Is it easy for you to depend on your partner or on others?     Y  N
8. Do you feel secure in your ability to deal with situations as they come up?     Y  N
9. Do you find it easy to get close to people?     Y  N
10. Is it easy for you to be affectionate with your partner?     Y  N

If you answered yes to six or more of these questions, chances are you fall within the secure attachment continuum.

## Part 2

1. Do you feel abandoned when your partner leaves to go to work?  Y  N
2. When you're upset, do you need to call someone to calm down?  Y  N
3. Do you have a hard time being alone?     Y  N
4. Do you believe that your partner or friends forget about you when you are not with them?     Y  N
5. Do you feel hurt when other friends go out without you?     Y  N
6. Do you have all-or-none thinking? For example, do you often think, "I'll never find a job I like" or "No one will ever love me."  Y  N
7. Do you feel the need to be around people a lot of the time?     Y  N
8. Are you afraid that your partner will forget about you?     Y  N
9. Do you often feel that something bad is going to happen?     Y  N
10. Do you get angry or upset when your partner is more than ten minutes late?     Y  N

If you answered yes to six or more of these questions, chances are you fall within the ambivalent attachment continuum.

### Part 3

1.  Is it difficult for you to keep eye contact with people?        Y  N
2.  Is it difficult for you to ask for help?        Y  N
3.  Is it difficult for you to trust people and open up?        Y  N
4.  Do you get startled easily?        Y  N
5.  Do you feel safer when you are alone?        Y  N
6.  Do you feel intruded upon when someone walks into the room?  Y  N
7.  Is it difficult to let people do things for you?        Y  N
8.  Do you usually hug with one arm?        Y  N
9.  Is it difficult for you to open up to your partner?        Y  N
10. Do you keep secrets from your partner?        Y  N

If you answered yes to six or more of these questions, chances are you fall within the avoidant attachment continuum.

***Your attachment style:*** _____

_____

_____

Now that you have identified your attachment style, you can go on to understand how it affected your developing brain. As you will see, some of your behavior is a *reaction* to how your brain was programmed to function, given your childhood experiences, as opposed to a *response* from your genuine self. There is a difference between an automatic reaction, which is mostly unconscious and is based on how your brain was programmed by childhood experiences, and a well-thought-out response, which is conscious and based on who you truly are and what you want in your life today as an adult.

# Conclusion

We are biologically programmed to attach to another human being from the moment we are born. The attachment style we develop, based on how sensitive our primary attachment figure was to our needs, is not a pathology or a diagnosis; it is a state of mind. I would love to see a world in which we could announce our attachment styles like we announce our names, not to label or diminish one another but rather to have a deeper understanding of the people in our world. If I understand that my partner is on the ambivalent attachment continuum, I won't take personally his need to call me and connect throughout the day. This will free me up to treat his need to connect with compassion and not to view it as controlling or suffocating. What a relief that would be!

In the interest of practicing what I preach and not keeping you guessing about the attachment style the psychiatrist was discussing on my trip to Tahiti—the one that described me and allowed me to make sense of myself:

Hi, my name is Dr. Shirley, and I come from an avoidant attachment style. Through many years of training, therapy, and self-discovery, I am happy to announce that I have pretty much earned my secure attachment wings. (I don't particularly like the term *earned secure attachment*, so I added the word *wings* because it does feel very liberating and free.) This is not to say that I never read into something that isn't there, always find it extremely easy to ask for help, or don't ever feel the *need* for alone time. However, I am more aware of my assumptions and behaviors and can readjust them a little easier now. I believe that learning and evolving is a lifelong process, and I will continue to learn and grow through my experiences and interactions.

As Dan Siegel says, "It's not what happened to you as a child, it's how you make sense of what happened to you." I share this information not so we can point fingers and blame our parents; this is not a "hate your mother and father" book. I share it with you so you can have a deeper understanding of who you are and why you behave and think the way you do. If learning this information requires you to work through some pain and hurt feelings from your past, then do so with honor and respect. The look of relief on my patients' faces when they are truly able to see their parents as human beings with their own shortcomings, and not the beacons of unconditional love we fantasize that they are supposed to be, is priceless. They can then begin to depersonalize and understand that their parents' behavior was not a reaction to their being defective, unlovable, or unworthy. I am certain at that point that they are on the road to earning their secure attachment wings. The ability to love your parents, but at the same time to feel angry with some of the things they did that affected your sense of self, is a necessary step in the healing process. The capacity to hold both love and anger toward another human being is invaluable.

## End-of-Chapter Exercise

Get to know yourself at an attachment level. The purpose of this exercise is not to blame anyone from your past. I guarantee that a heartfelt "I'm sorry" from a parent will help your current and future relationship with him or her, but it will do nothing for the past and the damage it may have caused you. The exercise is also not meant to define or label you; we are complex and cannot be reduced to definitions or general characteristics. However, understanding the way you attached to your primary caregiver and other adults in your childhood will allow you to understand yourself in a more profound way. Notice your reactions, feelings, and beliefs, not with judgment but with curiosity. How close do you feel to your partner? Do you look him in the eyes when you're making love? How long has it been since you were in a relationship? Are you understanding the "whys" better given this information?

## Chapter One Takeaway

If you have or interact with children, treat them with love, take care of their needs, and get to know them for the human beings they are, not who you want them to be. Spend quality time interacting with them. Quantity is less important. Help them navigate through their feelings. If they're feeling sad or mad, let them have those feelings and just validate them. Repairing is as important as doing it right the first time. If you lose your temper with a child, repair the damage right away by apologizing, validating her fear, admitting that you were wrong, and doing it better the next time. Notice the child's attempts to connect with you and try to make her feel "felt" by you. This will make a lifelong difference in her life. The dishes can wait; no one will remember if you did them at that moment or not. If your children read this book as adults, what do you want them to say about the way they were parented? What attachment style do you want them to have?

# 2

# Attachment and Your Developing Brain

*We do not see things as they are,*
*We see them as we are.*
—The Talmud

## The Story of Amanda

Karen and Michael had been trying to get pregnant for almost two years. Karen had given up on the idea and was a little relieved. She had been promoted to a position she really enjoyed that had her working long hours. She didn't feel she had enough energy to give to a baby. However, just before she was going to talk to Michael about it and start taking birth control again, she found out she was pregnant. When Amanda was born, Michael took a three-month paternity leave from his job. Karen went back to work three weeks after giving birth because she did not want to jeopardize her new position. Michael took over the responsibilities of caring for Amanda. When he went back to work, they hired a full-time nanny. Karen got home from work right before Amanda's bedtime. Sometimes she gave Amanda her last feeding and put her to bed, but many times she was too preoccupied with things at work or arguments with Michael. It was easier to let the nanny do it. Michael traveled extensively for work and could not be a stable presence in the home.

By Amanda's first birthday, it was clear that she preferred the nanny over Karen or Michael. Karen understood that Amanda spent more time with the nanny, so she tried not to take it personally. She attempted to spend more time with Amanda in the evenings and on weekends, but Amanda often got fussy, and sometimes Karen didn't have the patience to deal with it.

When Amanda was almost three years old, Karen and Michael started having problems communicating. They argued a lot, often in front of Amanda. When that happened, Amanda would cry, run into her room, and hide under her bed.

When Amanda was four, her world came crumbling down. Karen and Michael got a divorce, and the nanny quit. Amanda had to get used to seeing her daddy every other weekend, but only when he wasn't traveling, and she had to become familiar with a new nanny. Karen delved deeper into her work and spent less time with Amanda, often getting home after Amanda was asleep.

Amanda would become very clingy when Karen got home from work. At bedtime she would get irritable, no matter what Karen did, which usually resulted in Karen yelling at Amanda and Amanda crying herself to sleep. This situation annoyed Karen, but she assumed it was due to the divorce and didn't worry too much about it.

Amanda did not feel safe. She was being primed to develop ambivalent attachment due to the sporadic availability of her mother, the unpredictability of her father's schedule, the sudden loss of her first nanny, and the upset in her household. Throughout the book, we will follow Amanda and learn how her ambivalent attachment affected her beliefs and the way her brain developed, promoting dysfunctional patterns of behavior as well as a fear of failure. We will see how these unconscious behaviors permeated all areas of Amanda's life.

# The Brain and How It Works

Researchers studying brain development have come to the conclusion that the infant's brain is designed to be influenced and shaped by the experiences encountered in its environment. In his book *The Developing Mind*, Dan Siegel supports John Bowlby's theory of attachment by demonstrating how our attachment patterns become hard-wired in our brains, and how this hard wiring determines how we experience the world and how we behave in it. Our early life experiences create certain neural pathways in the brain, forming connections that are specific to each one of us.

Because the brain of an infant is malleable, it is imprinted, for better or worse, by the emotional and social interactions experienced from birth. This imprinting is like ski tracks that are left on fresh snow, eventually becoming hard-wired into the brain, creating neural pathways that influence our behavior and beliefs as we grow into children, and then adults. While infants are able to find ways to survive whatever they encounter in childhood, they are not naturally able to successfully deal with all of their experiences and interactions. If an infant's caregivers are sensitive and attuned, the infant can feel safe and develop an ability to shift between tense and calm states without too much stress. If the caregivers are insensitive and misattuned, the infant will develop defense mechanisms to survive childhood. These survival mechanisms should not be confused with resilience. Infants are not born with a capacity for true resilience. They are born with a capacity for survival. This distinction is crucial in understanding the long-term effects of attachment.

Studies show that our early experiences can also influence which genes get activated and which stay dormant. We each have our own genetic make-up, and our experiences do not change our genetic sequence, but they do influence the expression of our genes. This concept is huge. It suggests that, for the most part, our experiences can be just as influential in our lives as our genetic make-up.

You can begin to see how important experiences are to the developing brain. The sensitivity of the adults in a child's world, especially the person who holds the primary attachment position, will greatly influence how different parts of the brain function and connect to one another. Every part of the brain plays a critical role in how we think and behave. Understanding the significance of these parts will give you a clearer picture of how attachment styles affect the developing brain, how attachment styles become hard-wired—and how they can be reversed. Let's start with the right and left hemispheres of the brain.

### The Right and Left Sides of the Brain

The brain is that three-pound organ in our skull *and* the nervous system that runs throughout our body. The brain is divided into the right and left hemispheres. Each hemisphere of the brain develops at different times and has different functions. The right side is known to be more creative, intuitive, subjective, and visual. It understands nonverbal communication such as body language, eye contact, tone of voice, and facial expressions. People who are right-brain dominant tend to look at the whole picture. That is, they are interested in the meaning of an overall experience as opposed to the details. The right brain specializes in images, is artistic, and loves poetry and art. Emotions and gut feelings stem from the right side of the brain and can cause emotional reactions that have not been well thought out. Often, when right-brain dominant people speak, they know what they want to say but may have some trouble finding the right words to describe it. They can go with the flow easily, allowing for more spontaneity in their lives. Only the right hemisphere has a map of the body, so right-brained people have an easier time getting in touch with the sensations in their bodies but can also be overwhelmed by them. The right side is the keeper of autobiographical memories, which are memories of ourselves at different moments in our lives—for example, our tenth birthday party, high school prom, or first kiss. Consequently, when you ask people a question about an event in their past, they will tend to look to the left, activating the right side of their brain to help them recall the event, stimulating those memory circuits. If you notice them looking to the right, they may be telling an untruth, as looking to the right activates the left side of the brain, stimulating the logical circuits, which they would need to do to make up a story.

The left hemisphere is more linear, logical, and literal. It is interested in cause and effect and likes to dissect things in order to understand them.

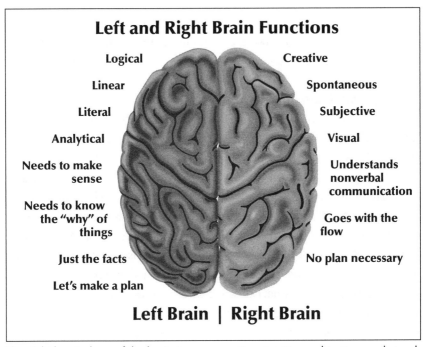

## Left and Right Brain Functions

**Logical**                                    **Creative**

**Linear**                                     **Spontaneous**

**Literal**                                    **Subjective**

**Analytical**                                 **Visual**

**Needs to make                                Understands
sense**                                        nonverbal
                                               communication

**Needs to know
the "why" of                                   Goes with the
things**                                       flow

**Just the facts**                             **No plan necessary**

**Let's make a plan**

## Left Brain | Right Brain

The right hemisphere of the brain is more creative, intuitive, subjective, and visual. The left hemisphere is more linear, logical, and literal. When balanced, these specialized functions enable us to choose the best response for the situation at hand.

It likes to analyze and needs to make sense of things; ambiguity is not a friend to the left hemisphere. People who tend to be left-brain dominant enjoy planning out their days, years, and lives, and leave little room for spontaneity. They are detail oriented and like facts. The left side of the brain is about approaching challenges and figuring out a solution. Resilience is a left-brain function. So when we notice that a child is being "resilient" after the death of a parent, she is in left-brain mode, since she might not fully understand death or have anyone to help her navigate and identify her feelings, a right-brain function. Resilience can often be a survival mechanism and not a healthy response.

Living only from the right brain can feel like emotional quicksand, and living only from the left brain can feel like an emotional desert. A balance between the two hemispheres allows us to use the best side, or a combination of both, for whatever life throws our way. It is imperative to understand how both sides of the brain work so we can invite the left side in when the right side is taking over or invite the right side in when the left side won't budge.

### The Reptilian Brain and Survival

The part of the human brain known as the reptilian brain has been with us for more than 300 million years. It is the most primitive part of the brain. It is called the reptilian brain because it is the same brain that reptiles possess. Evolution has not changed it much, since its function is essential for survival. The reptilian brain contains the brain stem and cerebellum. Damage to this part of the brain causes death, because it regulates breathing, heart rate, digestion, elimination, body temperature, reproduction, and balance. It also regulates the fight, flight, and freeze responses: the ways the body reacts to danger or threats. When we feel threatened and our life is in danger, a signal goes to this part of the brain. In seconds it decides if escape will require running (flight) or fighting. If running and fighting are not options, either because we are trapped or because these responses could worsen the consequences, the brain goes into a freeze response—a "deer in headlights" mode—which causes the outside of the body to become immobilized. Because the threat is still present, however, the inside of the body is still activated. The heart is pumping fast and breathing is shallow and hurried. If it is believed that death is near, the body goes into collapse mode, which slows down the heart, at times so much so that it can result in death. The reptilian brain is purely instinctual and programmed to react; it does not think.

### The Limbic or Emotional Brain

The middle section of the brain, still considered part of the primitive brain, wraps around the reptilian brain and is called the limbic brain. It is also called the emotional brain and is found in all mammals. This is the part of the brain that allows for the capacity to bond with others. While this may be obvious to some of you, I would like to point out that since this part of the brain does not exist in reptiles, they cannot bond with you. However, it is a psychological fact that once you name something, you automatically feel bonded to it. So the next time your friend insists that her pet snake

Greta loves her, you can enlighten her with your knowledge. If she insists and allows Greta to roam freely around the house, check on your friend often because to Greta, your beloved yet naïve friend is simply her next meal waiting to be enjoyed. Serously, it's a true story, so warn her.

The limbic region includes the thalamus and hypothalamus. The thalamus sits on top of the brain stem. It can be viewed as a relay station for nerve impulses carrying information from our senses (except smell) to the brain. It receives this information and determines which signals to forward to the higher-functioning parts of the cortex. The cortex is the last layer of the brain and the most evolved. The thalamus sends some nerve impulses from the body to the cortex because this is the "thinking brain." It is involved in making rational decisions. Let's say you burn your finger on the stove. The thalamus picks up this sensation and sends it to different parts of the brain to help you make the best plan of action given what has just occurred. The thalamus also helps regulate sleep and waking. The hypothalamus is responsible for our resting states, maintaining body temperature, nutrition, and hydration. It also controls the autonomic nervous system, which includes two branches: the sympathetic branch and the parasympathetic branch.

These two branches work together to keep us in a balanced state—not too aroused and not too relaxed, making adjustments whenever the balance is disturbed. The sympathetic branch is activated when something either internally or externally causes us to become aroused, kicking us out of a state of homeostasis. The word *aroused* might cause you to immediately think about sex, and you are right. This branch of the nervous system is activated during orgasm. However, arousal also involves any kind of excitement or fear and gets us action-ready when we detect danger.

During sympathetic activation, the neuroendocrine system is stimulated. It releases hormones to get the body ready for the fight-or-flight response. The adrenal glands release adrenaline, cortisol, and other stress hormones to give you the best chance for survival. Your heart rate goes up to increase blood flow to your muscles. The extra blood flow speeds up the conversion of glycogen into glucose, which provides energy, getting your legs and arms ready to work at maximum capacity to run or fight. Blood flows away from the digestive tract, as you don't want to be wasting energy digesting the sandwich you just ate while you're trying to run away from that huge dog that is chasing you. Blood also flows away from the skin, since you don't need blood there when you're running or fighting, which is why you turn as white as a ghost and feel cold when you're scared.

Your lungs and your pupils dilate to ensure that you get enough oxygen while you're running or fighting and are able to take in as much as possible visually—to be aware of that punch coming at you from the left. While all this is happening, your sweat glands open to cool your body down, which is why your hands and underarms get sweaty when you're stressed, and the flow of saliva is reduced, causing a dry mouth when you're scared. The contraction of your bladder and rectum is inhibited, causing you to urinate or defecate on yourself if the fear is severe enough. It is now easier to understand how and why our bodies deteriorate if we are under constant stress. Many gastrointestinal ailments and immune deficiencies are stress related and can be alleviated as soon as you learn to decrease your stress levels. More on this in chapter 5.

Once the brain determines that the threat is over, or that the activation was not caused by a real threat, the parasympathetic branch's job is to return your brain and body to a resting, calm state so you can recover. It slows down your heartbeat, stimulates the flow of saliva, increases blood flow to the digestive tract, constricts the pupils to allow for closer vision, and increases blood flow to the skin. This branch is also involved in the erection of the genitals, which explains why it is difficult to get in the mood when you're stressed.

*The freeze response and collapse mode:* As explained earlier, if fighting and running away are not viable options, the body has a third option to save you from danger: the freeze response. Under threat, the sympathetic branch of the autonomic nervous system is stimulated. But if we realize that we cannot fight off the threat or run away from it, the parasympathetic branch takes over, causing a sudden brake effect on the nervous system, stopping us cold and immobilizing our bodies in hopes of deterring the predator. This response is likened to playing possum, or playing dead, as a predator is less likely to attack a target that appears dead. The problem is that the threat is still there, so the sympathetic branch is still stimulated, causing your heart to continue to beat fast and your breathing to be shallow and hurried, resulting in a "deer in the headlights" type of paralysis. Have you ever been so scared that you couldn't move, but your heart was racing one hundred miles an hour? Remember that hide-and-seek game you played with friends as a kid? How hard was it to stay still and keep quiet so that you wouldn't be found, all the while feeling like your heart was going to jump out of your chest? If you were anything like me, all of a sudden you had an incredible urge to urinate, making the standing still part even harder. I never understood why that happened. I recall getting upset that, all of a sudden, I had to desperately go to the bathroom and interrupt my fun game. Now I know that the excitement of being found stimulated my sympathetic nervous system, causing the contraction of my bladder to be inhibited. Who knew?

If the threat continues, our brain assumes that death is near, causing an overwhelming helplessness to take over. Our bodies go into collapse mode. During collapse, two things happen: the body floods with endorphins, the body's natural morphine, causing a numbing effect; and dissociation occurs, allowing us to observe what is happening from outside of ourselves without feeling it. News stories tell of people who say they didn't feel pain when they were being mauled by bears, although they could see what was happening. Our brains are very kind to us in that way. However, research shows that we have body memory. Therefore, what the mind doesn't remember, the body does.

*The amygdala and hippocampus:* Also included in the limbic system are the amygdala and hippocampus, which play important roles in processing information that comes from our body. Both parts are involved in learning, emotion, and memory, but in very different ways. The amygdala processes memories of our emotions. Its basic function is to examine information that comes in through our senses by way of the thalamus and to decide if a situation is dangerous or not. If you experience a lot of things that scare you when you are growing up, your amygdala becomes very sensitive. As an adult, you might interpret danger in situations that are not dangerous. I call the amygdala our threat detector. If the amygdala decides that something is dangerous, it sounds an alarm signal, and the body prepares for danger. I envision it as a submarine telescope that is always scanning for potential threats.

The hippocampus processes information in a narrative way, allowing us to remember the how, when, and where of an event. It is involved in organizing and storing an event into memory, what is referred to as autobiographical memory, which is stored in the right brain. The hippocampus forms new memories and connects them to our emotions and senses, such as smell and hearing. Under threat, the hippocampus malfunctions, causing the event to be stored in a fragmented way. Some parts of the event are stored in our conscious memory, referred to as explicit memory, and some parts are stored in our unconscious memory, referred to as implicit memory. This explains why we may not remember certain events in our lives or can recount a horrific story from the past as if we were reciting the ingredients of a recipe. Studies show that people with a history of trauma have smaller hippocampi and larger-than-average amygdalae.

### The Neocortex, or Thinking Brain

The neocortex wraps around the limbic brain. It is the top layer and evolutionarily the newest part of the brain, referred to as the thinking brain. This layer is responsible for many functions, such as attuned communication, emotional balance, information processing, self-awareness, empathy, fear modulation, insight, intuition, and morality. The neocortex is also responsible for executive functioning, which is the ability to connect past experiences with present action, allowing us to manage time, make plans, strategize, organize, pay attention to and remember details, and keep track of more than one thing at a time. Conceptual thinking—thinking "outside of the box" or in an abstract way—is also a neocortex function. The neocortex is the part of the brain that can weigh the consequences of risky behavior, helping us determine if risks outweigh benefits in a specific situation or vice versa. In addition, the neocortex is involved in delayed gratification.

If you have teenagers, you will immediately notice that these are the exact skills they lack. There's a reason for that. Studies show that the teenage brain does not have sufficient connections between the neocortex (the thinking brain) and the limbic area (the emotional brain). These connections do not increase until approximately age twenty-five, which explains why teenagers sometimes make void-of-all-thought decisions. As it turns out, they are mostly reacting from their emotional brains and not from

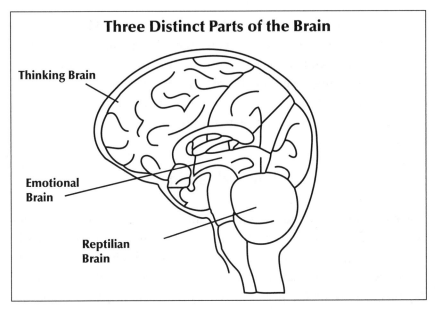

## Three Distinct Parts of the Brain

**Thinking Brain**

**Emotional Brain**

**Reptilian Brain**

In addition to the right and left sides, the brain is also divided into the reptilian brain, the most primitive and old part, the limbic system or emotional brain, possessed by all mammals, and the neocortex, or thinking brain, the youngest but most evolved part of the brain.

their thinking brains. I have no explanation as to why some adults act the same way, however, knowing this, I conclude that the connections that were supposed to increase and strengthen by age twenty-five for some reason got bypassed! The neocortex also controls voluntary movement and helps us regulate our emotions by inhibiting and managing the more primitive layers of the brain.

In their book *The Whole-Brain Child*, Dan Siegel and Tina Bryson refer to the neocortex, or thinking part of the brain, as the upstairs brain and the more primitive part, the emotional part, as the downstairs brain. They use this imagery so parents can help children learn about their brains to understand what happens when emotions take over. Siegel and Bryson explain that sometimes when you have big feelings, you can't make good choices because the downstairs brain takes over and blocks the upstairs brain from entering. Personally, I believe this is a great image for adults as well, to help us understand, in a basic way, what happens when we stop being present and become reactive. Simply put, the downstairs brain takes over and disconnects from the upstairs brain. We call this situation a tantrum in children and "I don't know what came over me, but I lost it" in adults. For me, understanding this piece alone helps me gain perspective when I notice myself losing it. I know in these moments that I have to find a way to reconnect the upstairs with the downstairs.

## Survival Is King

The most important and continuous function of our brain is to scan for danger. Studies show that the brain scans for danger every five seconds. That is how our species survived. Not only does the brain consistently scan for danger, but it also learns to anticipate what is dangerous based on past experiences. Given this, the brain is considered an *anticipatory organ*. The fear circuitry in our brain will never let us forget anything negative that has happened to us. Negative experiences stick to our brains like Velcro, holding on to the information and generalizing it to other situations to ensure our survival. Positive experiences tend to stay in the background, as our survival does not depend on them. This is why that one negative review on your job performance will stand out and be remembered more than the ten positive reviews you received. The brain's job is to keep us alive. It's all about survival! I'd beg to differ with the brain, however, in that our *emotional* survival does depend on our ability to hold on to positive experiences.

Imagine two cavemen friends out for a walk in the woods. An hour into their walk, a tiger appears. Never having seen a tiger before, they notice it but keep walking and talking. Suddenly, the tiger pounces on one of the cavemen. The other one screams as he watches his buddy being mauled and his fight-or-flight responses take over. He runs away horrified. Panting, he tells his tribe all about what just happened. From that day on, anytime he sees the colors orange and black, his heart starts racing and he takes off running as fast as he can without thinking. Thanks to the process of evolution, that reaction does not involve thought, because pausing and wondering if in fact that orange-and-black thing is really a tiger like the one that ate his buddy could cost him his life. When the brain perceives danger, the threat signal goes off, and we immediately go into fight, flight, or freeze mode. In this state, all communication between the primitive part of the brain and the neocortex—the thinking part—is cut off. We just react.

There are other bodily reactions whose original purpose was survival of the species as well. Have you ever wondered why some people get the uncontrollable urge to vomit when they see someone else vomit? Picture this: a caveman tribe is feasting on a recent kill that unbeknownst to them is past its expiration date. After his third bite, father caveman starts to vomit, which causes most of the tribe to spontaneously do the same. This seemingly spontaneous act of purging ensures the survival of the tribe, since the meat might be toxic. Have you ever wondered why you cannot even look at a bottle of tequila for weeks after getting sick from drinking too much of it? Your brain doesn't know that you chose to indulge. It just knows that something that looks and tastes like tequila caused you to get sick and throw up. It could have been toxic. It could have killed you. Your brain develops an aversion to tequila so you stay away from it in an attempt to keep yourself alive. That's your survival instinct at work.

Group exclusion also falls under the survival-of-the-species umbrella. Being excluded from a group is a very painful experience. Being rejected by a sorority, getting shunned by the popular kids at school, or not being asked to go for drinks after work with the gang hurts our feelings and causes us to feel sad or even mad. We can always depend on our concerned yet uninformed friends and family members to say something like, "It's okay. It's not that big of a deal" or "You didn't like them anyway." However, being socially excluded stimulates the *pain* circuits in our brains, causing these rejections to physically hurt, literally. Studies show that the pain circuits get stimulated even if you get excluded from a social group you didn't want to join. This indicates that social belonging is necessary for survival, which makes sense when you consider how vulnerable you would be walking alone in the savanna, versus walking with a group of your caveman family and friends, providing more pairs of eyes to help spot the approaching tiger. Ever wonder why public speaking is so terrifying? (Most people fear it more than death.) Let's break it down: If I am speaking in front of a group of people, I run the risk of saying something they will not like or agree with. That may cause them to boo me off the stage, laugh at me, or simply shun me. If they don't like me, I will be excluded from their group and I will be alone, and being alone increases my risk of dying. The brain can be quite melodramatic!

Since you now have this information, you can tell your well-meaning friends and family, "It *is* a big deal that I didn't get asked to drinks after work. It *does* hurt. It's *supposed* to hurt; that's how our ancestors survived. Just validate my feelings, and I'll be okay!" They will have no idea what you're talking about, but I'm sure they'll do what you ask to prevent your further downward spiral.

Survival brain mechanisms were extremely helpful and necessary in caveman days, when most of our stress was about *physical* survival: getting eaten; dying from poisonous berries or toxic meat; mistakenly walking into the black cave where the bears live and not the gray one where your family lives; and other very real-life threats. However, times have changed. In the modern world, stress can be brought on by things such as deadlines, traffic, and bad work reviews. Although compared to being eaten by a tiger, these stressors seem minor, they activate the same fear circuits in the brain. Once those circuits are activated, the brain cannot tell the difference between traffic and a tiger. Once the amygdala decides something is dangerous based on fact or memory, it does not have the ability to differentiate or categorize in order of degree. Unfortunately, the amygdala does not have the capacity to say, "Okay, traffic ahead, level 2 on the stress scale, no need to lose it or get your underwear in a knot. Hungry tiger coming at you with only dinner on its mind, level 10 on the stress scale, GO, GO, GO!"

Knowing your body well enough to notice even the slightest change is key to not overreacting in any situation. Being aware of your body will allow you to notice your heart beating faster, your chest getting tight, or your stomach feeling nauseous, which usually signals the threat response coming on. Once the threat response is activated, in a split second, the thinking part of your brain goes off-line and you are reacting from your emotional brain. Identifying the beginning of the fight-or-flight physical response will afford you enough time to keep your thinking brain engaged and to make a conscious decision about whether or not you are in a life-threatening situation. When danger is not immediate, if you can keep your thinking brain engaged, you can "short-circuit" the debilitating threat response, stop yourself from reacting, choose an appropriate response, and get yourself back to a balanced state.

I had a personal experience with this one day when I was working with a family in their home and about to start a family group session. We were all choosing our seats in the living room. As I was about to take my seat, I noticed the middle son sitting there with a huge snake wrapped around his neck. I am afraid of snakes, but until that moment I didn't realize how deep my fear ran. I felt my knees get weak and suddenly noticed my heart racing. I knew I had a split second to engage my thinking brain before my body went into collapse. I started talking to myself: *Okay, just get up and walk into the other room. Just keep walking, just keep walking.* Thankfully, everyone else was distracted by the twins fighting for one of the chairs, so I had some time to figure out my next move.

I decided to use a technique called systematic desensitization, where you use short exposures to the feared object to diminish the fear. I stood in the hallway and waited until my heart slowed down. Then I walked to the doorway that led to the living room and peeked at the snake, who was now about twenty feet away but looking in my direction and sticking out its little tongue as if to taunt me. I noticed that my heart started to race again, and I retreated back into the hallway. I did this four more times until my heart didn't race anymore when I looked over at the snake, who was still looking my way, taunting me. I proceeded into the living room and took my seat. I noticed that my heart began to race a bit at this point, but not as much as when I first noticed the snake. In the calmest voice I could muster, I asked the son to put the snake away.

If you're wondering why I said I had to engage my thinking brain before collapse took over, it was because apparently, my fear of snakes is so grand that my body was going to bypass fight, flight, *and* freeze and was a split second away from going into collapse, which our bodies will do when the fear is so great that we believe death is imminent. When fear is at its peak, our nervous systems can only take so much and we collapse, which we commonly refer to as fainting. Imagine the scene: the therapist who is there to help the family faints at the sight of a snake. Nice! Did I mention that *perceived* threat can get the fight, flight, freeze, or collapse reaction going too?

## How the Brain Interprets Threat

We perceive information from outside ourselves through our senses—sight, hearing, touch, taste, and smell—and we perceive information from inside ourselves through our viscera, or guts. As you now know, danger is the first thing our brains are designed to look for. If a threat is detected, the thalamus sends this information to two areas. First it goes to the amygdala, or threat detector, as I like to call it, which incidentally is also called the fear organ because if it is removed, a person does not experience fear. As soon as the amygdala receives the signal, it quickly determines whether the threat is real. During this decision-making process, the sympathetic branch of the nervous systems starts to mobilize and you may feel some activation because your brain still isn't sure if that spot on the carpet is just a spot or a spider.

The information is also sent to the thinking brain for a second opinion: "Is that really a spider?" The higher brain structures in the thinking brain help the amygdala assess whether it is a spot or a spider. Once the thinking brain determines that it is a spot and there is no threat, it sends a message to the amygdala: "Calm down. It's only a spot of wine on the carpet." The parasympathetic branch takes over, allowing the body to metabolize the hormones that were released during the sympathetic activation. It takes approximately eight to ten minutes for adrenalin to be metabolized.

In a person with a history of abuse, the amygdala is disproportionately reactive to small stimuli. This reactivity causes higher brain structures in the thinking brain to disconnect, rendering them unable to influence the amygdala to calm down, triggering a fear response. The amygdala's danger signals cause the sympathetic nervous system to prepare the body for fight or flight, flooding the brain with stress hormones and causing you to load your rifle to protect yourself from that spot of wine on the carpet. The emotional brain takes over as it is disconnected from the thinking brain.

Unfortunately, there are many people who walk around with an over-active amygdalae. This overactivity is sometimes felt as anxiety. Anxiety is caused by a continuous feeling of fear, whether conscious or unconscious, real or imagined. If you're feeling anxious, you're afraid of something. Thus your amygdala is on overdrive. This something could actually be nothing in the present, but if you've experienced many fearful events in the past, your amygdala is programmed to always be on the ready, with an inability to differentiate past threats from present calm. Your amygdala is always ready to sound the alarm and save you from the tiger lurking around the corner.

A patient of mine, Lillian, suffered from profound anxiety and said it was ruining her life. I explained to Lillian how her brain worked. We talked about how her amygdala was basically doing its job, however, because she had suffered so much abuse and unpredictability in childhood, her amygdala was basically on overdrive and on high alert at all times. Her nervous system felt like it was under the constant threat of danger, thus Lillian walked around in a perpetual state of anxiety. She spent a few sessions getting in touch with her anger at the unfairness of it all. But I also wanted Lillian to view her amygdala as an ally that just happened to be working overtime. We discussed different ways she could imagine giving her amygdala a break. We imagined her amygdala going on vacation or falling in love with another part of the brain (love always being so distracting), so that Lillian could feel small moments of calm in her otherwise anxiety-ridden world.

One day Lillian told me about a dream she had had the night before. In her dream, she was in Las Vegas with her friends, and they all decided to go to the hotel lounge for a drink. As she described the dream, Lillian started laughing. She said that a really creepy guy wearing a white polyester pantsuit, like John Travolta in *Saturday Night Fever*, with his shirt unbuttoned to his navel and gold chains around his neck, approached her and asked if he could buy her a drink. At this point in the story, Lillian began to laugh so hard that she couldn't talk and in between fits of laughter, she said, "Then he said his name was Francois Amygdala!" Apparently, she was so disgusted with her overactive amygdala that in her dream her amygdala had turned into a seedy lounge lizard. That visual got me laughing right along with her.

For Lillian, understanding how her brain worked and why it worked that way made a huge difference. It freed her up to feel more compassion for herself, since she understood that her brain was just trying to keep her safe, given the land mine she had grown up in. The humorous visual of her amygdala as Francois, the seedy lounge lizard, allowed her to feel more in control of her anxiety. I taught her to become an expert in her body sensations. Lillian got into the habit of noticing her body and when she felt her heart beating fast and her breathing getting shallow, she knew anxiety was coming on. Realizing that there was no tiger lurking around the corner, she'd immediately say to herself, "Calm down Francois. I'm safe."

## How We Remember

In his book *The Developing Mind*, Dan Siegel says, "Memory is more than what we can consciously recall about events from the past. A broader definition is that *memory is the way past events affect future function*. There are two types of memory: implicit, or procedural memory, and explicit, or declarative memory.

### Implicit Memory
Research has shown that before babies learn to talk, they have the capacity for remembering. They get excited when they see or hear a familiar face with which they have had positive interactions and cry when presented with a toy or a person with which they have had fearful interactions. This is called implicit memory, a type of memory that is not conscious. Implicit memory uses brain structures located in the primitive brain, in particular the amygdala. Consequently, it does not require us to be conscious of remembering or retrieving information, as we would a phone number.

Implicit memories are stored without conscious awareness and cause infants to begin to develop mental models of how the world works. Studies show that from the very beginning, the mind is able to create generalizations from experiences. This means the brain begins to anticipate what will happen next. If we have had a fearful encounter with a furry animal, the next time we see a furry animal, we will feel scared and attempt to protect ourselves by running away. By a child's first birthday, such repeated patterns of implicit learning are deeply encoded in the brain.

Infants with secure attachment have had many nurturing, attuned, and sensitive experiences with their caregivers, allowing an expectation of a safe environment to be formed. This expectation is encoded implicitly in the brain, and a generalized representation of what to expect from others is solidified and anticipated. An implicit memory is formed; namely, I can trust others and the world is a safe place.

Infants with insecure attachment experience less predictability, with possibly frightening and/or emotionally distant caregivers, creating an expectation of an unsafe environment filled with uncertainty and fear. This too is encoded implicitly in the brain, creating a very frightening internal world for the infant, imprinting the implicit (nonconscious) belief that people are disappointing and not to be trusted and that the world is not a safe place.

The effect that implicit memories have on us as adults is that anything can trigger them—a smell, a look, a color, a sound. Because we don't have a conscious recollection of the implicit memories, they do not feel like memories, so we can find ourselves reacting but not knowing why. If you were repeatedly hit with a blue paddle while your mother was making coffee, the color blue *or* the smell of coffee could trigger a feeling of fear and an urge to run or fight back. You might not recognize the feeling of fear but might notice your heart beginning to race or your palms getting sweaty, indicating that your sympathetic nervous system has been activated and your body is preparing to go into fight-or-flight mode.

### Explicit Memory

Explicit memory is the memory that most of us refer to when we talk about remembering. Explicit memory allows us to recall experiences from the past. It is separated into semantic (or factual) memory and episodic (or autobiographical) memory. Semantic or factual memory relates to facts we remember, such as numbers, letters, and state capitals. Episodic or autobiographical memories relate to the self at a particular time in the past—for example, your ninth birthday party. We are conscious of remembering and retrieving this type of memory. The hippocampus and parts of the thinking brain are responsible for the ability to have explicit memories. The memories begin by a child's second birthday, as these brain structures begin to mature.

If an experience does not produce too much fear, the facts of the event, processed by the hippocampus, will merge or consolidate with the emotional memory of the event, processed by the amygdala, which will result in you recalling the event itself and how you felt during the event. If stress or fear is involved, this process gets messed up, and the memory does not get stored in a consolidated manner.

Stress has a profound effect on memory. When we are under stress, our brain releases hormones that suppress the function of the hippocampus, which is involved in encoding explicit memories about emotional events, such as the day you brought home your first dog, your high school graduation, or getting your first driver's license. However, these same hormones do not affect the amygdala, which specializes in the processing and storing of emotions into implicit memory. They only affect the functioning of the hippocampus, causing us to process memories in a fragmented manner. Parts of an experience—for example, the facts of an event—will be encoded in explicit memory, but the emotions we felt while experiencing the event will not be consolidated. They will get stored in our implicit memory bank, allowing us to tell the horrific details of a traumatic experience without batting an eye. The emotional reaction to the traumatic event is encoded in the implicit memory bank, while the story—the event itself—is stored in the explicit memory bank. The two are not integrated. When the stress proves to be too much, hippocampus functioning is completely suppressed, and the amygdala takes over. In these cases both the story and the emotional aspects of the traumatic experience are encoded in implicit memory. This explains why every time you see a Doberman pinscher you panic, not consciously remembering that at five years old you were bitten by one.

Right out of graduate school, during my internship at a hospital, I ran a group with eight fairly functional women who were in a voluntary outpatient program dealing with issues associated with depression. There are many ways to run a group. To get the group going, some leaders like to begin with a theme that most group members can relate to. Others, like my supervisor and me, preferred the more silent approach, in which nothing is said, with the idea that whatever needs to happen will eventually happen and start the group off. You have to be very comfortable with silence and it allows for different characteristics of people's personalities to get triggered. Usually, the peacemaker of the group said something to get the conversation going, which irritated those who didn't like her goody-two-shoes tactics. The person who was most uncomfortable with silence sometimes started off, making an anxious attempt at a joke, which often fell flat but broke the ice.

On one particular day, I started the group as usual, by not saying a word. I'm still not sure if it was Let's Try to Make Dr. Shirley Really Uncomfortable Day or not, but no one else said a word either. Five minutes, ten minutes, fifteen minutes passed, and not one person said a thing. Thankfully, I'm very comfortable with silence because of my avoidant attachment, so I was in my own little world, probably visiting a Greek island, and I was able to stay calm. Twenty minutes into the silence, a group member named Trina spoke in an angry voice about how ridiculous this was, how bad a group leader I was, and how she was not learning anything or getting any better. Ordinarily, because I was so new at this and I questioned myself all the time, my insecurities would have taken over and I would have panicked. Instead, I think Sigmund Freud took over my brain. In an unrecognizable, calm voice I said, "What's going on inside of you right now?"

Trina went on to describe her anger as rage. I asked her to notice where she felt the rage in her body, and she immediately said her stomach. She described the rage as hot lava boiling up inside her. I asked her to close her eyes and focus on that sensation of hot lava boiling up inside her and just see what happened next. I knew her body was telling her something, and although having her focus on it could have made it worse, I felt it was important to see if she could figure out the message her body was sending. This is a skill I'm eternally grateful for having in my tool belt and one you will learn in chapter 5. I asked her to simply notice if the bubbling lava moved, got worse, or dissipated, or if a thought, image, or memory popped up.

After a few minutes, she suddenly opened her eyes and said, "It's my mother!" She proceeded to tell us how her father left her and her mother when she was six years old. She described having a very loving relationship with her father, who used to pick her up every day after school and, as they walked home, made up stories about adventures they would have together. After he left, her mother became depressed and was quick to anger. When her mother was angry with her, which could be for anything, she would stop talking to her. One time her mother did not talk to her for five days. You can imagine how utterly terrifying it would be to be a six-year-old who was abandoned by her father and left with a mother who gave her the silent treatment, essentially abandoning her as well.

The silence at the beginning of group triggered the implicit memory of how angry Trina felt about her mother's silence. Understandably, as a child she did not feel safe getting angry with her mother, because that might cause more silence, only terrifying her more. The terror from her mother's silence caused her hippocampus to malfunction, fragmenting the memory, sending the story of it to her explicit memory bank, a story she had shared with the group on other occasions. However, the anger she felt toward her mother had been stored in her implicit memory bank. The silence triggered her implicit memory, and that anger came to the surface without her knowing why she felt so angry when it seemed as though nothing significant had occurred. It is not uncommon for anger of this nature to be directed at the therapist, a concept we call transference. She had transferred the anger she unknowingly repressed toward her mother onto me. Now that doesn't mean that I wasn't a bad group leader, but because the anger was so intense and spontaneous, it was clear that even if she didn't like my group leadership skills, it pointed to something else going on inside of her.

Any time a reaction goes above and beyond the event at hand, it usually signifies that it has touched something inside that has more to do with unresolved feelings from the past, and not the present circumstances. Trina's ability to focus on the sensation in her body allowed the memory to pop up, causing the implicit memory to become explicit, thus integrating the memory. This is not to say that she would never be triggered by silence again, but if she were, she would know the "why" of the trigger and could now make a choice about how to respond without just reacting—a skill that I'm sure has served her very well.

The meaning of words is also related to our own personal brain firing patterns stored in implicit and explicit memory. When I think of the word *ruler*, I automatically get mental images in my head of my school, my father's drafting table, and the Bonaventure Hotel. Why the Bonaventure Hotel? Well, it was my first job right after high school and one year, the CEO gave all employees a big, heavy, gold-colored metal ruler with a picture of the hotel on it. I still have mine; I'm not sure why.

My friend Randy, on the other hand, thinks of the word *ruler,* and his heart starts to beat very quickly. For a split second, he becomes immobilized. When Randy was a kid, his father hit him with a ruler as form of discipline. His father kept the ruler on his desk and ordered Randy to get it when the need for discipline arose, just to add a little sadism to the mix. In Randy's brain, a ruler was associated with pain and was therefore scary. Because he couldn't run or fight back, he would freeze. This association between pain, fear, and the word *ruler* can be traced to a specific neural firing pattern in Randy's brain that does not exist in mine.

## Attachment and Brain Development

The brain goes through various critical periods of growth spurts, which can be detected by our behavior and developmental milestones from infancy to adulthood. Based on all of the wonderful and valuable brain research in the last decade, we now know that the brain is plastic. In other words, we can change the connections that have been formed by our experiences, regardless of age. Our brains are not like cement, and you *can* teach an old dog new tricks!

### The Brain and the Infant

In a baby's first two years, the growth and maturation of the right hemisphere is most active. When the caregiver is sensitive to the infant's needs during this time, she is stimulating the development of important right-brain functions that include the ability to adapt and cope with novelty and stress, the ability to regulate arousal and self-soothe, and the infant's overall emotional well-being. All experiences in the first two years of life are stored in the implicit memory bank, which begins to set the foundation for how the infant will function in the future.

At two months of age, the part of the brain that processes what we see is developing, so visual experiences will affect how this area of the brain matures. Communication during this time then is through the mother's gaze. When a mother looks at her baby and the baby looks back, the face-processing areas of the right hemisphere are activated. This gazing "exercise" lets the infant know she exists because at this young age infants have not developed a sense of self. The only way they know they exist is by being seen: "If someone sees me, I must exist." Additionally, the infant learns about herself and her worth by what is mirrored in her mother's gaze. Consequently, the self is borne out of the interactions within relationships. Because the limbic system (which contains the amygdala, the threat detector part of the brain) is maturing at this time, imagine the difference between what is being activated and imprinted in the brain of an infant with a mother who gazes into her baby's eyes with love, curiosity, and a smile ("I exist, I am loved, and I belong in this world."); the brain of an infant whose mother looks at her baby with a worried, depressed, or angry expression ("I exist, but people are not happy that I am here, so there must be something wrong with me."); and the brain of an infant who is never gazed at ("I don't exist."). A well-known saying among brain scientists is, "Neurons that fire together, wire together." In other words, the areas of the brain that are stimulated together become a patterned reaction that, as the years go by, turn into well-traveled, automatic paths. For the infant who wasn't seen, this may manifest into an adult whose life revolves around bringing attention to himself in order to ensure that he is "seen."

Have you ever noticed that an infant as young as two months old will intensely study her mother's face, especially her eyes? I often see this when a mother is feeding an infant. While eating, the infant studies her mother's face, as if trying to memorize every little detail. It is a shame that many mothers miss out on this crucial bonding moment by propping the bottle or talking on the phone while feeding their babies.

The tone of the mother's voice, her gestures, the movements of her hands and body, and her facial expressions also influence the development of the baby's right brain. Touch is very important at this age. Studies show that massaging infants of any mammalian species decreases the concentration of stress hormones and leads to less reactive behaviors and improved learning. Gestures, touch, facial expressions, and eye contact (gazing) are all right-brain modes of communication and activate the right hemisphere of the infant's brain. Secure attachment for the infant then is formed through direct right-brain to right-brain communication.

Let's imagine that Maria, a nine-month-old infant, begins to cry. Sonia, her mother, has no idea why, which is understandable since a nine-month-old can't tell you directly what's wrong. Sonia approaches Maria and in a soothing voice says, "What's the matter my sweet Maria?" Sonia picks Maria up and cradles her with gentle movements and a concerned look on her face. Sonia continues to talk to Maria as Maria starts to calm down. Sonia attempts to give Maria a bottle to see if she is hungry. Maria turns her head. Sonia, attuned to her daughter, gently says, "Okay, you're not hungry. Let's take a look at your diaper." As Sonia puts Maria down, they catch each other's eyes. Sonia smiles at Maria, causing Maria to smile back. Sonia takes this opportunity to expand this moment of positive arousal and begins to kiss Maria's stomach. This causes Maria to laugh and kick her arms and legs in excitement. Sonia does this two more times and then notices that Maria looks away. Sonia takes the cue that Maria needs a break from the stimulation. She stops, smiles, and continues to talk to Maria in a soothing voice while checking her diaper.

From a brain standpoint, something caused Maria to feel stress. She was either hungry, felt uncomfortable because her diaper was wet, got scared, or simply needed to feel a connection with her mother. At this age, babies have body sensations, not emotions. If they sense a shift in their bodies that doesn't feel right, it activates the right hemisphere, because the map of the body is located in the right. This activation evoked a sudden increase in the sympathetic branch of Maria's nervous system, resulting in an increase in her heart rate and blood pressure. Maria then began to cry, because that is the only way infants can communicate distress. Sonia's timely response caused a calming down in Maria's sympathetic nervous system, stimulating the parasympathetic branch to come on line, regulating Maria's system and bringing her body back into homeostasis.

Feeling calm allowed Maria to mimic her mother's smile. Noticing this, Sonia engaged in an activity she knew Maria enjoyed, the kiss-the-tummy game, which amplified Maria's feeling-good state. This shared interaction of play after stress expanded Maria's capacity to cope with future stressors. This sequence was experienced by Maria's brain as: "An activation of threat is followed by a calming sensation, which is then followed by a connection and a bonding experience." With repeated experiences of this type, this sequence will imprint in Maria's brain and allow her to tolerate stressful experiences in the future, because she will know implicitly that relief will soon follow.

This sequence can also be interpreted as nurturing Maria's sense of self-worth by demonstrating that she is cared for enough to be calmed and lovable enough to be connected with, strengthening her sense of belonging in the world. As this sequence is repeated, it becomes encoded as what Maria believes about her value and can anticipate and expect from the people in her world. Consequently, emotions won't scare her, because she knows that emotions are temporary and that she has internal and easily accessible external resources to help her through them. A secure attachment is forming and developing.

Right-brain development is experience-dependent. In other words, for the right brain to develop, it needs to be stimulated through human interaction. This is why the Walt Disney Company was sued for advertising that its Baby Einstein videos helped with language development—in other words, promising customers that their babies would learn to talk sooner. Studies show, however that watching TV is a two-dimensional activity that does not stimulate the brain. Consequently, they found that the Baby Einstein videos actually slowed down language development. Only three-dimensional activities have the capacity to stimulate the brain; live human interaction is a three-dimensional activity. Touching and hugging are activities that promote brain growth and are of the utmost importance during this stage of brain development and attachment. If interaction is minimal and an infant is left to fend for himself, the right side of his brain will become inhibited and development will be stunted. What is believed to happen is that the need for stimulation shuts down, planting the avoidant attachment seeds.

If you are an avoidantly attached adult, you may be extremely linear, logical, and literal because your right hemisphere is underdeveloped. Your capacity for encoding autobiographical memories, a right-hemisphere function, is impaired, which explains why people on the avoidant side of the attachment continuum have a difficult time remembering their child-hoods and often complain of having a terrible memory in general. People with avoidant attachment tend to be left-brain dominant, and people with ambivalent attachment tend to be right-brain dominant.

In ambivalent attachment, the right side of the brain is being stimulated because the mother does interact with the infant, at times being sensitive to what he needs. However, the mother is also insensitive and intrusive, and at times she disengages and becomes distant and unavailable. This situation is very frustrating and confusing for the infant, who becomes clingy in order to not miss an opportunity for attention from the mother, since he never knows when it will come. This devastating fear overwhelms the right brain. Continued experiences of this type dampen the development of the left brain during critical periods of left brain development. Consequently, the left brain's ability to calm down the right side is impaired.

### The Brain and the Toddler

Between the ages of two and four, the brain undergoes a large growth spurt. Right around two and a half, a part of the brain called the orbito-frontal region, part of the thinking brain and located toward the front, matures and develops. This area is believed to be important for attach-ment and is related to critical human functions. It connects crucial areas of the brain that have to do with social communication, regulation of emotions (the limbic area), empathy, and the capacity for knowing our-selves. The orbitofrontal region is said to function as a "reporter" to other areas of the brain. It basically gives information to other parts of the brain about the people in a child's world, creating a template for what the child is to expect of others. This template will also inform the child's sense of self. If the adults in a child's world were sensitive and responsive, his sense of self is healthy; if they were abusive or neglectful, his sense of self is tainted. As the child grows older and becomes an adult, his sense of self will affect his beliefs and behavior.

The senses are maturing, and by the end of this stage, children can pretty much see, hear, taste, touch, and smell at the adult level. The left hemisphere comes online, and this stage of development is marked by the acquisition of language. The left hemisphere, interested in the "why" of things, starts to develop, which explains why the word *why* becomes so prevalent in a toddler's vocabulary. This also explains why children of this age are so literal and have difficulty dealing with abstract concepts. Sarcasm, metaphors, and figures of speech make no sense to kids at this age.

At the risk of including a "TMI" (too much information) moment, I will share a very funny story that is a great example of the developing left hemisphere. My daughter, Sydney, was about four years old when she asked me why I did not sleep with underwear on. The question kind of caught me off guard and I flippantly said, "Because I like to let my butt breathe." About five minutes later, Syd came to me and said, "But Mom, butts don't breathe." I can only imagine her little brain trying to figure out how a butt breathes. Does it have a nose? Where is the nose on a butt? Maybe she even looked at her own little butt in the mirror and, at confirming that butts don't have noses, and therefore cannot breathe, came back to inform me that butts don't breathe! Just another Mother-of-the-Year moment. Try explaining what a figure of speech is to a four-year-old. Oh yes, I tried.

Developmentally, toddlers do not have the mental ability to think in complex terms. A three-year-old believes that as long as she stays out of her bedroom, it won't be bedtime. Because time is an abstract concept not yet understood at this age, the idea of bedtime is understood in terms of a more concrete place, her bedroom, which is why saying to a toddler at that age "in an hour" or "the day after tomorrow" is not helpful. If you have children, I am certain you have heard the question, "Are we there yet?" Did you feel baffled, like I did, when five minutes later they again asked, "Are we there yet?"

This stage of development is also filled with fantasy and magical thinking. It involves a lot of pretend play, which on the positive side allows children to believe in Santa Claus and the tooth fairy. On the not-so-positive side, the belief that there are monsters living in the closet or under the bed is just as real to them. Children at this age are also unable to take the point of view of other people and so they believe that everyone else sees the world as they see it.

### The Brain and the Child

Ages four to six represent a relatively slow brain growth period, mostly occupied with gaining experience and expertise in their newly acquired skills. The next fast growing brain stage is at age six to around age eight. Connections are being made between already existing neuronal groups. It is important to note that these new associations between networks can only be as sharp as the networks were when they were created and stood alone.

Nurturing secure attachment at this stage consists of being aware of where your child is developmentally and not expecting something that his brain is simply unable to handle. Instead of saying, "We are going to Disneyland tomorrow," it is better to say, "After you have dinner, you'll brush your teeth. After you brush your teeth, you will get into bed. After you get into bed, you'll fall asleep, and when you wake up, that's when we're going to Disneyland!" *Tomorrow* means nothing, but activities are concrete and have meaning to a young child's developing brain.

A patient once told me that his mother took him to a magic show when he was seven years old. Half-way through the show, the magician did the saw-my-assistant-in-half trick. The patient remembered that when he saw the assistant's body split in two, while her hand continued to wave at the audience, he was confused, sad, and scared all at the same time. He started to cry. He said that the assistant noticed him crying and kept waving at him, while sawed in half, which only made things that much more confusing. After the show, she came over to him to make sure he was okay and to show him that she was intact and in one piece. Obviously, the person who had planned the event did not know anything about the brain development of seven-year-olds!

Between eight and eleven years of age, children are able to start understanding logic and mental operations. Math gets easier, and they are able to put themselves in other people's shoes. However, they still have a difficult time understanding abstract or hypothetical thinking and still can't understand irony or sarcasm. Although eight to nine years is a slower growth period, at age ten the brain goes through another growth spurt, increasing connections and associations between neural networks while developing new skills. At this stage of development, children can use inductive logic, going from a specific experience to a general principle—for example, "My dog is friendly. Therefore, all dogs are friendly." But they have a hard time with deductive logic, using a general principle to figure out a specific event—for example, "All dogs are mammals. Therefore, my dog is a mammal." The mind is slowly starting to think in a more complex way. The next slow brain-growth period is from around age twelve to fourteen. This period is dedicated to practicing, perfecting, and consolidating new mental functions.

### The Brain and the Teenager

The teenage years are a pivotal time because the brain is going through a major reorganization, similar to that of a newborn. Additionally, there are fewer connections between the thinking part of the brain (the neocortex) and the emotional part of the brain (the limbic area) than in the adult brain. This is why teenagers truly believe that giving their friend a ride down the street on the roof of their car because they didn't fit inside is a good idea. Is your teenager's behavior starting to make sense? They are also more reactive because their amygdalae are running rampant without the thinking brain stepping in. Studies show that when teenagers are shown pictures of neutral faces, they tend to view them as negative or angry. In other words, teenagers are more reactive, which explains the "You're always mad at me!" accusation. This information is important to have because understanding your teenager's behavior and knowing that thinking takes a back seat to feeling and reacting in these years, is crucial to regulating your own arousal when your teenager is acting out. I know it helped take me to a place of understanding and compassion instead of frustration and the "What were you thinking?" place. Alas, she wasn't thinking. She couldn't. The connections weren't fully there!

Exposing the teenage brain to new experiences and challenges is important because, similar to the infant brain, connections made during this age will be imprinted. It is also a crucial "use it or lose it" time. Scientists estimate that the teenage primate brain loses about thirty thousand connections per second during these years. This is called pruning, as the weaker connections are eliminated and the stronger ones are kept and strengthened. If parts of the brain are stimulated, they will grow and connect. If they are not stimulated, they will die off. So it comes down to choosing whether you want your teenager to have a "sitting on the couch and watching TV" imprint to be strengthened or a "learning social skills and experiencing new activities" imprint to be strengthened as he moves forward into adulthood. Although navigating through social experiences causes some stress, it is essential for emotional and intellectual growth and development. Some challenges may become overwhelming, but a securely attached teenager with an internal ability to regulate her arousal due to the foundation set in the first two years of life can also reach out to her parents, teachers, friends, or relatives to help regulate her arousal, trusting that someone will be there to help. An insecurely attached teenager without the ability to regulate his arousal and who, additionally, can't trust that someone will be there to help, may become anxious or retreat into himself and isolate. So it is important for parents to encourage teens to socialize and to plan activities to get them out of their rooms.

If reading this has made you aware of the mistakes you've made because you didn't have this information and you are feeling the urge, as I did, to crawl into the nearest hole or jump off the nearest pier, fear not because repair is just as important as doing it right in the first place. Repair during the teenage years is of the utmost importance, since the brain of a teenager is about as malleable as that of an infant. However, repair works at any age and with any relationship. It is akin to owning mistakes in the moment and validating someone's feelings. As I mentioned before, our brain has evolved to remember the events perceived as threatening—that is, events that stimulate the sympathetic branch of the nervous system—in order to keep us safe. So if you repair as soon as you notice a shift in the other person that lets you know that what you just said caused anger, disappointment, frustration, or sadness, you will stimulate the parasympathetic branch of the nervous system and he will begin to calm down because he will feel understood by you. If repair happens immediately, the event will not be remembered as negative. The sympathetic arousal did not last long enough to flood the brain with stress hormones and what is most likely to be remembered is the outcome of the event, the feeling of being understood, losing the negative charge it would otherwise have had.

## It's All about Emotional Regulation

The healthy survival of an organism is dependent upon maintaining homeostasis in the face of internal body or external environmental stressors. It is important to point out that new experiences can cause stress as well. The brain likes what is familiar; new things and new experiences can produce enough stress to keep people from taking risks and keep them "inside the box," within safe limits. Attending to an infant's needs allows his brain to mature with the capacity to cope with stress, whether due to pain, fear, or novelty.

Keep in mind that the brain structures that help an infant cope are the same ones that help an adult cope, so the experiences an infant has with stress regulation has lifelong effects. Research shows that the most damaging effect of a mother's inability to be sensitive to her child's needs is the child's failure to develop the capacity to regulate his own emotions. And what are emotions? According to Jaak Panksepp (see chapter 1), they are simply a dysregulated nervous system!

When a mother is not sensitive to an infant's distress signals, the infant's nervous system reacts in two ways: hyperarousal followed by hypoarousal, or dissociation. In hyperarousal, the sympathetic branch is activated, which prompts the fight-or-flight response. The infant will cry, flail his arms and legs, and kick his feet—all attempts to get his mother's attention. However, the nervous system can only take so much activation. When it reaches a threshold, hypoarousal, or shutdown, occurs. The parasympathetic branch takes over, prompting the collapse response, which often leads to dissociation, or detaching from one's emotions, body, and immediate surroundings, because the world feels much too scary.

Initially, at the first sign of stress, the infant starts to fuss, then cry. If there is no one there to calm her, the crying intensifies and screaming ensues. The brain is flooded with stress hormones and panic sets in. This can result in the infant throwing up due to the intense level of dysregulation. Whatever the cause of the infant's dysregulation—a loud noise, you yelling "No" when she goes to touch an electric socket, her falling down and hurting her knee—repair occurs when you are there to calm her down. You are repairing the rupture in the homeostasis of the child's nervous system. This is what is meant by repair. When no one comes to help the infant calm down, terror is at its highest level. Since we are biologically programmed to survive, the body cannot stay in a dysregulated state for too long, so it shuts down. This switch from hyperarousal to hypoarousal, or dissociation, occurs when the infant's brain determines that there is impending danger that cannot be avoided and there is no way to escape. Helplessness sets in, and the infant surrenders to it in an effort to detach from an unbearable situation.

Repeated experiences of this type can create what psychologists call learned helplessness, where a perceived inability to control the outcome of a situation can cause someone to stop trying to better their circumstances. In other words, when an infant gets scared, he begins to cry. If no one comes, the crying intensifies, panic and terror set in, and the infant feels helpless in his environment. As an infant, he actually *is* helpless, and at that point his only recourse is to shut down and dissociate. If this sequence happens often enough—fear, crying, no one comes to sooth him—the infant begins to believe that he is helpless and will stop trying to better his situation by bringing attention to himself by crying. "I am helpless to whatever my environment brings" becomes a core belief that the passage of time will not change. In fact, the passage of time actually makes the belief in his own helplessness stronger, because the "helpless" circuit in the brain gets reinforced every time he feelse scared and doesn't do anything to help himself. It becomes a well-traveled path that he is not aware of but will follow automatically. It always baffles me when people say, "He's fifty years old. When will he get over it?" as if the passage of time somehow erases childhood traumas and beliefs without the need for any intervention or awareness. Age doesn't inherently bring awareness. I would be out of a job, and my profession would not exist, if on our eighteenth birthday, not only would we become adults in the eyes of the law, but, like magic, all bad experiences to that point would be erased from our

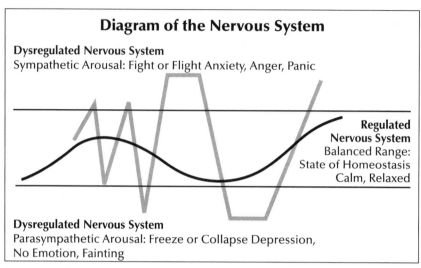

## Diagram of the Nervous System

**Dysregulated Nervous System**
Sympathetic Arousal: Fight or Flight Anxiety, Anger, Panic

**Regulated Nervous System**
Balanced Range:
State of Homeostasis
Calm, Relaxed

**Dysregulated Nervous System**
Parasympathetic Arousal: Freeze or Collapse Depression,
No Emotion, Fainting

In a healthy functioning nervous system, the sympathetic and parasympathetic branches work together to keep the body balanced, or in a homeostasis state. If there is too much activation, the nervous system becomes dysregulated and can become hyperaroused, causing the fight or flight response. When this activation becomes too much for the nervous system to handle, hypoarousal, or shut down, occurs, causing the freeze and collapse response.

memory banks and we would all be able to enjoy the benefits of secure attachments from then on.

Learned helplessness affects people's ability to seek out new strategies and different choices when faced with environmental demands that alter their homeostasis. People with learned helplessness view themselves as victims of their circumstances and their environments. You've probably heard people say things like, "I've tried that before, and it didn't work" or "What's the point? It won't change anything." Trained elephants are sadly a great example of learned helplessness. When they are young, they are tied to large trees with heavy chains. Initially, an elephant will try to walk away. But after a while, it realizes that it can't. Once that happens, the trainer replaces the chains with a rope, which the elephant could easily break. However, the elephant will no longer try to walk away. It has learned, "Why bother. I've tried it before and it doesn't work." The elephant's past experience is now dictating its belief system. It has learned helplessness.

### *Ambivalent and Avoidant Attachment and Emotional Regulation*

As stated earlier, infants and children who are being primed for ambivalent attachment have a parent who can sometimes repair their dysregulated nervous systems, sometimes cannot figure out how to calm them down, and sometimes are unavailable for repair. These infants and children appear fussy and clingy and are not easily soothed or calmed. As adults they tend to be hypersensitive to their emotions because they never learned how to calm or soothe themselves. This causes their amygdalae to go into overdrive and they feel as if they are in a constant state of anxiety. Some may be stuck in the past, worrying about past choices and what they could have or should have done, in a desperate attempt to fantasize a present calm. Some are stuck in the future, worrying about every tiny decision in hopes that making the right one will provide calm. Such worries stop these people from moving forward and only serve to perpetuate the belief that there is something wrong with them.

Constant worry without an opportunity for rest prevents the brain from strengthening its "calm" circuits, diminishing its ability to tolerate a calm, regulated state. If your childhood was full of worry, or if you weren't taught how to calm down, you have a huge capacity for anxiety. Even though it doesn't feel good, it is a familiar state of mind. Your capacity for a calm state of mind is limited. You must build up or expand your "container" for a calm state in order to tolerate it. In extreme cases, some people experience relaxation-induced anxiety. They are so used to feeling anxious that feeling calm, even for a little while, will in and of itself cause them to jump back into anxiety.

Infants and children who are being primed for avoidant attachment have caregivers who are not there physically and/or emotionally. To protect themselves, they learn to bypass hyperarousal or attempts to get their mother's attention and automatically go into hypoarousal, or shutdown. They stop trying to use others to help them feel safe and instead dissociate from their feelings to cut themselves off from intense emotions that they do not know what to do with or how to navigate through. This process causes an erroneous belief that they don't have needs or emotions, and do not need anyone for connection or to provide comfort.

For adult avoidants, almost everything is "no big deal" and, in truth, most of the time, they do not know what or how they feel about things. But the reality is: Emotions are an inescapable part of being human. If you don't feel emotions, it doesn't mean you don't have any. It just means you have become skilled at burying them very deep. Because avoidants don't have the faintest clue what to do with emotions, they don't like drama, don't care for surprises, and they try to avoid conflict at all costs in an attempt to keep their nervous systems in a homeostasis state. This also explains why transitions are difficult for them, as transitions cause the nervous system to go in and out of homeostasis. But avoiding emotional dysregulation does not give the brain an opportunity to develop the circuits necessary to transition from dysregulated states to regulated states with ease.

## Do Not "Ferberize" Your Children

Dr. Richard Ferber, a well-known pediatrician, came up with a method to teach infants as young as four months old to "self-soothe" and go to sleep on their own. The strategy is to put your infant in his crib alone and leave the room, allow him to cry for a predetermined amount of time, enter the room, and pat his back. You are instructed not to pick him up and after a few minutes to leave the room again, this time for a longer period of time. Dr. Ferber advises that every night you wait for longer intervals of time before going into the room, even if your infant cries. He admits that at times, infants will become so upset that they will throw up. In such cases, he instructs parents to "*matter of factly*" clean up the child and leave the room. This process is supposed to continue every night until your child falls asleep on his own.

Unfortunately, this is still a very popular method, but it is, in fact, abusive. With the knowledge you now have about how infants attach and how attachment affects brain development, I am certain you can realize the absurdity and cruelty of this method. I would love to say that Dr. Ferber has revised his training method since learning about the latest brain research showing that allowing an infant to cry does *not* teach him how to self-soothe, but, rather, it reinforces the fear circuits in the brain. That is not the case, however, and he still believes that his method is valid.

We now know what happens in the brain and nervous system when an infant is afraid and his system becomes dysregulated. Dr. Ferber claims that eventually an infant will learn to self-soothe and will go to sleep on his own. But the only reason an infant quiets down after being forced to cry himself to sleep is because he is *dissociating*, not learning to self-soothe. If the only thing I accomplish in this lifetime is getting people to stop using the Ferber method with their infants and children, I will feel as if my mission is complete.

Imagine the terror an infant feels when he is alone in a room crying, needing the person he is supposed to trust and who is supposed to protect him and love him unconditionally, but that person comes in for only a few minutes, and then leaves. When the parents comes in, the parasympathetic branch of the nervous system is stimulated, sending a signal of relief throughout the infant's body: "Yes! I'm safe! Thank you, thank you, Mommy and Daddy!" But when the parents leave again, within seconds, the sympathetic branch of the nervous system is stimulated, sending the signal: "Oh no! Why did they leave? I'm scared! I'm scared! I'm in danger!" This process sends such confusing and conflicting signals to the infant that it is no wonder he collapses and dissociates after a few days of this method. Oh, and the only reason why the infant or toddler *appears* fine the next morning when he wakes up is because the terror of the experience is stored in his implicit memory bank and he doesn't have a conscious recollection of it—*not* because it did not affect him. The traumatic effects of this experience can show up later as sleep disturbances in adulthood.

Emotional dysregulation does not feel good. Whether you're feeling too upbeat due to excitement or agitation, or too down due to depression or numbness, the need to feel regulated or to stay in a regulated state becomes vital. If you have not learned how to regulate yourself in an adaptive way, you might unknowingly use other methods that may or may not be healthy. Socially isolating is a way to keep ourselves in a regulated state. In other words, if we do not engage with others, we do not have to worry about dealing with the anxiety that shyness can bring, or the emotions that misunderstandings can create. Yawning is also a way to regulate our nervous system. Although yawning is associated with drowsiness or boredom, it actually increases your heart rate by 30 percent; it's the nervous system's way to wake itself up. I find that sometimes when I'm working with people of avoidant attachment and we begin to discuss a topic that is too activating (keep in mind avoidants tend to go into hypoarousal, or collapse, so they can shut down easily), they unknowingly start yawning in an effort to bring themselves back up from a collapse-like state.

Drugs are often used to self-medicate in an attempt to regulate the nervous system. Marijuana and alcohol are usually the drugs of choice for people who tend to be anxious, as they calm them down. Cocaine is the drug of choice for people who tend to be in more of a collapse state, as it helps to energize or wake them up. Cutting can also be a form of regulating the nervous system. Physical injury releases endorphins, our brain's natural painkillers, and induces a pleasant feeling, providing a temporary relief from intense feelings such as anxiety, depression, and stress. People who describe a feeling of emptiness or emotional numbness may use cutting as a way to stimulate their nervous systems to feel *something*.

These, however, are destructive and painful ways to regulate the nervous system, and they can often lead to other problems such as addictions. The key is to learn how to regulate your arousal in healthy ways, whether you need to calm it down if you are too aroused or stimulate it if you are too down. So, regardless of what life throws in your direction, you can keep yourself balanced. Regulation techniques will be taught in chapter 5!

## The Body Remembers Everything

Emotional regulation starts in the body. We have cranial nerves that connect the brain to the body. Research shows that only 20 percent of these nerves send information from the brain to the body; and 80 percent of the cranial nerves send information from the body to the brain. This means that information from our body informs our brain of how we are feeling. If my muscles are tense, my heart is beating fast, and my stomach is in knots, my brain is getting the message that something is wrong, I don't feel safe, and a threat may be near. Studies have demonstrated that when the body is tense, people interpret neutral stories as more negative.

Another study showed that when people were made to hold a pencil with their mouths, forcing the mouths to form a "smile," neutral stories were interpreted more positively. So even the muscles in your face will influence how your brain perceives what you are feeling, influencing a more positive or negative outlook.

### Somatic Experiencing Therapy and Stuck Impulses

The influence of the body on the brain became apparent to me one morning when I was sitting at a coffee shop, reading an article on Somatic Experiencing Therapy, written by its developer, Dr. Peter Levine. This type of therapy centers on the brain and nervous system. It uses the body as a guide to help restore emotional well-being. I was engrossed in the article, as I had just started my Somatic Experiencing Therapy training.

In the article, Dr. Levine explains that when we perceive danger, the nervous system gets activated. It prepares the body to go into fight-or-flight mode. If we are not able to complete the fight-or-flight response, perhaps because we are trapped, the freeze response takes over. This activation in the nervous system produces a kind of energy. If this energy is not released, it gets stuck and becomes locked in the nervous system and the body's muscles. Unless it is given the opportunity to be released, this locked energy doesn't go away. It gets buried deep within the body. Since 80 percent of our cranial nerves send information from the body to the brain, the brain is consistently getting messages from the body and is very aware of what the body is feeling at any given moment. If, due to stuck impulses, the body is consistently telling the brain that there is danger, we can find ourselves in a perpetual stressful state. This constant stress stimulates the release of cortisol and other substances, which weakens the immune system and wreaks havoc on our physical well-being. You will learn how to release stuck threat responses in chapter 5. Getting to know your body and recognizing body sensations are important first steps in learning to release trapped impulses.

Adults can be more prone to responding to stress with either a fight, flight, or freeze response. This could be due to a variety of reasons, for example, temperament or an accumulation of stuck past experiences that required one of these responses. In other words, if as a child you found yourself in unsafe situations, where freeze was your only recourse because you couldn't defend yourself or run away, you may have an inclination to freeze in dangerous situations as an adult. There may be a fight-or-flight response underneath the freeze, since our body's natural initial reaction under threat is to fight or run away, but until you work through the freeze response, it will more often be your go-to reaction in dangerous situations. In the present, when a stressful experience triggers an old, "stuck" fight, flight, or freeze response, the old implicit memory piggy backs on the new, in-the-moment experience, causing us to overreact to the present situation. Implicit memories do not feel like memories because we are not conscious of them, so we do not realize that we are reacting to a memory in addition to a new event.

As I was reading Dr. Levine's article, the waitress stopped by my table to take my order. I ordered two eggs over hard. I asked the waitress to tell the cook to break the egg yolks, so the eggs would be cooked through, because I like my eggs very well-done. I then decided that telling the waitress to give the cook step-by-step instructions was a bit obnoxious, so I said that she should just ask him to burn them. She looked at me with a "You're kind of weird. They're just eggs" look and said, "Sure, no problem." I went back to reading my fascinating article.

Dr. Levine went on to explain that depending on how much trauma we have experienced, whether through abuse, neglect, accidents, medical procedures, or shock traumas (such as natural disasters or assaults), we can be stuck in fight, flight, or freeze responses. These responses can show up in the way we talk, the words we choose, our posture, and our reactions. Just as I started to read how to recognize when someone was stuck in fight, flight, or freeze, the waitress came by and put my food down. I continued to read that people who are stuck in fight mode will use language that describes an urge to yell or hit others when they tell stories. For example, they might say, "I wanted to tell her off" or "I was so angry I felt like beating him up." They will describe body sensations that feel like a volcano bubbling or erupting inside. Physically, their muscles are tenser, their heartbeats are faster, and their hands form fists more often than normal. They are in fight mode and can go there quickly. As I cut into my eggs, the yolk oozed out, which really grossed me out. I was annoyed, but

I didn't want to overreact. (Hello! Clue?) Ever so controlled, I pointed to the ooze and said, "I need this cooked more." The waitress took my plate and said, "Okay, no problem!"

I continued to read, but noticed that I couldn't focus because my mind kept going to thoughts of yelling at the waitress: "Did I not *tell* you I wanted the cook to burn my eggs? What part of *burn* don't you understand? Was I not clear?" Suddenly, I noticed my heart racing and my blood beginning to boil. I truly wanted to tell the waitress off as images of me yelling at her invaded my brain. It then hit me (yes, I'm a little slow) that my reaction was way over the top for what had just happened. I realized that what I had just read had my name written all over it.

*Being stuck in the fight response:* Having had some training in Somatic Experiencing Therapy and reading about it at that moment I knew what to do. I closed my eyes to go into my body because I had no idea why I was so enraged. However, I did understand that oozy eggs shouldn't have put me in that state. With my eyes closed, I first noticed my heart racing, and I decided to focus on that. Then my attention went to my hands, and I noticed they had formed fists. I thought, "Really? You want to hit someone because the eggs were runny? Really?" I noticed I was judging myself, so I went back to just focusing on my fists, which had straightened out. I noticed that my fingers were moving slightly. I heard a plate being put down on the table and opened my eyes to see my eggs and the waitress staring at me. I put a fork in the eggs and noticed that the yolk was still not cooked through. Because of the exercise I was taking myself through, I was highly in touch with my body. I noticed a bubbling volcano about to erupt in my stomach as soon as I saw the yolk, which was not runny but still not fully cooked. I mustered every ounce of control I had and said to the waitress, "A little more done, please." I immediately closed my eyes and went right back to noticing what was happening in my body.

This time I focused on the bubbling volcano in my stomach, and an image of me as a little girl came to mind. I was red in the face and angry as hell because I was not being heard. An actual memory did not come to mind—just the image of little me with this familiar erupting volcano in my stomach and this overwhelming desperate feeling of not being heard or seen and wanting to scream in response. As I noticed this image, I noticed my hands tingling. I started to imagine yelling at the waitress and hitting her, saying over and over, "Listen to me! Listen to me! I want my eggs burned! Well-done! Why won't you listen?" As I imagined yelling and hitting her, I noticed my body shaking—not in an extreme way, more internally, but certainly in a way I had never experienced before. I felt a tingling sensation down my arms and in my hands. I let myself feel this, realizing that my nervous system was releasing old stuck fight responses. At this point, I didn't care if my eggs were back or if anyone was looking at me.

Waves of shaking and tingling went through my body. As they started to subside, I noticed my heart beginning to beat more slowly. I began to take deeper breaths. I allowed myself to calm down and began to recall other times when I had not felt heard and consequently had not felt seen. I remembered how angry it made me feel. With much embarrassment, I admit that I have lost it over things as simple as undercooked eggs. In that moment, I realized how any event could trigger a reaction because of an unconscious implicit memory stuck in my body. Although the actual memory did not appear, I'm sure that yelling at or hitting my parents was not something I could have done. Even if I had gotten mad about not being heard, they were at best not sensitive to my feelings, which caused me to feel unheard and unseen. I hadn't had the opportunity to release the fight response, causing it to get stuck in my body. Those childhood experiences, although anger-provoking, did not scare me enough to bring the freeze response on, so I stayed in a stuck fight mode. According to Dr. Levine, for reasons that are still unknown, the shaking, trembling, and tingling sensation, even if very subtle, appears to be the nervous system's way of resetting itself. It happens as the nervous system shifts and comes out of shock.

After my enlightening episode was over, I felt a sense of calm and empowerment at this newfound information that came from noticing and tracking my body sensations and just allowing them to guide my attention. Upon opening my eyes, there sat my fully cooked eggs. The waitress came by and asked how they were. I answered with a huge smile, "They're perfect!" I felt compelled to apologize to her for all the things I had said and done to her in my mind, but I didn't want to seem even stranger than

I undoubtedly already seemed to her. I thought, "What she doesn't know, she doesn't know." I happily ate my very well-done eggs.

*Being stuck in the flight response:* People stuck in the flight response will make references to running away, escaping, and wanting to hide. This reminds me of the movie *Runaway Bride* with Julia Roberts. I wonder if the writer knew anything about being stuck in the flight response. People stuck in flight mode have nervous energy. They tend to be fidgety, moving their legs or feet while sitting, never quite feeling relaxed, always looking over their shoulders or always on the go. The associated sensation is one of feeling trapped and needing to "get out of here." When they tell stories, they speak of wanting to run away from it all or escape to a deserted island.

*Being stuck in the freeze response:* The freeze response takes over when fight or flight isn't an option. It is not a conscious choice; it happens when the brain perceives that there is no way out, but the threat is still there. Many times a fight-or-flight reaction is underneath the freeze. Once you release and "melt away" stuck freeze responses, you might find trapped fight-or-flight sensations, since fight or flight is the body's natural reaction to threat. Repetitive exposure to situations that cause the body to freeze results in problems storing information in the brain, given the fragmented way the hypothalamus stores memory into our explicit memory banks under stress. Thus people in freeze mode don't have a lot of memories—either from childhood or from the recent past. They might reference not wanting to move around, wanting to stay put, and not enjoying anything that takes them out of a frozen-like state. Their body sensation is one of numbness, and they feel disconnected. Other than feeling numb, they have a difficult time being aware of any body sensations. Many have no idea how to respond to the question, "How does that feel?" Often, a sense of helplessness pervades. Physically, they may often describe feeling cold and having cold hands or feet. They might lack muscle tone on their faces, with an overall flat expression.

### Body Sensations from Past Trauma

Stuck fight, flight, or freeze impulses are how the body remembers everything that has happened to us, even if our mind doesn't remember. The actual memory may not be one that can be put into words, but the body sensation and consequent emotions are there, waiting to be released. I now know that my nervous system was primarily stuck in the fight response although through this work, I have released stuck responses in flight and freeze, as well. My parents, unintentionally, were not sensitive to my needs and did not have the ability to help me navigate through my feelings, which led to enormous amounts of frustration and stuck responses. I understand now that they did not know how to navigate through their own feelings, much less help anyone else do it. I remember my father's parting words when I left for college: "Study hard and don't get into a relationship; emotions are a waste of time." And that, my friends, is but a mere window into what my childhood must have been like when emotions arose. Being of avoidant attachment, I do not have many childhood memories. By the way, I believed him!

I am now able to see that I was a very sensitive kid; I'm still a sensitive adult. However, before having this knowledge and the guidance to work through and release what was locked in my body and nervous system, any minimal frustration led to me yelling, which is part of the fight response. That was my go-to place, and I went there often, many times scaring the people around me. I isolated myself because I didn't like this part of me, and I did not feel in control of it. Having this knowledge and the ability to notice what my body is feeling, and therefore what my body is "saying," allows me to take a step back, keep the thinking part of my brain online, and choose a response as opposed to just reacting. This allows me to be the person I truly want to be, not the defended person I had become. Sometimes yelling is the best response; at times no response is the best response. The key difference is that it is a *chosen* response and not an automatic reaction. I gauge my progress now on these signs:

- how often I keep my thinking brain online when my body gets triggered, and choose a response as opposed to reacting from anger
- how often I realize that something that would have made me angry in the past does not make me angry at all
- how often I still get triggered and lose it

When I lose it, I know that repair is just as important as my initial reaction. Having the expectation of never getting triggered again, because theoretically I have the knowledge to get past it, sets me up to fail. I am who I am, came from where I came from, and was wired the way I was wired. It takes time to rewire the brain, and I know I contribute to that every time I respond differently than I would have before I had this information—when I was sleepwalking through life. The important thing is acknowledging how often it is *not* happening versus the fact that it still happens on occasion.

## Conclusion

Brain development at every stage is dependent on the previous stage. Think of it as similar to building a house. If the foundation of the house is faulty, everything that is built on it will be insecure as well. If a child is made to feel safe and loved, his primary innate need for self-preservation—to stay alive—is satisfied. He can then pay attention to other necessary external learning, such as exploring his world, walking, talking, and the other naturally unfolding developmental milestones. However, if a child does not feel safe because he does not trust that he will be protected, his brain will remain stuck in this early stage of development: staying safe, which will prevail over all other learning and disrupt his natural development.

With secure attachments, the parent is attuned to the infant which allows the areas of her brain that control arousal regulation to be well developed. Additionally, the infant learns that when she is distressed, someone will respond and take care of her needs. Interpersonal stress is low and, over time, because of her mother's response to her distress, the infant learns to regulate her own arousal state to calm herself down. When the infant's sympathetic nervous system is aroused, the mother's sensitive attention activates the infant's parasympathetic nervous system, calming her down. We learn to soothe ourselves by the way our parents soothed us. If your parent holds and comforts you when you are hurt, you learn that after feeling upset, you can feel safe again. You form a secure attachment. The right and left hemispheres of the brain develop in a balanced manner.

The thinking brain communicates well with the emotional brain. Stress hormones aren't being over-produced and running rampant. The fight, flight, and freeze responses aren't held for long periods of time before repair by a sensitive adult occurs. This repair restores the nervous system back to equilibrium. Consequently, as secure adults, we employ methods to self-soothe and are better able to deal with the stressors that come up in our daily lives. We are able to transition from states of arousal back to calm states in a smooth, minimally stressful manner.

With insecure attachments, whether avoidant or ambivalent, the infant may be abused, scared, or ignored. The sympathetic nervous system gets activated, and the fight, flight, or freeze response takes over. When there is extreme upset without any comforting, the child reaches a physiological threshold and the parasympathetic nervous system takes over, dramatically slowing down all body processes, resulting in collapse or dissociation in order to not feel pain. These nervous system reactions, without repair, wreak havoc on our bodies, and cause stress hormones to flood the brain. Stress hormones are toxic to the brain and damage brain cells. This repeated sequence causes the amygdala to go into overdrive, perceiving threat where there may be none, resulting in the person living in a hypervigilant state. The right and left hemispheres of the brain are not well developed and are not in balance. The thinking brain and the emotional brain do not communicate well with each other.

The insecure adult, whether avoidant or ambivalent, is operating in the world with a brain and nervous system that are primed to over- or under-react. He lives under the false assumption of constant, inescapable danger. This causes him to develop defenses that create an illusion of safety. However, this is the defended self, not the authentic self.

In the next chapter, we'll explore how our attachment style and consequent brain development affects our behavior, beliefs, and the defenses we use to create an illusion that keeps us feeling safe. Can you even imagine walking around the world feeling safe and calm? What would that look like? What would be different? What would be the same?

## End-of-Chapter Exercise

Ask a friend to say the word *no* slowly five times in a regular tone of voice. As your friend is speaking, just notice how your body feels. Do you feel tightness in your chest? Is your heart beating a little fast? Then have your friend, in the same tone, slowly say the word *yes* five times. Notice how your body feels again. More often, our bodies relax at hearing the word *yes*. The tense sensations we felt while the word *no* was being said suddenly become more apparent. This is an example of how the nervous system reacts to our environment. The word *no* activates the sympathetic nervous system, while the word *yes* activates the parasympathetic nervous system.

## Chapter Two Takeaway

Know that you can affect the brain development of your children and also rewire your own brain. Look at your children with a loving gaze. Try to communicate with your eyes: "I'm happy that you're alive and in this world." A loving gaze gives children their sense of self and belonging. Practice being sensitive to what your child is feeling, even if you don't understand it. Just name the feeling; that's enough for your child to feel understood. If you don't have children, practice this with the adults in your world. If you mess up, know that repair is just as important as doing it right in the first place. The best gift you can give to yourself and the people in your world is the ability to regulate your own nervous system. More on that later.

# 3

# How Your Brain Affects Your Behavior

*The mind is everything; what you think, you become.*
—Gautama Buddha

## Amanda Growing Up

Amanda was now a fifth-grader. Because of his travel schedule, Michael's every-other-weekend visits had been reduced to once a month or every six weeks. Neither Karen nor Michael was very involved in Amanda's school. They often missed open houses and other special events. When Amanda brought this to their attention, Karen usually said she had gotten caught up in meetings and simply forgotten. Michael told Amanda that she hadn't given him enough time to change his schedule. Amanda was tall and pretty, like her mother, but she didn't think so. She felt like the ugliest girl in the class.

Her nanny picked her up from school, and she did homework all afternoon. At night Amanda waited by the window. As soon as Karen got home, Amanda bombarded her with stories about school, the results of her tests, and other things she thought her mother would be proud of. Initially, Karen listened, but often she became irritable and short with Amanda. Soon Amanda went off to her room and sulked. Every night at around eight, Amanda got very clingy with the nanny, knowing it was time for her to leave. Once the nanny left, Amanda sat on the floor against the front door and cried. This behavior irritated Karen, who didn't understand why Amanda acted this way. After all, this had been the routine since Amanda was a baby. Karen figured Amanda was just doing it to get attention and that if she ignored the behavior, it would eventually go away.

Amanda worked hard in school to get straight A's. She hoped this would make her parents proud and want to spend more time with her. Unfortunately, it only caused them to believe that all was well and there was nothing to worry about.

Amanda's clingy behavior came from a fear of abandonment. She did not feel loved and was getting the clear message that she was forgettable and not worth her parents' attention. Additionally, she felt that other people's behavior, such as her father missing her school functions, was her own fault. She was being programmed to expect rejection when she tried to get close to people and to believe that she was easily disposable. Her amygdala was primed to see the danger of rejection all around her, causing her to behave in ways that guaranteed rejection.

## How the Past Affects Your Present

Past experiences affect adult behavior in myriad ways. Our view of our parents and their perceptions of us are among the most influential factors in adult behavior. Many psychologists believe that the same-sex parent teaches us how to be in the world, and the opposite-sex parent teaches us our value. How many women whose fathers were not around—emotionally or physically—date men who fear intimacy and won't commit? This situation is a direct mirror into the value these women place on themselves. They expect to be abandoned, so they unconsciously choose men who will abandon them or, at the very least, are unable to commit. By choosing this type of man, they reconfirm what they have been programmed to believe—that they aren't good enough or are undeserving of being loved by a truly loving and committed man, even though they may talk forever about how they wish they could meet a guy who wants to get married and have a family. How many women who were raised by a narcissistic father only date narcissistic men because they are accustomed to being devalued and ignored? They are operating on emotional autopilot.

How many people were told by a parent that they would never amount to anything, and lo and behold they don't? How many people were dismissed by a parent and grow up with a need to constantly tell people about their accomplishments to get the validation they lacked as children? How many people grew up with an alcoholic parent and end up marrying an alcoholic? These are all examples of sleepwalking through life.

To break the chains that bind you, it is incredibly important to understand how the people in your life and your experiences have influenced the beliefs you have developed about yourself, other people, and the world. In chapters 1 and 2, I gave you information on how these seeds were planted based on your attachment style and its influence on brain development. The beliefs that were formed as a reslt of this influence your behavior, what you react to, and what you do to protect yourself from perceived danger. In this chapter I show you how your nervous system is primed to react given the experiences from your past. The chapter also discusses defense mechanisms—psychological strategies we use to keep us safe and help us cope with reality. You know from the last two chapters that what is reality to you may not be reality to me, given the immeasurable differences of our past personal experiences. Consequently, the defense mechanisms we use to keep us safe and help us cope with our own perceived reality might in fact be getting in our way.

## The Nervous System and Your Behavior

To understand how the past affects the present, let's start with the nervous system. You know from chapter 2 that your amygdala, or threat detector, sends an alarm to ready the troops the moment danger is perceived (activating your sympathetic nervous system), getting your body ready to fight off the threat or to run away from it. How does the amygdala decide if something is threatening? Fantastic question! The answer? We don't always know. Many times reactions can be traced to a specific experience, but often we react to something and have no idea why. It can be *anything* given the countless experiences we have had since birth. Because the information stored in our implicit memory banks is out of our conscious awareness, virtually anything can set the alarms off. Add to that the fact that stimulation of the sympathetic nervous system is involuntary—in other words, we cannot control when it gets activated—and this can be a recipe for disaster. The good news is that we *can* control calming it down once we notice it has been activated, giving us a better chance of choosing a response and not reacting without thought. This is key. Tools to help you notice your body and calm down are provided in chapter 5. It is imperative that you become familiar with what makes you tick and why. The more you know about yourself, your attachment style, your brain, how your nervous system works, and the defenses you have developed given your experiences in life, the more you will be able to prevent being hijacked by your amygdala.

To put all these ingredients together, start by simply noticing your reactions to things. Awareness starts the whole process off. How do you feel when someone gets close to you and invades your personal space? Do you get nervous? How do you know? Does your heart start beating faster? Does your breathing get shallow? Do you look away? This is your nervous system telling you: "Warning! Danger! Too close!" If you are on the avoidant attachment side, this, or a version of this, depending on where you fall on the continuum, is how you would most likely react. You would notice your body relaxing when the person walks away and gets out of your personal space. Someone on the extreme end of avoidant attachment will feel a huge relief when another person walks out of their personal space. A person with mild avoidant traits will feel slightly calmer when someone walks away from them.

On the other hand, if you are on the ambivalent attachment continuum, the closer the person, the calmer you feel. As the person begins to walk away, your heart will begin to race, and you will begin to feel anxiety and panic. This is your nervous system saying: "Please come back. Don't leave me. I'm scared!" Those on the extreme end of ambivalent attachment have fantasies of *merging* with another to ensure that they will be with that person forever. On the other end, people with mild ambivalent traits might prefer to be in the company of others and might feel slight anxiety when they are alone.

### Moving Toward and Away

Given that the most important function of the brain is to keep us safe, our nervous systems are innately programmed to approach or avoid after assessing a situation and deciding whether it is safe or dangerous. Neurobiologist Steve Porges, a psychiatry professor at the University of Illinois–Chicago, studied this area in depth. He came up with the term *neuroception* to describe the nervous system's ability to continuously evaluate the environment for risk from a variety of external and internal cues outside the realm of our conscious awareness.

If our nervous systems have determined that an environment is safe, the social engagement system (part of the parasympathetic nervous system) activates. It keeps our defenses down, allowing us to feel calm, interact freely with people, talk, hug, look people in the eye, and feel good doing it. If we neurocept danger, the amygdala sounds the alarm, the sympathetic branch of the nervous system gets activated, and the body prepares for fight or flight. If we cannot fight or run away, we go into freeze mode. Keep in mind that neuroception means detection without awareness. As I mentioned before, myriad things can trigger the amygdala to perceive threat.

According to Porges, sometimes we have no idea why our nervous systems react the way they do. But whether or not we are consciously aware of it, there are reasons for our reactions. Our nervous systems react to certain situations based on our attachment styles, ages, temperaments, past experiences, and whether or not we have strong support systems. Are you one of those people who cannot be in confined places and is terrified by the thought of getting in an MRI machine? You *know* you're safe, but your body is telling you that you're not. Maybe you had a traumatic experience in an enclosed place at some point in your life that you don't consciously remember. Your body still reacts to it and gets triggered by the MRI machine, as if a tiger is ready to pounce on you. Porges points out that some medical procedures can trigger the fight, flight, or freeze response. At times doctors might need to hold patients down, particularly children, to give an injection or to do painful procedures such as surgeries or dental work. You might not recall that when you were five years old and given an anesthetic to have your tonsils removed, you had a feeling of being trapped right before the anesthetic took effect. Your body remembers, but your conscious mind might not. Now, as an adult, that MRI machine might be triggering the trapped feeling, and your body is responding to that implicit memory.

This would have been great information for me to have had years ago and reminds me of another "Mother of the Year" moment. My daughter, Syd, was about eight years old, and she was helping me make dinner one night. She was slicing a lemon, missed the lemon, and cut the web-like connection between her thumb and her pointer finger. The enormous amount of blood from the cut led me to believe that it was a serious injury, so I wrapped up her hand and drove her to the nearest emergency room. The doctor took one look at the hand and decided stitches were in order. Well, in case you have never had stitches, they hurt. To calm the pain, they insert a needle containing anesthetics *inside* the wound to numb the area, so getting the stitches won't be painful. This seems a little counterintuitive, but that's how it works.

The nurse came in with a huge needle and attempted to insert it into my daughter's wound. As you can imagine, the screams that came from my daughter's mouth were deafening, and rightfully so. What did Mother of the Year do? I proceeded to get on top of her, all the while yelling over her screams, "It's going to be okay," and *holding her down* while the nurse injected her open wound. The irony is beyond ridiculous. I am practically hiding under the table in sheer embarrassment as I type this. Knowing now what I know about the brain, I am horrified at the thought of her being held down by the very person she was supposed to trust. Her amygdala had pushed the panic button and prepared her body for fight or flight, while her own mother rendered her immobile. I have since forgiven myself; what we don't know, we don't know. The important thing is behaving differently once you have the information.

Which brings me to three years later, when Syd broke her arm while in-line skating on our street. It was her birthday weekend. She had friends over for a night of pizza, movies, and fun. I went outside to tell the girls to come in. Syd pleaded with me to let them stay out a little longer. She said, "One more time, Mom!" as she took off up the street in her skates. As she was skating back down, I noticed that she had picked up quite a bit of speed. I put my hands out and grabbed her hands to slow her down, but I ended up twirling around, and she slipped out of my hands, falling face first onto the street. I will spare you the gory details, but suffice it to say that when she stood up, her left arm was not the shape it was supposed to be. Again we drove to the emergency room. This time, however, I knew about medical trauma, and I was not having it.

The x-rays showed that she had broken both bones in her forearm, and they had lodged under her wrist. The doctor suggested very calmly that I bear hug her from behind, holding down her right arm while he pulled her left hand in an attempt to dislodge the bones and straighten her arm. Well, I got on my soapbox and proceeded to explain to him the traumatic effects of certain medical procedures, especially holding someone down and immobilizing her while her body is going into fight-or-flight mode given the perception of danger from a painful procedure. I insisted that she be given a general anesthetic, practically accusing him of being a barbarian for suggesting such a thing. He didn't buy it and in the most condescending tone he could muster said, "You know, anesthetic could kill her!" I responded in the most dramatic tone I could muster, "I'll take my chances!" After many kisses and "I love you's," they took her in, gave her general anesthesia, and adjusted her arm. Syd came out with a blue cast and a smile. Good one, Mom!

Trauma researchers agree that trauma is not in the event itself. An experience becomes traumatic when it overwhelms a person's capacity to cope, stimulating the primitive part of the brain to go into fight, flight, or freeze mode. This explains why some soldiers come home with post-traumatic stress disorder (PTSD) and some with similar experiences do not. It also explains why people react differently to potentially traumatic events, such as a bank robbery. Some people can chalk the experience up to being in the wrong place at the wrong time. Others cannot enter a bank again without feeling a sense of panic and reliving the event. PTSD can occur after you've seen or experienced a traumatic event that involves the threat of death or actual death. The symptoms can be around for years and may include flashbacks, where your body responds as if you were reliving the event; repeated nightmares; avoidance of anything or anyone that reminds you of what happened; difficulty sleeping; and hypervigilance, which means you are constantly scanning the environment, expecting threat, and can overreact to things, especially loud noises.

### Universal Reactions of the Nervous System

While it's true that we all react differently based on our life experiences, according to Porges, the nervous system has built-in, universal reactions to certain things. Sound is one of them. Low-frequency sounds or deep tones are interpreted by our nervous system as predatory and cause us to feel an urge to run away or brace for possible danger. This is why every scary movie includes music with low-frequency tones right before a scary scene. The music unconsciously puts the nervous system on alert or in fight-or-flight mode, making the scary scene that much scarier. Sorry Steven Spielberg, the cat's out of the bag! You may have noticed that babies cry when they hear low-frequency tones, sometimes even the voice of their own father. It is the low-frequency sound they are reacting to, not the person. If this is occurring in your household, dad adjusting his pitch should help.

High frequencies are interpreted by our nervous systems as pain prompting us to stop and look toward the noise, reacting in a "Someone-is-in-danger; maybe-I-can-help" manner. When you hear a dog or cat screech, you will notice an impulse to go toward the animal, not away from it. The sound of an ambulance siren is not random; it is purposefully high pitched to make sure it is heard. When we hear a siren, we usually try to see what direction the vehicle is coming from, so we can move out of its way. If the siren had a low-frequency tone, it would scare you. You might react without thought by trying to get away, and this automatic reaction may put you in the way of the ambulance, slowing it down. A siren's high-pitched sound, although irritating, makes us orient toward it and then respond (which requires thought, and is not automatic) by moving out of the way.

The phrase "It's not what you say; it's how you say it" is actually biologically true. The pitch in your voice is critical. It will determine if the nervous system of the person you're talking to detects safety, stimulating his parasympathetic branch, bringing his social engagement system online, and calming his defenses, causing him to want to come toward you; or if his nervous system detects danger, stimulating his sympathetic branch and triggering his defenses, causing him to feel the need to protect himself and walk away.

Music can change our physiological states instantly. The soft melodic tones of Johnny Mathis, James Taylor, Neil Diamond, Barry Manilow, and Frank Sinatra, to name a few, allow the nervous system to drop its defenses and put us in a more open state, because we feel a sense of safety. It is not a coincidence that rap music, which usually tells the story of a dangerous world, has more low-frequency tones; and if you pay attention, you'll notice that it does not put you in a loving, open mood.

Try this experiment: listen to very different types of music. As each song is playing, notice what your body does. Does your chest or stomach tighten? Do you feel the urge to look over your shoulder to make sure you're safe? Do you feel calm and relaxed? Do you feel a burst of energy that makes you want to get up and dance? Try something else: the next time you and your partner are having an argument, turn on "your song"—the one you fell in love to. Do you notice your nervous system calm and the anger dissipate, even just a little?

Faces also speak directly to our nervous systems. They say the eyes are the windows to the soul. In biological terms, they are the windows to our nervous systems. Constricted pupils can cause people to move away from you because they are perceived as dangerous. Beady eyes, which appear suspicious, do not invite people to come toward you. Pupils become dilated when the sympathetic nervous system is stimulated and in a social environment, and dilated pupils can signify the excitement of sexual attraction. In one study, people looked at what appeared to be the exact same picture of a person—except in one picture the person had dilated pupils and in the other the pupils were constricted. When asked to choose the more attractive image, study participants chose the picture with dilated pupils. The participants did not notice the difference in pupil size. They just saw two pictures of the same face and picked the one they liked better.

The muscles around our eyes also make a difference in how we perceive and are perceived by others. When we are scared, there is less movement around the eye area. The muscles around the eyes lose tonality, producing a flatter look. This look will be detected as unsafe to others, and people will most likely feel like moving away from us. Wrinkles around the eyes produce a "moving toward" impulse; wrinkles appear when we smile a genuine smile, not a forced one. The expression "smiling eyes" refers to this look, and it signifies safety to others. So basically the Botox I have been paying a lot of money to have injected around my eyes helps me look younger but causes people to avoid me because their nervous systems perceive me as unsafe. Ironic, isn't it?

In his lectures on communication and the nervous system, Steve Porges always references the song "The Look of Love." Although he's not sure if Burt Bacharach and Hal David were privy to the workings of the nervous system when they wrote it, the song speaks to the way our nervous systems communicate with each other:

*The look of love is in your eyes*
*The look your heart can't disguise*
*The look of love is saying so much more*
*Than just words could ever say*
*And what my heart has heard*
*Well it takes my breath away . . .*

When someone is in fight-or-flight mode, cheek muscles drop and have less movement, looking flat and less animated. The eyelids droop, lips become tight, the face looks tense, and facial movement is less fluid.

These are all examples of the subtle things we neurocept about others without our awareness. What we might be aware of, however, is a feeling of wanting to move toward or away from someone, causing us to say, "I really liked her, but I'm not sure why" or "I'm not sure why that person gave me the creeps." Although you cannot control whether your pupils constrict or dilate, if your eyes appear droopy or your check muscles drop, as you will learn in chapter 5, you can learn to calm your nervous system, which will automatically drop your defenses and you will appear safe for others to approach.

A feeling of safety allows your nervous system to calm down, creating a relaxed look on your face. That relaxed look is actually your nervous system easing the muscles in your face as it detects safety in the environment and peace from within. This allows your defenses to calm and be present in the moment, without the distraction of worrying about that lurking tiger. This state allows others to perceive you as safe and want to move toward you. Going back to the Burt Bacharach and Hal David song:

*You've got the look of love*
*It's on your face*
*A look that time can't erase . . .*

People who come from abuse and neglect tend to walk around in a perpetual defensive state, which causes their faces to look tense and appear unapproachable to others. Additionally, they are less sensitive to others' attempts to socially engage them. Certainly this is out of our awareness, however, it can explain why some people make friends easily and are approached more often than others, whether they are the most beautiful person in the room or not.

Understanding this is key. Feeling safe is necessary to establishing any type of relationship, whether romantic, friendly, or professional. Porges teaches this formula as the building blocks of healthy relationships:

SAFETY + PROXIMITY + CONTACT = BOND

You have to feel safe to want to get close to someone in order to connect with them and form a bond. When we feel safe, we are more likely to make eye contact, talk with a rhythmic pitch and flow, and display friendly facial expressions that are animated and congruent with the conversation. We are also able to tune in to other people and notice subtleties in them. Modulation of voice, eye contact, and a relaxed facial tone make people feel comfortable, causing their defenses to calm, giving them the ability to interact with us and not feel the need to protect themselves. In other words, when we have our social engagement systems on, we invite people to come toward us. Nervous systems then feed off each other, making for an enjoyable interaction. Social situations become a negotiation between approach and avoid, moving toward and running away.

## Moving Toward and Away Exercise

Dr. Stan Tatkin, an innovative psychologist, has developed a technique for working with couples based on attachment theory, the brain, and the interplay between the nervous system of one partner and the nervous system of the other. An exercise he calls Toward and Away demonstrates nervous system reactions—without thought involved—based on the attachment style of each partner. Test it out: ask your partner to stand about fifteen feet away from you and then start walking toward you slowly. Notice how your body responds. If you are on the avoidant side of the attachment continuum, you may notice your heart beating a little faster. You may start to feel uncomfortable, with an urge to move back. You may even feel somewhat intruded upon, as your partner gets closer. If you are on the ambivalent side, you may find yourself feeling calm, happy, and excited as your partner gets closer. Once your partner is about one foot away from you, ask him to turn around and walk away slowly. Again, notice how your body reacts.

When I do this exercise with couples, the reactions are quite extraordinary. I can actually see avoidants relaxing their whole bodies when their partners walk away. Conversely, I have had people on the ambivalent side break into tears as their partners walked away. These reactions are involuntary; they do not require any thought. They are nervous system reactions that have nothing to do with the partner per se but do relate to the partner's role in the other person's life.

Your partner represents your next primary attachment figure. You may have chosen someone who has traits that are similar to one or both of your parents in an unconscious effort to resolve childhood issues. This happens because our brains like what is familiar, even if it attracts us to situations that aren't healthy, such as the woman who grows up with an alcoholic father and then marries an alcoholic. There are very specific reasons why we choose our partners. Although we don't always make these choices consciously, they are not coincidental. Unfortunately, because of this, our partner often becomes the person we feel the need to protect ourselves from, as opposed to what they should be: the person we feel safest with—our go-to person—above and beyond anyone else.

## Defense Mechanisms

Another way we attempt to keep ourselves safe from perceived danger is through the use of defense mechanisms. We all use defenses to adapt to difficult situations. When my mother passed away, my sister and I went to the funeral home to make the arrangements. She and I spoke with the director of the funeral home in a very businesslike manner. Some very emotional decisions were made, and we completed the task in front of us. In that moment, we used a defense mechanism called suppression. We made a conscious decision to hold our feelings at bay while dealing with the director and that situation. Later that evening, when I spoke to my sister, we realized that we had both cried all the way home. We had allowed ourselves to release the emotions we held back while talking with the director.

Defenses are psychological strategies we use to keep us safe. They help us cope and reduce our anxiety. Sometimes, as in my situation at the funeral home, these defenses are conscious and functional. More often, however, they are not in our conscious awareness. They inhibit our ability to adjust to particular situations and be our genuine selves, leading to maladaptive behaviors. As you read in chapter 1, given our experiences and interactions with caregivers, we learn to anticipate the intentions of others as a way to keep ourselves safe. However, as adults, our perceptions of reality might be distorted. They might not truly reflect what is happening in a particular situation because without awareness, we are still operating as if we are helpless infants and toddlers. Consequently, the defenses we use are not always a response to current reality. Rather they can be a response to our *perception* of reality. This distorted perception is unconscious. Therefore, our defenses are not really adaptive. That is, they do not always help us cope with real danger but with perceived danger.

People with insecure attachments, whether ambivalent or avoidant, may use defenses more often than others. Although someone might be prone to using one defense over another, given their attachment style, there is no direct correlation between a defense mechanism and a particular attachment style. When we use defense mechanisms unconsciously, we are not in tune with the reality in the moment or how and why it is affecting us. We are operating from a protective armor of past needs that remain unmet, which can cause significant problems in our relationships with partners, family, and friends, and in how we function at work and in our everyday life.

Unless these unconscious defenses are pointed out to us *and* we have the ability for insight, we have no idea they exist. Sigmund Freud, the father of psychoanalysis, the first psychologist I learned about in high school and my first love, came up with the idea of defense mechanisms—techniques we use to distance ourselves from unpleasant thoughts, feelings, and behaviors that we do not feel safe admitting to, whether we are conscious of the process or not. Working through past trauma and learning better ways to cope with stress can reduce the unconscious need for defense mechanisms.

### Primitive Defense Mechanisms

Psychologists have categorized defense mechanisms based on how primitive they are. The more primitive the defense mechanism, the more unconscious it is, the younger we were when that particular defense came about, and the more negatively it can affect our lives. The following are seven primitive defense mechanisms:

*Denial:* This is a refusal to admit or accept reality. People with avoidant attachment are prone to using denial when it comes to feelings. Keep in mind that needs and feelings get buried deep inside because there was no one around to help a child navigate through them. "I'm okay," "It's no big deal," and "It is what it is" are common sayings from those on the avoidant attachment continuum who use denial as a defense. Many times, people become so good at burying their feelings that they really *don't* feel them. However, the feelings always come out somewhere, somehow. A person who is in denial about how angry she is at her spouse for taking a job in another city, causing the family to move, may start having affairs as a way to unconsciously unleash her anger toward him. At times, this behavior is masked with a label of sex addiction. In reality, it could be that admitting to angry feelings toward a spouse seems unacceptable. The anger splits off from conscious awareness and gets dressed in different clothing, in this case an affair.

Minimizing is a watered-down version of denial. It is a way to technically accept what has happened or what you're feeling, but not completely. You say you'll get over losing your job and you probably will, but can you let yourself feel the emotions associated with this loss? You're putting your toe in the water but not jumping into the pool.

*Regression:* This occurs in the face of stress, when a new challenge, feeling, or thought seems so unacceptable that we revert to an earlier stage of development. For example, a huge stressor at work can cause us to think about ditching work and going surfing. We may have watched someone who is fifty years old behave as if he's twenty; that's regression. Sometimes trauma can cause a person to be fixated or regressed at the age the trauma occurred. I recall a forty-five-year-old patient who had been sexually abused as a child and whose voice sounded like that of a little girl. She was fixated in childhood. A common form of regression occurs when children who feel anxiety at starting a new school become clingy or start exhibiting earlier childhood behaviors, such as bed-wetting or baby talk. A popular saying among psychologists is, "When under stress, we regress." Someone with ambivalent attachment may regress when their partner leaves to go on a trip and may get clingy before they leave, as a child would on their first day of school.

*Dissociation:* This is a way to disconnect from the here and now. We all use dissociation at one time or another. At times, it is not used as a defense mechanism; it happens because an activity does not require much thought. For example, people tend to dissociate while driving. It is not uncommon to drive someplace and not remember the drive, because driving has become second nature and your mind goes somewhere else.

However, many times dissociation is a defensive strategy used to keep us safe. As I have mentioned before, when we find ourselves in a dangerous or life-threatening situation, the brain uses dissociation to save us from feeling extreme pain. Dissociative identity disorder (DID), also known as multiple personality disorder, is an extreme example of dissociation. In DID, the brain finds a way to separate a traumatic experience from conscious awareness by creating different identities that keep memories from coming to the surface. In extreme cases, people with an avoidant attachment style might dissociate from their needs and feelings. As adults, they do not feel the need to connect with others. They isolate from people, living a loner existence.

*Projection:* This is when we put our unconscious thoughts or feelings onto others. If I am angry with you but unconsciously do not feel safe enough to admit it, or don't even know the anger is there, I might accuse you of being angry with me. This accusation will most likely start a fight, thus allowing me to get my anger out in an indirect way. People also use projection when they cannot admit something about themselves that they dislike and thus project it onto someone else as a characteristic the other person possesses. If I am very critical but unable to admit it, I might accuse you of being overly critical, even when you're not.

Jealousy is a form of projection. If I have an unconscious fear that I am not good enough to be loved, I may accuse you of flirting, being too friendly with others, or downright cheating on me. Someone with an ambivalent attachment style is prone to feel jealous given their fear of being abandoned. Paranoia is also a form of projection. If my amygdala is on overdrive and I am on constant "tiger watch," I might project a belief onto people that they are out to get me, when it's just good old Francois Amygdala (see chapter 2) working overtime.

*Acting out:* This can show up in the form of addictions to repress overwhelming feelings or thoughts, such as "I hate my mother" or "I wish my father were dead." These thoughts can be so terrifying, even if they live in the unconscious, that we use sex, drugs, alcohol, gambling, going out every night, or not going to work or school to distract and alter our brain function, so we can keep the feelings locked down and not have to admit to or feel them. Both ambivalents and avoidants can use acting out as a defense mechanism, since they have had profound disappointment with their caregivers, and residual feelings may be living in their unconscious.

*Reaction formation:* This is when we switch an unwanted or seemingly dangerous thought, feeling, or impulse into its opposite. For example, if you hate your boss, instead of allowing those feelings into your awareness, you become overly kind and generous toward her. You've probably heard news reports about someone who vehemently speaks out against gay rights and is then found to be having an affair with someone of the same sex. Or someone who is publicly critical of extramarital affairs is found to be having one. This is reaction formation at its finest. It is amazing how our minds can compartmentalize in this way. You can work through this defense mechanism by noticing if a reaction, behavior, or belief is extreme. For the most part, any over-the-top behavior, reaction, or belief usually has something hidden underneath. Time to look under the hood.

### Less Primitive Defense Mechanisms

The following defense mechanisms are less primitive in that they are a little more sophisticated. They can live in the unconscious or can be within conscious awareness. If within conscious awareness, they can help us deal with our feelings, stress, and anxiety, but they are still not ideal ways of coping.

*Repression:* Repression involves burying painful thoughts, feelings, and memories so they are out of conscious awareness. The problem is that the thoughts, feelings, or memories don't go away. They continue to unconsciously affect our decisions, reactions, and behaviors. Thankfully, becoming healthy does not require uncovering everything that is repressed, but it does require noticing when we have a reaction to something—when we have been triggered—so that we can choose how to respond to it, rather than becoming aware of the reaction after the fact, without a sense of how we got there. In the oozy eggs story I told you in chapter 2, I had repressed my anger at being ignored and not being heard by my parents. Therefore, I almost lost it with the waitress who brought out my order incorrectly. The anger I had buried deep down, which I was not aware of, came out when an action triggered my feeling of being ignored and not heard. This was an important realization that enables me now to be more aware so I don't walk around the world reacting to repressed feelings.

*Displacement:* This is about redirecting negative thoughts and feelings about one person onto a less intimidating person, making it less scary to deal with those feelings. For example, children who are feeling ignored by their parents might displace their anger toward their parents onto a younger brother or sister. Being angry with a parent is too scary, so the younger sibling, who has nothing to do with what is happening, gets the brunt of the anger. As a parent, it is important to notice and understand this behavior and to spend special time with the older child. Displacement can also occur with a partner. For example, if getting angry with your boss is too intimidating, you may take your anger out on your significant other. Bullying is an example of displacement. More often than not, the bully is a victim himself, but his tormentor is too big and intimidating to confront, whether it's a parent, an older sibling, or an older neighbor kid. So the bully displaces that anger onto someone less threatening.

*Intellectualization:* This involves removing all emotions from an emotional experience. For example, you might be given the diagnosis of cancer and instead of allowing yourself to feel sadness and anger, you jump into learning about cancer from an objective perspective. You explore every possible cure, whether helpful or not. This is not to say that being informed is a bad idea, but a balance of allowing the feelings and exploring the medical possibilities proves to be the healthiest response. People with avoidant attachment are prone to use this defense mechanism and the next one, rationalization.

*Rationalization:* This is a close cousin of intellectualization. It occurs when we are so afraid of feeling pain, disappointment, or guilt that we make up a logical argument to reduce these feelings. Examples of rationalization include saying things like, "I didn't really like him" to deflect the hurt of someone breaking up with you, or "I'm glad the store was closed because I need to save money" to avoid the disappointment of your favorite store being closed when you got there, or "I really shouldn't eat that much red meat anyway" to deflect the anger about a restaurant running out of the steak you wanted to order. You can still conclude that the outcome was in your best interest, but it is okay to feel hurt, disappointed, or angry as they are just feelings. When you rationalize, you're just missing out on the important step of acknowledging the feelings associated with an experience.

### Mature Defense Mechanisms

Defense mechanisms that are considered mature are healthier ways of dealing with our feelings and thoughts. They are often within our conscious awareness and can prove to be adaptive and helpful in certain situations.

*Sublimation:* This is how thoughts, feelings, and impulses that feel unacceptable or overwhelming are redirected to behavior or activities that are more acceptable. Maybe you got into a huge argument with your husband and felt the urge to punch him out, but instead you went to a kickboxing class at the gym. The Amber Alert system came about as a result of sublimation. After a little girl named Amber was abducted and murdered in Texas in 1996, her parents developed People Against Sex Offenders. The group collected signatures to force the Texas legislature to pass stricter laws to protect children, saving hundreds of children's lives. After his only son, Adam, was abducted and murdered, John Walsh helped found the National Center for Missing and Exploited Children in 1984. He then created the TV show *America's Most Wanted,* another example of the use of sublimation. This show has helped capture more than eleven-hundred dangerous fugitives and has brought home more than fifty missing children. These examples show that as long as you allow yourself to feel the emotions associated with difficult circumstances, sublimation can be used in healthy ways.

*Compensation:* This is a way to counterbalance perceived weaknesses by emphasizing strengths in other areas. Someone might say, "I'm not a great driver, but I'm a great navigator." She is purposely compensating for a weakness with a strength. However, when compensation is unconscious, it can become exaggerated. People who use big words in casual conversation might be overcompensating for a deep-rooted belief that they are not very smart.

*Suppression:* This is when you consciously hold back, or suppress, feelings or thoughts. My sister and I used suppression when we visited the funeral director to make arrangements for my mother's burial. I also use suppression when I purposely distract myself from thinking about a scene in a scary movie while I'm trying to go to sleep. People with secure attachment, and those earning their secure attachment wings, often use this mechanism to get through difficult situations. Suppression is very different from denial. It is a conscious suppression of feelings or thoughts to get you through a situation—for example, trying to get to sleep.

As I said earlier, if used with awareness and for a specific purpose, defense mechanisms are not always dysfunctional. Some defense mechanisms, such as sublimation and compensation, can be healthy ways of dealing with thoughts, urges, and feelings.

### Other Defenses

Besides the above defense mechanisms, people use other methods to protect themselves from vulnerability, to keep a sense of safety, and to deflect, avoid, or simply deny unwelcome feelings and thoughts. The following is a list of some of them. Based on your new understanding of defenses, you may be able to identify others not listed here that you've noticed yourself or others using to keep from feeling vulnerable to perceived danger.

*Defensiveness:* Defensiveness, or being defensive, is a reactionary behavior that occurs when we believe our sense of self is being attacked. Some people become defensive when they feel criticized, questioned, or accused, whether real or perceived. Others live in a defensive state, constantly feeling the need to protect themselves from anticipated criticism and threats to their ego or sense of self, fearing that their shortcomings will be exposed. Defensiveness is an indication of low self-esteem. We cannot control what others say about us. The only reason to be defensive is if we believe what they are saying. Although criticisms and accusations, whether true or false, never feel good, if we feel a strong need to defend, at some level we must believe the criticisms or accusations to be true. Otherwise, they would sting, but we wouldn't feel the need to become defensive. If you're reacting too strongly, it's time to look under the hood.

*Passive aggressiveness:* Passive aggressiveness is very difficult to work with because the sender is usually not aware of being passive aggressive. This behavior hits the receiver out of nowhere, like a sniper hiding in the trees. It is an aggressive act that is passive in its delivery. You don't see it coming, but it stings when it hits you. If you react, you look like the person with the issues—that's the passive part. Suppose your coworker, who you thought didn't like you, offers to bake a cake for your going-away party. You don't fully trust that she has no hidden agenda, but you second-guess yourself, think maybe she does like you, and reluctantly agree. At the party, in comes your coworker with the most beautiful cake ever. Everyone oohs and aahs. Now you're sure that your perception that she doesn't like you is just your imagination—until you cut into the cake.

The cake is chocolate, and you hate chocolate cake. You know she knows that, because when she offered to bake it, you told her you didn't like chocolate, and you heard another coworker remind her of that the day before. You feel your blood pressure rising and your face get hot. You are angry. If you say, "I told you I don't like chocolate," you will be perceived as ungrateful. To your relief, the coworker who reminded her blurts out, "But she doesn't like chocolate!"—to which the cake baker says with a smile, "*Oh my God,* I forgot. I'm so sorry!" You know she didn't forget. Instead of expressing her negative feelings about you directly, she's doing it passively. She's not comfortable confronting you about whatever made her angry, so she hurts you in an indirect way. Passive aggressiveness is extremely underhanded and usually provokes an intense reaction from the recipient. Reacting causes the eyes to be on you and not the aggressor. You were right all along: she doesn't like you.

A patient of mine came in furious one day. He was always angry about something, so I didn't think much of it. This time he said, "It's my mother again!" I asked what happened. He hadn't shared too much about his mother in the past, but from the little he did share, I knew they had a strained relationship. In fact, in our first session he said that he had moved clear across the country so he would not be anywhere near her. When he told me that, he looked at me with an angry expression, but I had noticed a sadness in his eyes.

He went on to say that his birthday had been the week before, and he had received a package from his mother. I noticed he was breathing heavily, but I didn't know why. I looked at him with anticipation. After a pregnant pause, he announced, "It was a huge box of mixed nuts." He looked at me with expectant eyes, waiting for me to react. At this point I still didn't understand his anger. I thought, "Did I hear him correctly?" It certainly wasn't the most personal or exciting gift—but to elicit such anger? After a few moments, noticing that I had not caught on, he said, in the numbest of voices, "I'm anaphylactic." That meant he had a severe, possibly deadly, allergy to nuts. At hearing this I gasped—an unplanned reaction. Apparently, my reaction brought to the forefront the sadistic maliciousness of his mother's actions and her passive aggressiveness. For the next thirty minutes, he just sobbed. I later found out that that was the first time he let himself feel the pain of her actions.

*Identifying with the aggressor:* Another defense used to stay safe is called identifying with the aggressor. It is an attempt to bond with an abusive attachment figure, usually a parent. As a way to find something in common and to connect with the abusive parent, children begin to treat themselves in an abusive and vicious manner, mimicking the aggressive behaviors used by the parent. As I have mentioned, we are biologically programmed to connect, and our psyches will come up with innovative ways to accomplish this.

Stockholm syndrome is an example of identifying with the aggressor. Stockholm syndrome occurs when a hostage cannot escape, is isolated, and is threatened with death or other harm, but at times is also shown acts of kindness by the captor, such as being fed or allowed to use the bathroom. Someone held captive under these conditions will attempt to keep his captors happy to stay alive. He will become obsessed with learning the captors' likes and dislikes, sympathizing with the captor. It takes approximately three or four days for this psychological shift to occur.

Some people are kidnapped, found years later, and admit they had opportunities to escape but didn't. In 1974 Patty Hearst was kidnapped and tortured by the Symbionese Liberation Army. At some point during her capture, she bonded with her captors and joined their cause, changing her name and helping them rob banks. Jaycee Dugard's story is a more recent example of this phenomenon. Jaycee was abducted at age eleven and found more than eighteen years later. Like Patty Hearst, she admitted to feeling a significant bond with her captor. Battered spouses also bond with the abusive partner because of a biological need to connect. In these cases, there is usually a history of child abuse, and these two issues prove to be a dangerous combination. Self-esteem is low, a sense of deserving mistreatment exists, and when a bond is created, leaving the situation is often not within the realm of options or possibilities.

In addition to attempting to bond or connect with an abuser, some children go from a passive role to a more active role. They take on the characteristics of someone who causes them extreme anxiety to reduce that anxiety. Going from victim to offender is much less frightening than remaining a victim. One of my patients, Sara, who had a very abusive mother, identified with her aggressor as a defense mechanism. Sara's first childhood memory was from age six. She was in the hallway between her mother's room and the bathroom. She was walking to the bathroom when her mother came out of her bedroom and started yelling at her, saying how stupid she was for forgetting her scarf at her friend's house earlier that day. Sara's mother yelled at her a lot, and during that time, it seems like she forgot things often. Sara began to feel there was something wrong with her. (Yes, she was living in a fight-or-flight state, which affected her ability to remember things.) She distinctly remembers that when she was ten years old, she decided to be worse to herself than her mother was to her. Every time she thought she did something wrong, she'd anticipate her mother's yelling voice and would yell at herself in the same manner. Sara, then, treated herself in the same way that her mother treated her, taking some of the fear and power out of her mother's yelling. When Sara became an adult, her mother's critical voice lived in her head and was louder than ever.

Many of us use this defense mechanism on a smaller scale. If one parent put you down, didn't believe in you, or simply ignored you, planting a belief that you were unimportant or undeserving, notice if you now have a little critical voice in your head that puts you down, questions your ability, or reminds you how unspecial you are. If you do, you have identified with the aggressor and continue his ugly torment. Look at yourself in the mirror. You're an adult, and the tormentor isn't there. It's time to say good-bye to the little tormentor in your head. Chapter 5 will show you how.

*Humor and sarcasm:* Humor and sarcasm are two very common ways to deflect, avoid, or simply deny feelings and thoughts. When humor is used to deflect feelings, it usually comes right after an emotional moment that brings sadness, anger, or disappointment. I recall a session where a memory of abuse came to one of my patients. I felt such sadness and hurt that I knew he felt the same. After a few seconds he said, "And you thought I was going to be an easy patient." Chuckle, chuckle. I knew he saw the feelings that had come up for him reflected in me, so I simply asked, "How is it for you to just sit with these feelings that are coming up?" This question brought about a wonderful exploration of his feelings and an enlightening conversation about how frightening it was for him to let himself feel emotions. One of my finer moments!

Sarcasm is always hostile. Although I usually avoid words such as *always* and *never,* in this case they apply. There should be no room for sarcasm, especially when communicating with children or teens. If you analyzed every time you used sarcasm, you would almost always find anger, hurt, or disappointment underneath. Under a sarcastic "good job" lies, "I'm angry that you didn't do a good job." Under a sarcastic "Really?" lies, "I'm hurt and cannot believe you just did that!" Under a sarcastic "I hope you didn't injure yourself bringing the groceries in" lies, "I'm disappointed that you don't help out more around the house."

Because sarcasm is an indirect form of communication, it leaves you unsatisfied and the recipient uncomfortably angry. Nothing changes, but now there is tension in the air. Sarcasm is the opposite of honest, open communication. When people say something sarcastic to me, I have fun with it. I break it down to what I surmise they might be feeling and simply ask them a direct question, such as, "Are you letting me know that you're angry with me because . . . ?" This usually makes people feel initially uncomfortable and they may try to deny it. But more often than not, a more honest communication ensues. I don't like sarcasm.

## The Four Fears

There are four basic fears—fear of failure, fear of success, fear of abandonment, and fear of engulfment. These fears can also be viewed as defenses, or ways we protect ourselves from emotional pain. As we learned in chapter 1, insecure attachments, whether ambivalent or avoidant, result from childhood experiences in which our caregivers, for one reason or another, were not sensitive to our needs, causing us to develop inaccurate and distorted beliefs about ourselves and our worth. Not feeling worthy, lovable, or deserving can influence behavior, choices, and decisions in ways that we may not be fully aware of and that might cause us to stay stagnant and not move forward in our lives.

These fears are the manifestations of beliefs we developed in childhood and experiences that we unconsciously processed into adult behaviors. Fear can stop us from taking risks. People with secure attachment are more able to face their fears because for the most part they have a healthy sense of self and do not let fear get in their way. This is not to say that they don't feel fear, but they are able to forge forward, believing they can attain their goals. If things don't work out as planned, they know they will be able to tolerate the pain that comes with disappointment. People with insecure attachments, whether ambivalent or avoidant, many times do not have the confidence to face their fears or the tools to tolerate and process disappointment.

### Fear of Failure and Fear of Success

Los Angeles psychologist Dr. Lu Katzman-Staenberg, whom I was lucky enough to have as a mentor, once said to me, "Honey, fear of success and fear of failure stem from the same place—a fear of growing up." She is absolutely right. Although everyone has fears when venturing into new projects, sometimes the fear is so great that it stops you from trying, whether consciously or unconsciously. A fear of failure can stem from parents who put you down and said you would never amount to anything. Consequently, you don't try, because you are too afraid to find out if they were right. A fear of failure can also stem from never having been taught how to navigate through uncomfortable feelings, such as disappointment. Certainly, failing at something brings about disappointing feelings, and confronting those feelings can become overwhelming.

Parents who did too much for you and never let you do anything on your own may have unknowingly planted a belief that you are not capable of doing anything for yourself. In this situation, fear of failure becomes overwhelming, because you have never had a chance to experience failure and realize that you can survive it. Fear of failure can also stem from the fear of being rejected. It is not a stretch to say that no one likes failure, even though some of the most profound learning can come from failing or being rejected. However, from a survival standpoint, successful people get all the attention and glory. People want to be around them, and survival is more likely in groups. Rejection brings with it the fear of being alone: "If I fail, no one will like me. If no one likes me, I will die alone."

Best-selling business author Seth Godin says, "The cost of failure is not that a saber-toothed tiger will eat you . . . the cost of failure is nothing." Godin understands how the brain perceives failure as a serious concern, with life-or-death consequences. Remember, the brain likes what's familiar. If working through feelings of disappointment is not familiar, the brain can't be sure the process won't be life threatening, thus causing panic. Fear of failure, however, can become a self-fulfilling prophecy. If you are too overwhelmed with fear to try, you will stop yourself from moving ahead. You will feel like a failure when you see everyone around you progressing, paralyzing yourself even further.

When you have a fear of success, you know the steps to take to get what you want, but you can't seem to muster enough energy to take them. This situation comes from feeling bad about yourself ("I am bad or defective") and believing at some level, conscious or not, that you can't be bad *and* successful. The fear of success, then, stems from what I call an unconscious incongruent confusion. Simply put, success is celebrated and valued. Successful people get attention; other people want to be around them; they are asked to speak at functions; they are invited to the White House; they get knighted by queens (think Paul McCartney). So how can you be bad or defective *and* successful? It makes no sense; it's incongruent; it's confusing.

If a child is abused or ignored, it affects her sense of self, worth, and value. In the case of abuse, the interpretation is most likely, "If I were good, they wouldn't hurt me. So I must be bad." In the case of neglect, the interpretation is most likely, "I'm not significant enough to be paid attention to. So I must be defective."

When your core belief is that you are bad or defective, reaching success is going to require you to redefine yourself and change the core belief about your worth and sense of belonging in the world. Otherwise, self-sabotage will be your unwelcome companion. Some people reach success only to sabotage themselves and lose it all. Others reach success and retain it, but they never embrace it because they feel uncomfortable and guilty for having it.

One very successful woman I worked with in therapy had been denying herself the pleasure of her success for years. Although she lived in a large house and drove an expensive car, she felt very guilty. She suffered extreme pain from feeling as if she didn't deserve what she had and what she had worked hard for. After about one year, we started to uncover how underserving she really felt. One day she casually mentioned that at times her emotional pain was so great that she slept in the doghouse alongside her dog, because sleeping in her opulent bedroom was too overwhelming. She couldn't stand the guilt feelings. It was only then that I realized the depth of the discrepancy between her sense of self and her level of success.

Going back to what Dr. Katzman-Staenberg said, fear of failure and fear of success are both fears of growing up, because the feelings that you're bad, defective, and worthless developed early in childhood. But you're not that little kid without choices anymore. You're an adult, the world is your oyster, and your brain is plastic. Change is most definitely possible!

## *Fear of Abandonment*

Fear of abandonment most often stems from ambivalent attachment, because your primary caregiver was inconsistent in meeting your needs. People with avoidant attachment have this fear as well, but their emotions are buried so deep that it is not as apparent. As you learned in chapter 2, your brain is programmed for survival, and being alone doesn't feel safe. The fear of abandonment, however, takes it to another level—an over-the-top place that signifies that something is going on underneath. People with fear of abandonment are controlled by this fear. Most of their thoughts revolve around how to avoid being abandoned, which often causes that very thing to happen, because the people around them feel drained.

The fear of abandonment can be triggered if you invite people into your life who are prone to leave you because *they* have a difficult time trusting others and therefore keep everyone at arm's length. One would think that someone with a fear of abandonment would never invite these types of people into their lives. It is not uncommon, however, to unconsciously re-create what we already know because it's familiar, even if it doesn't feel good. If your primary caregiver left you or met your needs sporadically, those are characteristics you are prone to invite into your world. The fear of abandonment can also be imagined, because you anticipate or even assume people will leave you. You analyze every detail of another's behavior to be prepared for what you consider to be inevitable. If a friend said they were going to call and didn't, you replay everything you said and every move you made to see if there was something you did to upset them. You may think you noticed your boss paying extra attention to your coworker and begin to obsess that you are going to get fired. You may feel pressure to be the life of the party to ensure that you are fun enough to be invited again.

As I mentioned in chapter 1, partners especially trigger this fear, as a partner takes the position of the primary attachment figure in your life. Most everything that was unresolved from childhood gets triggered with your partner. Nice, huh? Someone with a fear of abandonment has an unconscious belief that if he is not right in front his partner, he will be forgotten and his partner will instantly fall in love with someone else. The core issue is that he believes himself to be forgettable and disposable. If your partner comes home after work and doesn't say hello, anxiety shoots up. The "tiger" is lurking around the corner. You feel danger. Something is wrong. Your partner doesn't love you anymore, and you're breaking up! While it may be rude to come home and not say hello, this reaction goes way beyond a reasonable response to rudeness. That surge of anxiety causes the thinking part of your brain to go offline. You are now coming from your emotions and worse yet, your amygdala, the threat detector. The thinking brain has disconnected from the emotional brain and chaos ensues. The worst is imagined, when all that really happened was your partner had to go to the bathroom and couldn't hold it in long enough to say hello first.

The urge to ask your partner, "Do you love me?" or "How much do you love me?" comes from a need to feel connected and safe. What's behind the classic question, "What are you thinking?" is a need to know if your partner is unhappy in the relationship, upset with you for some reason, or is thinking about breaking up with you so you can be prepared and his leaving you won't catch you off-guard. Words calm you down more than behaviors do, because like little Dora, the fish from Disney's *Finding Nemo*, you cannot retain the words. You need to hear them again and again and again.

As you can imagine, living like this is exhausting, so sometimes people with a fear of abandonment will leave the relationship first, finding any excuse to get out of it. After the break up, they will almost always feel relief, because their anxiety will have automatically decreased, since they are no longer being triggered by the fear of their partner leaving. Many times, however, this sense of relief mistakenly leads people to believe that they made the right choice in breaking up. Although there is always something we can find not to like about our partners, it is important to differentiate between a conscious choice and an unconscious reaction.

### Fear of Engulfment

People on the avoidant side of the continuum can usually relate to fear of engulfment. Children who have been neglected develop a belief that they are damaged goods. Being around people causes anxiety because the more they are around people, the more likely their defectiveness will be found out. Additionally, because they were left alone a lot, being alone becomes familiar and comfortable. Consequently, they tend to be loners or at the very least really enjoy and feel relaxed being by themselves. Fear of engulfment can also stem from having to submerge your own identity, needs, sense of worth, or personal safety because your parent took up all the space and needed all the attention. There was no room for you or your needs. This situation causes a severe mistrust of people and their intentions. Consequently, being around people increases anxiety. Fear of engulfment can also be brought on by parents who are controlling, smothering, or extremely overprotective. Consequently, an exaggerated need to have your own space, your own stuff, and privacy become high priorities.

It is not so much that people with a fear of engulfment don't want to be in relationships or don't want to feel connected to others. It's just that they feel safer when they are alone. One patient told me that she felt the safest when no one knew where she was. She could be in a sea of people, but the idea that her husband, kids, other family members, and friends didn't know her exact whereabouts brought about a peace that she didn't quite understand.

Unlike people with a fear of abandonment, whose anxiety gets triggered when they are alone, people with a fear of engulfment have increased anxiety when they are with the people they love, especially their partners. There are many reasons for this; one is that having needs brings about shameful feelings. Being around people may start to feel good, causing needs to start popping up, making the person very uncomfortable. A person with a fear of engulfment might also think the people around him will notice how worthless he is and leave him. Because people who have been neglected push their needs so far deep inside, most of the time they don't know what they are feeling. Being around others when you're quiet, especially if it is your significant other and she is on the ambivalent attachment side, may beg the question, "What's wrong?" to which, most of the time, you will have no idea and not have an answer. Not surprisingly, the other person will take it personally and believe you are upset at them or are shutting them out, which does not feel good to them. This can cause an argument that you have no idea how you can resolve, since you still don't have a clue about what got you there in the first place. As with fear of abandonment, the significant other takes the primary attachment role. Whatever is unresolved from your own past gets triggered in the relationship.

As I have mentioned, it is very common for someone with a fear of abandonment to fall in love with someone with a fear of engulfment, and vice versa. This is a match made in heaven that is going to take you into the bowels of hell, because your thoughts, beliefs, behavior, and needs will trigger her thoughts, beliefs, behavior, and needs, and vice versa. It seems counterintuitive for the two types to meet, find things in common, *and* fall in love. One would think that two people with fear of abandonment would recognize one another and live happily ever after, attached to each other's hips, and that two people with fear of engulfment would live happily ever after, residing in separate homes and seeing each other on occasion. But no, that would be too easy and stagnant. We have an innate pull toward psychological healing, which may be why two people from seemingly opposite ends of the attachment spectrum often meet and fall in love. If both are willing and able to work through unresolved issues and create a safe space for each other, healing can certainly take place. They can grow together, nurturing a healthy balance of togetherness and independence. This process creates a secure attachment within the relationship. I have seen it happen many times.

## What Do Your Defenses Look Like?

Regardless of attachment style, we have all used defense mechanisms at some point in life. As I explained, some defenses are conscious choices and used in healthy ways. It is important to recognize your defense mechanisms to better understand their origins and to ensure you are conscious and aware of them.

Write down five different scenarios where you used a conscious defense mechanism to help you through a specific situation:

| Scenario | Defense Mechanism | Result |
|----------|-------------------|--------|
| 1. | | |
| 2. | | |
| 3. | | |
| 4. | | |
| 5. | | |

Write down five defense mechanisms you have used unconsciously, but that you now recognize. As I have stated many times throughout this book, learning the "why" of your behavior and examining your life with this new information will allow you to bring unconscious behavior into conscious awareness. This awareness will offer you the opportunity to make different, purposeful choices. If you can't think of any examples, ask friends to give their input. We all use some defense mechanisms we are not aware of.

| Newly Recognized Defense Mechanisms |
|--------------------------------------|
| 1. |
| 2. |
| 3. |
| 4. |
| 5. |

# Conclusion

Understanding how you behave based on your attachment style and the development of your brain is crucial to understanding yourself. Learning about the nervous system and my automatic reactions based on my past was invaluable to me. I not only began to understand myself but also my contribution to how others reacted to me. I felt empowered with this information, knowing that first I needed to feel safe in the world and then to help those around me feel safe to change the way we interacted.

Through many years of my own therapeutic work, I made many discoveries and became aware of things inside me that I had no idea existed. Outside of the therapy room, I started to do things that helped relax my defenses and keep my social engagement system on. I began by listening to soothing music before going out, and I purposefully kept an image that calmed me in the forefront of my mind while I engaged with others. The saying "You can catch more flies with honey" makes biological sense if we define honey as having a relaxed look on your face that decreases the neuroception (unconscious detection) of danger from others and invites them to move toward you.

Behavior that compels us to approach or avoid begins to make sense when you recognize that the nervous system is innately programmed to keep us safe from that lurking tiger, which now may exist only in our minds. This danger actually did exist when we were infants, toddlers, and children if our primary caregivers did not provide the safe environment we needed to thrive and move through our developmental stages with ease and expertise. This early environment and its side effects become such well-traveled paths in our brains, that as adults we continue to live as if we are still bound by the chains of our past. Our interactions become unconscious negotiations of safety or danger, approach or avoid.

Defense mechanisms are examples of behaviors we use to stay safe from emotional vulnerability. If we are not conscious of the defense mechanisms we use, they can actually create exactly what we fear the most: abandonment. The exercise in this chapter will help you bring to the surface the defense mechanisms you may not be aware of using, giving you the choice of whether you want to continue to use them or face whatever is hiding under your defenses. When we use our defense mechanisms consciously, they can be useful tools to get us through difficult moments. However, awareness is key.

Like defenses, fears help us adapt to the current environment. But we might be still living in the past, unaware of what the current environment really looks like. Fears of success and failure guarantee mediocrity, because they stop us from stepping outside of our comfort zone and taking chances. Fears of abandonment and engulfment stop us from being free to love and to be loved with reckless abandon.

Underneath these fears is a worry of not being able to handle the end result: "What if I fail?" "What if I succeed?" "What if I'm abandoned?" "What if I lose myself?" It is the fear of looking around the corner and being face to face with that tiger that drives much of our behavior. A wise man once told me this story: A father tried to scare his son by telling him that monsters lived in the closet. The boy opened the closet door. That is the key. The boy opened the closet door and did not find any monsters. He faced his fear and did not let fear of the unknown control his life. The truth is that even if you fail, succeed, get abandoned, or feel engulfed, you *will* be able to handle it. You just need the tools to do so. You can't build a house without a hammer. Tools are provided in chapter 5.

My goal with this book is to help you have the ego strength and belief that you can handle anything that comes your way, without having to use preventive measures such as a primed-for-danger nervous system or unconscious defense mechanisms. My goal is for you to have enough tools in your tool belt to use *after* something happens—if it does—as opposed to actively protecting yourself from something that no longer exists, hasn't happened yet, or may never happen.

## End-of-Chapter Exercise

The next time you go out with your spouse, family, or friends, think of someone or something that brings an immediate smile to your face or a calm within. It can be a favorite place, a favorite song, a pet, your child, your niece, your nephew, or anyone else you are particularly fond of. Usually pets or people do the trick—but whatever works for you is okay. Keep this thing or person in your mind's eye when you walk into your destination, whether it is a restaurant, a nightclub, or a party. Remind yourself of this happy thought every few minutes. This will cause your face to soften and your defenses to subside. Notice how people respond to you. Do they smile? Are they friendlier? Notice how often you are approached or spoken to. Chances are, if you are in a more relaxed state, people will read that as safe and want to come toward you. You will have your social engagement system on.

## Chapter Three Takeaway

While your demeanor and approach toward other people (relaxed versus tense) may initially be influenced by your past, you can change that. Exploring the past can be a painful process. However, it is just that—the past. To make the future look more like you want it to, it is important to get to know yourself in the present and to understand what makes you you. Approach this information with curiosity, as if you are learning a new language, without judgment or reproach. Learn to have compassion for yourself and who you have become given your experiences and consequent defenses. Scientists say that when we believe we are under threat, the compassion circuitry in our brains shuts down. Compassion is a state of mind, not something you have or don't have, which means you can turn it on or shut it off at any time. Forgive yourself for what you didn't know. Do not continue where your parents left off. You are an adult now who gets to choose exactly how you want to live. Begin to explore that choice and the possibilities it brings.

# 4

# Are You Sleepwalking?

*So often times it happens that we live our lives in chains and
we never even know we have the key.*

—From "Already Gone" by the Eagles

## Amanda the Young Adult

By age twenty-four, Amanda had grown into a tall young woman.
She had dark hair that she tied back in a bun and a nice figure
that she hid inside baggy suits and dresses. She lived alone and
worked at a brokerage house. She'd been there three years and
was still an assistant—not because she wasn't offered the opportunity to move up but because she was afraid to take a more challenging position and possibly fail at it.

She had been in three relationships, but her current one, with
Howard, seemed like the real thing. He was a divorced broker at
her firm and liked the same things she did—ordering in Chinese
food, watching old movies, and taking long walks. Initially, he was
very attentive, calling her often and bringing her flowers. When
he started traveling a lot for work, he *only* called twice a day: in
the morning to wish her a good day and at the end of the evening

to talk about the day and say goodnight. Amanda felt invisible to him, like she didn't exist. She worried that he would forget about her throughout the day and find someone he liked better. Consequently, she called him many times a day, accusing him of not loving her. She could calm those thoughts only when he repeated over and over that he did love her. This began to irritate Howard, who explained to Amanda that although he thought of her throughout the day, he was too busy to speak with her. Amanda's anxiety about losing Howard rendered her unable to stop this behavior, causing him to feel smothered and that his needs were not important. Eventually, he broke up with her.

It took Amanda a long time to get over Howard. It seemed like every time she let herself get close to somebody and begin to trust him, he would back off and eventually break up with her. She wanted someone who loved her, respected her, and wanted to spend time with her, but she was starting to think that those types of men didn't exist. It got to the point where Amanda was scared to date anyone.

Because of her ambivalent attachment, Amanda feared abandonment above all else. This fear permeated her thoughts and caused her to behave in ways that guaranteed abandonment. Her poor sense of self, coupled with the belief that she was unlovable, did not allow her to believe that Howard would remember her even if they were not in constant contact. She projected these beliefs onto him. She lived with a conviction that she was dispensable and that unless she reminded people of her existence, she would be forgotten. These beliefs caused her to assume things that weren't true and to see things that weren't there. This combination would set up anyone she dated for failure, and no one would be able to meet her needs. Without an awareness of how her past affected her present, she was going to be telling a similar story in twenty years.

## Everyone Develops Unconscious Patterns

We are all creatures of habit. We like the familiar, even if it isn't best for us.

We create a dance and dance that same dance over and over again, at times wondering why it doesn't yield the results we want. How often do you change the way you argue with your partner? Does the current way you argue work? Do you walk away feeling heard and understood or unheard and distant? If you answered the latter, has it ever occurred to you or your partner to communicate differently?

This chapter will help you gain insight into your life and areas that are not going the way you want them to go. Is your work or career the problem? Your friendships? Your romantic relationships? Think about your friends. Do many of them exhaust you emotionally? Are they mostly takers? Are you there for them emotionally, but they disappear when you need them? Do you find yourself without a friend who can give you as much comfort as you give her? How does your life now resemble what was missing in your childhood? Can you relate the things you have learned about your attachment style to the way you're living your life now?

Think back to your childhood. Were there times when you felt the same way you feel with your friends today? Did you have to take care of a parent who should have been taking care of you? Did you feel like you couldn't express your needs in your own home? If so, you may have been programmed to be the caretaker and now unconsciously attract friends who keep you in that role—friends who need to be taken care of. Intellectually, you may complain about it and wish you could find friends who were more reciprocating. Unconsciously, however, you seek out the friends you have because it feels familiar. You have become so used to *taking* care of that you don't know what it feels like to be *taken* care of. Thus you don't attract people with the ability to reciprocate or empathize, or your own behavior won't allow someone to be there for you. For instance, you might often say, "No, I'm fine. Don't worry." Could it be that you feel so insignificant that you don't want to burden your friends with your problems, so unknowingly you never give them the opportunity to be there for you?

When Peter first came to see me, he was stuck in "taking care of" behavior. He only dated women who were in some type of emotional distress, whom he could swoop in and save. He loaned money to many of his friends and had never been paid back by any of them. Friends always asked him to help them move or drive them to the airport, but never once had he gotten a ride to the airport from anyone besides a cab driver. None of his friends had ever offered, and he had never asked.

Peter knew something was missing in his life, but he truly had no idea what that might be. I helped him see that he was so used to giving, saving, helping, and caring for others that he didn't really know what it felt like to have someone give, support, help, or care for him. He told me that he was the eldest of three children. His father had died when he was eight. From that point on, Peter took on a patriarchal role. He began caring for his mother and two younger siblings. His own needs became unimportant. In fact, he couldn't remember a time when his mother took care of him. As a child, he wondered how anything he was going through could compare to the utter devastation his mother had experienced in losing her husband and having to take care of three little boys all by herself. Peter had denied his own needs for so long that he actually didn't realize he had any needs at all—until we began to work together.

During therapy, I helped Peter see that he was a fully entitled person, with every right to not only have needs but to also try and satisfy them— his need to be loved, his need to have fulfilling reciprocal relationships, his need to be listened to and understood, and so much more. This work took a while, because after he accepted that he had needs and it was okay to try and meet them, he felt guilty for having them. I needed to help him through that guilt so that he would know he wasn't doing anything wrong by noticing a need and meeting it.

I mentioned earlier that emotions should be a source of information and not a source of fear. In other words, they should not be something to run away from or try to deny. Peter's guilt is a great example of this. Do you know what guilt is? Well, let me tell you. It is not something we choose. It is a built-in mechanism that just shows up. Guilt is the way we punish ourselves when we believe we have done something wrong. Guilt doesn't feel good. It's uncomfortable and stops us from doing things that make us feel guilty. Guilt is a powerful emotion that has been used to manipulate people for centuries. It is the basis of many religious groups and cults. Unfortunately, many times parents use guilt to get their kids to do the things they want them to. Certainly, as with most things, a healthy balance is the way to go. If I purposely said something hurtful to someone or stole from a store, guilt is the appropriate emotion to feel. As I mentioned, because guilt doesn't feel good, in order to avoid it, I will stay away from doing things that create this feeling. However, if we were made to feel a lot of guilt as children, it is now programmed in us and can stop us from doing many things that are *not* wrong, especially when it comes to taking care of ourselves and meeting our needs. This was the case with Peter.

Had Peter's mother noticed that he was not grieving and was *acting* resilient, she could have helped him identify his feelings and given him "permission" to feel them. She might have said, "It's okay to feel sad about Daddy dying. Sometimes I even feel mad at Daddy because he died. I know it's not Daddy's fault. He didn't choose to die, but sometimes I miss him so much that I feel sad and mad." Now, an eight-year-old isn't going to sit there and say, "Wow, Mom, that's exactly how I am feeling. Let's grab a cup of coffee and continue this conversation. It's amazing how you know exactly how I feel!" However, rest assured that if she would have said that, or something like it, Peter could have been able to make more sense of the feelings that were coming up and feel okay for having them. In fact, if his mother had had all of the information I am sharing with you, she could have taken it a step further and said, "Sometimes sadness feels like a huge weight on my chest. Sometimes when I'm mad I feel a volcano in my tummy. How does it feel for you?" Teaching Peter to equate emotions with body sensations would have helped him become aware of what was going on in his body. This would have helped dissipate his emotions quicker, as opposed to letting them run rampant in his head, increasing their control over him or causing him to feel the need to dissociate from them. Connecting emotions with body sensations is a skill you will learn in chapter 5.

The best way to reduce the feeling of guilt, if you happen to be prone to this emotion (even if you haven't done anything wrong) is to ask yourself exactly that: "Have I done anything wrong?" or a version of this question. Remember that guilt is a built-in mechanism to make us feel bad, or at the very least, very uncomfortable, when we do something wrong. If the idea of going to your favorite restaurant, getting a manicure, or spending a few hours reading your favorite book comes up and you say to yourself something like, "I better not," ask yourself, "Why? Am I doing something wrong?" If the answer is "no," then push yourself to do the activity, even if it causes you some anxiety. A change in your behavior will start to change your brain, and feeling guilt for things that you have no business feeling guilty about will be a thing of the past!

Going back to Peter—little by little he began to recognize his needs and that it was okay to have them. Soon he started to set boundaries with his friends, which was very difficult for him. He was still there for them, but no longer at his expense. He didn't want to lose the part of his personality that genuinely cared for people. He wanted to be there for his friends and help out when he could. Those are very good qualities to have. However, he had to find a balance. Peter began to take care of his own needs, as well as those of others. He started living a more fulfilling life.

### How Patterns Reveal Themselves

Patterns show up as things we do over and over again, even though we often don't notice that we are doing them. Some people have behavioral patterns at work. For example, I was working with a woman named Sara, and early on in her therapy, as I was taking a history of her work life, a pattern showed up. It seemed that every time she got close to a promotion that would put her at the head of the finance department, she left the job and found another. She always had a good reason for leaving— an opportunity with a better company, an increase in salary, a move to a city she preferred to live in—which is why she hadn't noticed the pattern. However, the moves always took place right before her promotion to finance department head, a position she said she wanted. I suggested that we explore this pattern a little deeper to see if there was something under the hood, so to speak.

Sure enough, Sara had a fear of success that was stopping her from moving forward in her career. She explained that she was an only child. She didn't have a lot of memories from childhood but did recall that her parents were not around much and that even when they were, they were not very interactive or engaged. At times she believed they forgot she existed. I remember she told me once that her favorite song was Carly Simon's "That's the Way I've Always Heard It Should Be." If you are not familiar with it, look up the lyrics. They'll give you a window into how lonely her childhood must have been. I'll give you just the first verse:

*My father sits at night with no lights on*
*His cigarette glows in the dark.*
*The living room is still;*
*I walk by, no remark.*
*I tiptoe past the master bedroom where*
*My mother reads her magazines.*
*I hear her call sweet dreams,*
*But I forgot how to dream.*

Our favorite songs and our favorite films can tell us a lot about our dreams, our pain, and our beliefs. As you might have already guessed, Sara was on the avoidant side of the attachment continuum. She felt forgettable and unimportant. Being the head of any department is an important position, where many people look up to you. The head of finances, in particular, can make or break a company. Her quitting right before being promoted to the position she *said* she wanted was beginning to make sense. Sara unconsciously felt that she didn't deserve the success or the attention that went along with this promotion. She was treated as unimportant as a child, so she sabotaged these opportunities at work.

Look back and see if your patterns include quitting something right before succeeding, not doing the best job you know you can do at work, showing up late to important meetings, or always being the bridesmaid but never the bride.

Many patterns emerge in the realm of relationships. I've worked with people who get into relationships, love being in them, but right around the third year something always happens that causes a break-up. Many times, when we take a look back, they notice that they have done this over and over again. This pattern then becomes something important to explore. Our choice of a partner is no coincidence. A friend of mine always chose the same type of women—not based on how they looked but on how they behaved. Every single one of them would end up cheating on him. He would ultimately laugh and say his "picker" was broken, because every woman he "picked" ended up doing the same thing. My friend, who was not very insightful and used rationalization as a defense mechanism, had a huge fear of intimacy and unconsciously *purposely* chose women who would give him a very real and rational reason to break up with them. Our psyches are quite amazing that way!

Psychologist Dr. Harville Hendrix developed a type of couple's therapy called Imago Relationship Therapy, which has as its premise the long-held belief that our unconscious mind chooses the partners with whom we form relationships. According to Hendrix, our unconscious scans the candidates we meet to match an image formed in childhood. This image, or, *imago*, is a composite of the negative traits of our caregivers which had the most profound wounding effects on us. The theory is that the agenda of the unconscious is to repair the damage from our childhoods by choosing a partner who displays similar deficiencies, or what our caregivers didn't give us, resembling either one or a combination of both parents to correct the damage and therefore heal that wound. "If I can get my partner to really love me, that means I am okay," thus healing the wound of feeling unloved by a parent. Freud called this phenomenon *repetition compulsion* in his 1920 essay, "Beyond the Pleasure Principle." He believed that people have a compulsion to repeat traumatic events in an attempt to gain mastery over their feelings of an experience, attempting to heal the wounds of that experience. However, if we remain unaware of this process, we will continue to repeat these patterns, and the wounds will remain open. We will continue to choose unavailable people or people with intimacy issues who cannot love us because of their past experiences, which only perpetuates our feelings of being unlovable. There is no opportunity for healing. How many times have you said or heard someone say, "It's like I married my father [or mother]!" Now they chase you for a reason as well. With awareness you can help each other in the healing process.

More often than not, the type of partner we are attracted to fits a pattern established in childhood based on the type of attachment we had with our caregivers. We will either choose someone who will perpetuate the environment we came from, keeping with what is familiar, or we will choose the exact opposite, running away from familiarity to the other extreme. Either way, this is not a conscious choice, even if it feels like one; it is a reaction. As I mentioned before, many times an avoidantly attached person will fall in love with an ambivalently attached person. Consequently, the ambivalent will invade the avoidant's space continuously, triggering the avoidant and causing the avoidant to run away, thus triggering the ambivalent and causing the ambivalent to cling even more strongly. Neither one is aware of this dance or why the person he or she fell in love with has become such a source of irritation.

The goal of our conscious mind is to find acceptance and happiness. Our unconscious mind wants healing and growth. Many times the two seem to be at odds with each other, because the path through healing and growth can be trying and difficult. However, reaching the acceptance and happiness destination is always well worth it.

This is not to say that everyone who didn't have loving and supportive parents will end up in dysfunctional relationships. However, many of us may be repeating patterns we are unaware of that could be working against us, whether in our relationships, careers, or even in the way we present ourselves to others. It's time to start living consciously. The first step is to figure out what your behavior patterns are and why they developed. Answer the questions in "What Are Your Patterns?" (see sidebar) to gain insight into how your past has affected your behavior as an adult and your perceptions about other people and the world.

## What Are Your Patterns?

Let's connect the dots between your attachment style, your brain, your defenses, and your behavior and figure out your patterns. The choices you've made in life thus far are often not choices at all. They might be reactions to the programming of your past.

The following questionnaire will help you identify your patterns. Each category contains a series of questions. For the first question in each category, write your own short answer. For the questions that follow, circle Y for yes and N for no. For all other questions, fill in the blanks.

### Relationships

What do you want from a relationship that you don't already have?

Do you always end up with the same type of partner?          Y   N

Are you missing a solid commitment in your relationship?    Y  N
Do you feel smothered by your relationships?    Y  N
Do you feel emotionally detached from your partner?    Y  N
Do you feel ignored?    Y  N
Do you feel jealous?    Y  N
Do you feel disrespected in your relationship?    Y  N
Do you feel dissatisfied sexually?    Y  N
Do you trust your partner?    Y  N
Do you feel the need to be with your partner all the time?    Y  N
Can you be honest with your partner?    Y  N
Do you feel judged by your partner?    Y  N

### Friends
What do you want from your friends that you don't already have?

_____

Do you feel you have enough friends?    Y  N
Do you believe that your friendships are reciprocal?    Y  N
Do you ever feel used by your friends?    Y  N
Do you feel left out by your friends?    Y  N
Do your friends respect you?    Y  N
Can you trust your friends?    Y  N
Can you be honest with your friends?    Y  N
Do you feel judged by your friends?    Y  N
Do you believe that your friends are happy when you succeed?    Y  N
Do you believe your friends have your back?    Y  N

### Career
What do you want from your career that you don't already have?

_____

Are you happy with your career choice?    Y  N
If not, what would be the career of your choice?_____
How many times have you quit a job versus been fired? Quit ___ Fired ___
Is your workplace chaotic?    Y  N
Do you constantly find yourself solving your employee's
    personal problems?    Y  N

Do you have friction with your boss?                                          Y  N
Do you get along with your co-workers?                                        Y  N
Do you find yourself at the center of a lot of drama at work?                 Y  N
Do you feel challenged by your work?                                          Y  N
Do you always end up with the same type of issues no matter
    what type of job you take?                            Y  N
Do you feel respected and/or valued at work?                                  Y  N
Did you ever miss an opportunity for advancement because
    of a "good reason"?                                    Y  N
Do you find yourself just not giving your very best to your work?  Y  N
Do you find yourself not seeking out opportunities to get you
    where you want to go?                                  Y  N


Write down the issue(s) you've identified (if any):

Relationship: _____
_____

Friends: _____
_____

Career: _____
_____

Name 3 favorite songs: _____
_____

Name 3 favorite films: _____
_____


### Discovering Parallels

To the best of your memory, answer the following questions about
    your childhood:
Name three adjectives that best describe the following from your childhood:
You (as a child) _____
Mother _____
Father _____
Stepmother _____
Stepfather _____

Siblings _____

Which parent were you closer to and why? _____

_____

| | | |
|---|---|---|
| Did you have a relationship with your mother? | Y | N |
| Did you have a relationship with your father? | Y | N |
| Did you have a relationship with your stepmother? | Y | N |
| Did you have a relationship with your stepfather? | Y | N |
| | | |
| Did you grow up in a chaotic household? | Y | N |
| Is your environment, in any area of your life, chaotic now? | Y | N |
| Does chaos seem to follow you around? | Y | N |
| | | |
| Was there a lot of friction between your parents? | Y | N |
| Is there significant friction between you and your partner, now or in the past? | Y | N |
| Did your parents drink or use drugs excessively? | Y | N |
| Is your partner an alcoholic or drug addict, now or in the past? | Y | N |
| | | |
| Was there physical violence in your home? | Y | N |
| Does your partner become violent at times, now or in the past? | Y | N |
| | | |
| Was there verbal or emotional abuse in your home? | Y | N |
| Does your partner verbally or emotionally abuse you now or in the past? | Y | N |
| | | |
| Were your siblings jealous, mean, or disinterested? | Y | N |
| Are your adult friends jealous, mean, or disinterested? | Y | N |
| | | |
| Were you raised to believe that work could not be enjoyable? | Y | N |
| Do you hate your current job? | Y | N |
| | | |
| Did you feel nurtured and taken care of by your parents? | Y | N |
| Do you feel nurtured and taken care of by your partner? | Y | N |
| Do you feel nurtured and taken care of by your friends? | Y | N |

| | |
|---|---|
| Did you parent your parent(s)? | Y  N |
| Do you act like a parent with your friends? (always the designated driver or the advice giver) | Y  N |
| Do you act like a parent with your partner? (nagging him/her to do things, he/she depends on you for almost everything) | Y  N |
| | |
| Were you made to feel guilty for feeling sad, mad, or happy? | Y  N |
| Do you have a hard time expressing your emotions now? | |
| Do you have a hard time knowing what you're feeling? | Y  N |
| | |
| Did you feel like an important part of your family? | Y  N |
| Do you feel important to your friends? | |
| Do you feel important to your partner, now or in the past? | Y  N |
| | |
| Did you feel respected by your parents? | Y  N |
| Do you feel respected by your partner, now or in the past? | Y  N |
| Do you feel respected at work? | Y  N |
| Do you feel respected by your friends? | Y  N |
| | |
| Did you feel valued by your parents? | Y  N |
| Do you value yourself? | Y  N |
| | |
| Were you the peacemaker of your family? | Y  N |
| Is it hard for you to allow your partner, friend, or child to feel anger? | Y  N |
| Do you feel an immediate need to "fix it?" | Y  N |
| | |
| Did you feel emotionally supported by your parents? | Y  N |
| Are your friends and partner emotionally supportive of you? | Y  N |
| Are you supportive of them? | Y  N |
| | |
| Did you feel belittled by your parents or siblings? | Y  N |
| Do you allow others to treat you badly? | Y  N |
| | |
| Were you told that you would never amount to anything? | Y  N |
| Are you unhappy with whom you've become? | Y  N |

Were you ever told that you were stupid?                                Y   N
Do you underestimate your abilities?                                    Y   N


Were you disciplined with violence?                                     Y   N
Do you live in "fight or flight" mode?                                  Y   N


Were you shamed as a child?                                             Y   N
Do you have a hard time accepting or believing compliments?             Y   N


Go back to your answers and notice what cluster of questions you answered yes to. Take a moment to think about the parallels between your life as a child and your life as an adult. Write down these parallels in the spaces below.

### Parallels Between Childhood and Adulthood
(Use the prompts if you find them helpful)
As a child I used to, or I was told, or my environment was: _____
_____

As an adult I now: _____

Your attachment style:_____

Use the information in the previous chapters and the answers you just gave to identify your fear(s). Circle all that apply.

Fear of success              Fear of abandonment
Fear of failure              Fear of engulfment

Given all this information, what beliefs do have about yourself?

### Negative Beliefs
Circle all that apply.

I am defective.              People don't like me.
I am not worthy.             I can't do anything right.
I am not lovable.            I'm no good.
I am damaged.                Other:_____

## Positive Beliefs
Circle all that apply.

I matter.

I am a good person.          I am loved.

I am worthy.                 I'm good at some or many things.

I am nice to others.         I am valuable.

People like me.              Other: _____

## Which defense mechanisms do you use most often?
Circle all that apply.

| | |
|---|---|
| Acting out | Projection |
| Compensation | Rationalization |
| Defensiveness | Reaction formation |
| Denial | Regression |
| Displacement | Repression |
| Dissociation | Sarcasm |
| Humor | Sublimation |
| Intellectualization | Undoing |
| Passive aggressiveness | Other: _____ |

Your life should start making a little more sense after you complete this questionnaire. This is just a simple exercise to help you increase your awareness. The parallels you have identified are not coincidental. You may have created your adult environment to resemble that of your childhood. If your friends, romantic relationships, or career choices are in any way similar to your family of origin, you probably set it up that way because it is familiar, not necessarily because it is what you want. You are an adult now. You can choose whatever environment you want to live in. You do not have to re-create the past. It is time to bring the unconscious into conscious awareness.

I would like to repeat that this is not to suggest that we blame our parents or caregivers for all our troubles. The past is the past, and we have already lived it. However, figuring out how our beliefs and patterns of behavior developed gives us the information we need to heal our wounds and begin anew with different behaviors that will increase the quality of our lives.

## How to Change Your Patterns

In the exercise "What Are Your Patterns?" you took the first and most important step in changing behavior that isn't working for you anymore. You began to figure out what your patterns of behavior are and the "why" of your patterns. When you can make sense of why you do things and understand your behavior, you can begin to make changes and stop sleep-walking. Discovering the "why" offers the choice.

One of the most important steps in changing patterns is realizing what negative and harmful beliefs you have developed about yourself, based on your past experiences and relationships. Changing negative beliefs is not easy, especially before you are even aware of them. Or you might be aware of your negative beliefs but have no idea where they came from. You have not connected the dots. It is certainly a wakeup call when you come to the grim realization that these beliefs have formed the foundation on which you have lived your life.

A sixty-year-old patient of mine once asked me why she had never had a marriage proposal. I asked her if she believed that someone could fall madly love with her. Without skipping a beat, she responded, "No," to which I responded, "That's why." This woman was beautiful, witty, and highly intelligent—a Sophia Loren or Raquel Welch type. But at age twelve she was forced to live alone in an apartment because her parents were too busy living their lives and didn't have time to parent her. The message she had received her whole life was that she was not lovable or worthy of anyone's time. When she was a child, the attention she got was sporadic—sometimes there, sometimes not. She was on the ambivalent side of the continuum and yearned to be loved but she did not believe that she was lovable. Need I say more? Discover the negative beliefs you have about yourself and how they relate to your childhood experiences. Begin to notice how they influence your life.

Adding all these ingredients together, it may not be so surprising that your life isn't the way you would like it to be. I want to stress that the purpose of the exercise "What Are Your Patterns?" is certainly not designed to reduce, define, or label you. That would just be adding to the baggage you are already carrying around. We are complex beings. Who we are today is a compilation of every experience we have encountered in life, the good and the bad. The purpose of the exercise is to gain a better understanding of who we are, our beliefs, our patterns, and how this all came about. If one or all areas in your life aren't working—whether work, friendships, or romantic relationships—you *do* have the power to change it. You may start noticing that your life, the people who are around you, your job, or possibly your partner aren't all that random after all. Yikes!

## *Setting Boundaries*

If you want to start changing your patterns, setting appropriate boundaries is a great place to begin. This is the process of letting people know what is acceptable and not acceptable to you. More often than not, when I mention boundaries to patients, they immediately think they have to be tough and aggressive to set boundaries. They view boundary setting as a confrontation. This is certainly not true. At times, you might need to confront someone to set a boundary, but even confrontations do not have to be communicated in an aggressive manner. Some boundaries can be set silently, without anyone noticing. Do you feel obligated to answer the phone every time it rings? Do people expect you to? Deciding *not* to answer the phone while enjoying lunch out with a friend is setting a boundary for yourself. It allows you to enjoy the moment. As with most things, there are exceptions. At times we may not be able to follow through with boundaries we have set. For example, if you are waiting to hear if your friend made it through surgery, you will probably take her phone call at lunch. However, such situations should be the exception and not the rule.

Boundaries can also be set in a loving and calm manner. If your husband makes plans without consulting you first and that bothers you, it is your responsibility to let him know. Together you can then find a compromise that works for both of you. The idea that "he should know" not to make plans without you works only if he is psychic, and even then, his accuracy will never be 100 percent. If his planning doesn't bother you, then it isn't a problem. Many times we think things *should* be a certain way or *should* bother us, even when they don't. Why? Who wrote the book on "shoulds"? The rule of thumb in any scenario, whether it be with friends, family, or partners, is that if something bothers you, it is your responsibility to say something. If it doesn't bother you, you don't need to say anything.

How do you know if something bothers you? If you can't stop complaining about it to your friends or find yourself going over and over it in your mind, it bothers you. Figuring out why it bothers you is the next step. I call it the "series of why" questions. (Three-year-olds know exactly what I'm talking about!) You can do this on your own or have a friend help you. Think about an incident and notice how your body feels as you are thinking about it. Can you feel your heart begin to race, your stomach get queasy, or your face get flushed? That means something about it is bothering you. Then ask yourself, "Why does this bother me?" Notice the first thing that comes to mind. If nothing comes to mind, focus on your body. Your body knows what your mind may not remember. A sensation in your body might trigger a memory, thought, or feeling. Maybe you noticed sadness or anger. If you did, ask yourself, "Why am I feeling sad or angry?" Again, notice the first thing that pops into your mind. Continue asking why until you get to the root of the problem, all along paying attention to the reactions in your body and noticing if a memory, thought, or feeling comes up. Eventually you will get to the bottom of the "why." More often than not, you will discover that it is a reaction to something that happened in the past. It doesn't matter if it would or would not bother your sister, friend, mother, or society. There are no "shoulds" in life—only how things feel to you.

## The "Why" Exercise

Event that bothered you:

_____

Body sensations:

_____

Emotions that come up:

_____

Why does this bother me?

_____

What are my beliefs about myself?

_____

Why do I believe that?

_____

What is my reaction to the person(s) involved with the event?

_____

Why did I react that way?

_____

What are my thoughts (assumptions) about myself?

_____

Why do I have those thoughts (assumptions) about myself?

_____

What are my thoughts (assumptions) about others?

_____

Why do I have those thoughts (assumptions) about others?

_____

As I have repeated many times, when you have a strong reaction to something, it is triggering something else in you. In the interest of getting to be an expert on yourself, it is important to figure that out. This exercise will help you break down a strong reaction into its most primitive form, or its foundation. Once you understand the "why," that "aha" moment gives you the opportunity to choose a response.

*Why setting boundaries can be so difficult:* Valuing yourself enough to ask for what you need is a necessary ingredient in setting boundaries. If you have a hard time setting boundaries, ask yourself—you guessed it— "Why?" Is it because you believe that people won't stick around if you set boundaries? Are you too afraid to test it out? Are you used to viewing yourself as a victim and have a hard time seeing yourself as a doer? Do you remember your parents teaching you to stand up for yourself? Did they stand up for themselves, or did they let people step all over them? How did they react when you told them how you felt about something they did? Did they get mad? Did they validate your feelings, or did they make you feel foolish for having them?

I was working with Sandra on setting boundaries, and she told me about her friend Kelly, with whom she had a particularly difficult time setting boundaries. Sandra had paid the last three times they had gone out. They were about to go out again, but Sandra did not want to get stuck with the bill. However, she was having a difficult time at the thought of confronting her friend, even just to ask her to pay for her half. I asked her "Why?" Sandra looked at me with a lost look on her face. She had no idea why, so I asked her to say the first thing that came to her mind. Sandra responded, "I'm afraid she'll get mad at me." I asked, "Why does the possibility of her getting mad at you scare you?" Sandra responded, "I don't know." I then asked, "How did it feel when your mom or dad got mad at you?" figuring it may be traced back to an experience she had had with one of her parents. She said, "Well, my dad was not around too much. When he was, I usually had fun with him, and we didn't argue much. My mom was the disciplinarian in the family. She would get mad a lot and yell at me." I then asked, "How did it feel when she got mad at you?" Sandra responded, "Not good." I asked, "Why?" She said, "It made me feel scared." At the risk of sounding like a three-year-old, I asked, "Why did it make you feel scared?" This time she answered spontaneously, "Because I didn't feel safe when she was mad at me." Bingo! That unsafe feeling associated with Sandra's mother getting mad at her was stuck in her implicit memory. Consequently, the possibility of any person getting mad at her triggered that unsafe feeling. And who wants to feel unsafe? Remember that from a brain standpoint, feeling unsafe *feels* life threatening, so we avoid it, consciously or not, at all costs. Sandra's fear of confrontation made sense.

Moving over to the left brain, or logic, for a moment, you may be thinking, "But she's an adult. Other than it being unpleasant, a friend getting mad at you is not the same as your mom getting mad at you when you are a kid. As an adult, it shouldn't feel unsafe." And you'd be right. It isn't the same, because even if your friend got violent when she was mad, as an adult you have many choices to protect yourself. You could walk away, call 911, or never talk to her again. However, when we are children, those options are not available or even realistic. When Sandra was a child, her mother got mad at her in a way that scared her and made her feel unsafe, stimulating her sympathetic nervous system, causing her body to go in to fight, flight, or freeze mode. Mom getting mad was associated or coupled with feeling unsafe in a scary, life-threatening, five-year-old way. In the fight, flight, or freeze response, her amygdala (threat detector) was activated and her hippocampus (associated with memory) was deactivated, causing those experiences to get fragmented, lodging parts of them into her implicit memory bank: the *association* of Mom being mad and her feeling of not being safe. Consequently, she avoided any situation that might cause someone to get mad at her because these situations triggered this implicit memory and thus were dealt with in a five-year-old kind of way: "Avoid confrontations at all costs." The fact that she was adult did not come into play. (See chapter 2 for a more detailed explanation.)

Remember that events that get locked into our implicit memory come up unknowingly when they get triggered. Because we are not aware that we have been triggered and are reacting to an unconscious memory from the past, we behave as if it is about the situation at hand. In this case, the possibility of someone getting mad at her triggered Sandra's five-year-old feeling of being unsafe, causing her to avoid confrontation at all costs, even at her own expense. Consequently, Sandra shied away from setting boundaries. Without asking "Why?" she would have never understood the connection and would have gone about her life sleepwalking and not feeling very fulfilled or empowered, always seeing herself as a victim to others' behaviors.

Having this information enabled Sandra to face her fear of setting boundaries. Now that she knew where it came from, she talked herself through the fear and set the boundaries anyway. More often than not, Sandra realized that her friends were willing to respect her boundaries and the association with her mother and the feeling of being unsafe as a child eventually decreased, thus, rewiring her brain.

Keep in mind that when you change the dance you have been dancing with your friends, family, partner, or coworkers, you will encounter resistance—not necessarily because they don't want you to be happy but because we are creatures of habit. We don't like change. This is not a reason to give up. You need to persist until the other person responds in a positive way. If they don't the ball is in your court. You get to decide whether to stay connected or to redefine the relationship. As with anything else, things are not always black and white. They include a lot of gray, and that is when compromise comes in. The important thing to remember is that your relationships—at home, at work, and in the social arena—should be reciprocal. If a sense of balance is missing, you may need to change something about your behavior that is contributing to the imbalance.

### Treating Yourself with Love and Compassion

Just as important as setting boundaries is noticing how you treat yourself. Do you treat yourself with love and compassion or with judgment and impatience? Think back. Where did you learn to treat yourself in that manner? Did a parent treat you that way? Did you see your parents treat each other that way? Is this the way you really want to treat yourself? If the answer is no, figure out where you learned the behavior. Some behavior is simply role modeled and learned from our parents or a significant adult in our lives, such as a teacher or a coach, that we eventually adopt as our own.

Very often we realize that we are treating ourselves in the exact way someone else treated us, even if we remember not liking it. This falls into the "identifying with the aggressor" defense mechanism. It almost seems like an automatic process—we take over where the aggressor left off. Do you remember a parent calling you stupid and now you find the word *stupid* coming out of your mouth when referring to yourself? Do you ever judge your feelings like your older sibling used to? Do you belittle yourself like the bully at school used to? It is important to pay attention to that voice in your head and to identify whether it is yours or it belongs to someone from your past. The good news is that role-modeled behavior or habit can be changed once you figure out that it is how you *learned* to do something from observing someone else, and it is not necessarily *your* choice.

Being aware of it is the first step. Notice how you treat yourself and decide if it serves you or if it hurts you. Ask yourself, "Do I treat my friends the way I treat myself?" Sometimes it's easier to gain perspective on an issue when we take ourselves out of it. If the answer is, "No. I treat myself worse," it is time to ask yourself the series of "why" questions from the previous exercise. I have no doubt that you will be able to trace your behavior to an event or events in your childhood that planted the seeds. Being mean to ourselves does not come out of thin air. It was taught through interactions we had with the significant people in our lives based on the things they said, did, or didn't say or do. You do not have to take over where they left off. Did I hear you say, "It's easier said than done"? You're right, but you have to start somewhere. Try this: imagine how you would treat your friend. Then treat yourself the same way. If your friend got laid off, would you tell her it was because she's good for nothing and lazy? If your friend's mother died, would you tell him to suck it up and suggest he not take time to grieve? That sounds pretty harsh, but you'd be surprised how harsh you can be with yourself when you start to listen.

Another technique is to talk to yourself the way you would talk to a child. If an eight-year-old got a bad grade on a test, would you call him an idiot, or would you acknowledge his putting forth his best effort and try to work with him to figure out what type of help he may need? If your ten-year-old niece forgot her lines in the school play, would you ridicule her and tell her she should never try out for another play again, or would you point out her courage for acting in the play in the first place? Learning to treat yourself with love and compassion shouldn't be difficult, but for many of us, it is one of the most challenging things we will ever do. It is not an easy task to change behavior, but it is certainly well worth it.

### Communication Is the Key

This brings us to the next most important area of focus to help change your patterns: communication. Whoever said that communication is an art was absolutely right. Many times it's not *what* you want to say but *how* you say it that makes all the difference. In addition to how you say something, how you *listen* to whomever you're communicating with is just as important. Your number one goal in communicating is to make someone feel "gotten" by you. Notice the relief and comfort you see in her when she says, "You get me." Recall how you felt when someone made you feel completely understood. That feeling of being "gotten" by someone goes beyond feeling understood, heard, or listened to. It goes deeper—into that primal attachment bond. If you recall in chapter 1, I mention that Daniel Stern refers to attunement as a parent's ability to be sensitive to the verbal and nonverbal cues of their child and to put themselves *into* the mind of the child as a way to be synchronized with them. Imagine feeling so deeply "gotten" by another person that you feel "felt" by them.

*Validate others' feelings:* Validation is key in making someone feel heard. Validating what someone is saying or feeling does *not* mean you agree with her or even understand her. By validating you're simply saying, "I hear what you're saying and how it makes you feel," not "I agree with what you're saying, and it's all my fault." How many times have we said or heard someone say to a child, "Don't feel scared. It's okay." We think we are comforting the child or helping him realize he will be all right. In reality, we are confusing and frustrating him. For whatever reason—a big dog just barked at him or a jack-in-the-box just jumped in his face—he is feeling scared. Saying, "Wow, that was scary!" or "That scared you, didn't it?" validates his feelings, and doesn't make him believe that what he is feeling is wrong because an adult he admires just told him not to feel scared.

My friend Jack was struggling with his six-year-old son Greg, who was a very sensitive child. Jack was the poster Marlboro Man. If you're too young for that reference, it comes from a time when they actually had cigarette commercials on TV. The Marlboro Man was the quintessential rugged male, with a thick mustache (it was the 1970s). He was a doer and a fixer, riding off into the sunset on his horse while smoking his Marlboro brand cigarette. The Marlboro Man did not give the impression that sensitivity and feelings were his area of expertise. Jack was not the most sensitive male either and was truly at a loss as to how to comfort his son. I gave him this little pearl of wisdom: "Less is more. Mirror the feeling. Don't try to fix it in this moment. Save that for later." One week later, Jack called me astounded, saying, "It works! I can't believe it, but it works like a charm!" He was putting Greg to bed when Greg started telling him about a friend at school who said something mean to him. Greg started to cry, and Jack said, "That must have really hurt your feelings." Jack explained that Greg looked into his eyes, grabbed his face with both little hands, and said, "That's exactly how I felt Dad." Jack told me that Greg then calmed down and fell into a sound sleep. Jack excitedly said, "It even works with my teenagers!"

The following is an example of a very common conversation that, more often than not, leads to an argument:

BILL: Why do you have to go out with your girlfriends once a week? [Question]

SALLY: I like spending time with them. Why do you ask? [Answering the question without defensiveness and being curious about the question]

BILL: It makes me feel like you'd rather be with them than with me. [Sharing information about oneself with the other person]

SALLY: Does going out with my friends make you feel like I don't care about you? [Looking under the hood at the feeling being shared and not taking it personally]

BILL: Yeah, I know you care about me, but that's what I feel. [Reiterating that it is not an accusation but a sharing of information]

SALLY: Okay, let's reach a compromise. How about if I go out with them twice a month instead of every week? [Coming up with a compromise]

BILL: You would do that for me? [Clarifying question]

SALLY: Absolutely! [Answering the question]

I know what you're thinking: Nobody talks like that! I purposefully made the conversation extreme to make my point. The truth is that learning to talk like this or a close version will more often than not result in actual communication and less arguing. Sally not taking Bill's question personally, figuring out the feeling behind what Bill was saying, and validating the information he was sharing about himself allowed Bill to feel heard and understood. Mind you, Sally may not have agreed with Bill or even understood why he felt the way he did. Maybe Bill's question even annoyed her a bit. But she did not take it personally as though he was saying that she was doing something wrong. Not interpreting his question as an accusation and simply hearing what he was saying, without judgment, let him know that she heard him. When we take things personally, we assume we are being accused of doing something wrong and immediately go into defense mode.

Additionally, Sally chose to be with Bill. It should matter to her how he feels, whether she believes his feelings are reasonable or not. That doesn't mean she should stop what she is doing, given that there is nothing wrong with going out with girlfriends, which doesn't deliberately hurt Bill. However, coming to a compromise was important to help him feel heard and taken care of, and therefore safe, and was important to keeping the peace in the relationship, which ultimately reduces stress for both of them.

The conversation could have gone like this:

**BILL:** Why do you have to go out with your girlfriends once a week? [Question]

**SALLY:** What? Why do you care? What's the big deal? [Defensive]

**BILL:** It just makes me feel like you'd rather be with them. [Information]

**SALLY:** Oh brother, are you kidding? There is nothing wrong with me going out with my girlfriends for God's sake! [Defensive]

**BILL:** Does it have to be *every* week? [Not feeling heard and escalating]

**SALLY:** Oh, now you want to tell me how often I can see my girlfriends? You're such a control freak! [Assumption and name calling]

**BILL:** No I'm not! Why are you even with me if you can't stand being around me? [Protecting]

And off they go into Never Never Land, where amygdalae run wild and free!

*Don't make accusations:* When communicating, it is very important to stay away from accusatory language. "You always make plans without checking with me first" is an accusation. You can almost see the protective shield go up, causing the recipient of this accusation to feel the need to defend herself. For all you know, the person thought she was doing you a favor by making the plans. "I know it's not intentional, but it makes me feel disrespected when you make plans without checking with me first" is a very different statement. It allows the recipient to hear you because you are not accusing her. You are giving information about you that she may not be aware of. Although you do not have any control over how the person will respond, if you have communicated in a nonaccusatory way, you get to choose, given her response, if you want to continue to associate with her or not. If you continue to associate with a person who does not hear you and continuously crosses a boundary you have attempted to set, the ball is back in your court. The operative question to you is—wait for it—"Why?" Why are you with this type of person?

Following are three examples of making an accusation versus communicating a feeling. You can see which behaviors work and which ones create problems.

*Communication I*
JANET: I can't believe you made dinner plans with Sara and Bill without checking with me first! [Accusation]
DAVID: What's the big deal? Cancel them if you want! [Defensive]
JANET: That's not the point! [Frustration at not being heard]
DAVID: What is the point? [Defensive]
JANET: What do you mean, "What's the point?" I can't believe you don't get it. [Frustration at not being heard]
DAVID: Oh boy! Here we go again. I *never* get it! I must be the biggest idiot in town! [Defensive]
JANET: Well, if the shoe fits! [Fighting words]

The conversation goes nowhere from here because their neocortexes (thinking brains) just went offline. David and Janet are now operating from their amygdalae (threat detector/emotional brains), and off they go into defend-and-protect mode, better known as fight mode—unless David or Janet abruptly leaves, going into flight mode. Keep in mind that *under stress we regress*. This means that when we are coming from our emotional brain, we will regress to the nonthinking, reactive way we used to deal with stressful situations. Someone coming from an ambivalent attachment style will be more prone to "act out" by becoming anxious and yelling or screaming, whereas someone coming from an avoidant attachment style will act out by "acting in" and will become quiet, walk away, or isolate himself.

If I am working with a couple whose arguments often end up this way, I have them choose a neutral word that either one can say out loud. It is a signal that one of them needs to walk away and take a thirty-minute time-out, or break, before continuing the conversation. Usually, the person who is less activated (upset) will be most likely to use it, but the agreement is that once the word is said, talking needs to stop immediately, and the partners need to walk away from each other. At times, the couple will choose a word that is funny, which helps break the tension and lower defenses, increasing the possibility of a resolution. Sometimes, if you are not as activated as your partner and you notice your partner regressing, stop engaging and let her have her feelings. This can be difficult, because many times our own discomfort brings up an urge to interact, point out, and fix. Not engaging and giving her some space, however, can be the best response in situations where the amygdala has taken over.

It takes twenty to thirty minutes for the sympathetic nervous system to calm down. When you take a time-out, make sure you engage in something that will help calm you down—listening to music, taking a walk, or playing with your pet. If you take thirty minutes off but spend them thinking about what you are going to say next, you will keep your sympathetic nervous system aroused, and the arguing will continue.

*Communication II*
JANET: Honey, I really enjoy going out with our friends, but it makes me feel dismissed when you make plans without checking with me first. [Prefacing a concern with a positive and stating a feeling, not making an accusation]

DAVID: Oh, I just knew you were free, and we had been talking this week about seeing Jane and Chris. [Offering an explanation; not defending himself]

JANET: I know. I don't think you did it to intentionally hurt me, but I really would like us to have a conversation first before making plans. [Hearing his explanation and restating her boundary]

DAVID: Okay. [Hearing her]

Even though David did not validate that Janet felt dismissed, he responded in a way that made her feel heard and did not make her feel the need to protect herself. The information was shared, and Janet felt heard by David.

*Communication III*
(Let's throw a monkey wrench in it!)

JANET: Honey, I really enjoy going out with our friends, but it makes me feel dismissed when you make plans without checking with me first. [Prefacing a concern with a positive and stating a feeling, not making an accusation]

DAVID: What's the big deal? You were free, and we talked about getting together with Jane and Chris. [Acting defensive and minimizing her feelings]

JANET: Well, it's a big deal because it makes me feel dismissed, and then I start to feel angry. [Keeping calm and restating her feelings]

DAVID: I don't get angry when you do it. [Defending and shifting the focus]

JANET: I understand that, but I'm letting you know how it makes *me* feel. [Keeping calm and bringing the conversation back to the original point of the communication]

DAVID: I really don't think it's a big deal. [Still defending and minimizing]

JANET: I appreciate that you don't, but I'm sharing with you how it makes me feel. Can you hear that? [Staying calm and going back to the original point of the communication]

DAVID: Yes I can, but I just don't see why it's such a big deal. [Trying to hear her but still feeling the need to defend and minimize]

JANET: I'm not trying to make it a big deal. However, I just don't feel heard by you right now. I love you. I'm not accusing you of anything. I'm just sharing with you how I feel and asking if we could do this differently in the future. [Getting that he is feeling accused; addressing his feelings and helping him feel safe; going back to original point of the communication: expressing how his action made her feel and suggesting a resolution]

DAVID: Okay, I'm sorry. Next time I'll check with you first. [With the threat of being accused gone and safety restored, he can now hear her.]

JANET: Thanks! [Feeling heard]

This time, Janet stayed away from accusations and accusatory language, but David still heard her words as an accusation. Janet did not take his defensiveness personally. Once she figured out that he was hearing her communication as an accusation, she addressed it and took care of his feelings. This calmed him down enough for them to have a successful exchange of information.

Three important points were illustrated in the previous example. The first was that Janet noticed that David was feeling accused, even though Janet was not accusing David. The way we hear things can sometimes be due to unresolved issues from the past. In this case, the fact that Janet was not using accusatory language but David kept feeling accused by Janet was an indication that David had been triggered and was reacting to something from his past. He might have been accused or blamed often in his childhood by his parents, siblings, or friends and expecting an accusation, he might hear all communication through this filter. Janet, catching that his defensiveness had nothing to do with her, did not take it personally. She took care of his feelings and helped him feel safe in the exchange.

In chapter 3, I discuss Steve Porges's work on how our nervous systems are primed to approach or avoid to keep us safe. In all communication, especially when sharing a difference of opinion or setting a boundary, it is of utmost importance to notice if the other person begins to feel threatened. You can tell he is going into defend-and-protect mode because his voice may get louder and his emotions may start to escalate. His nervous system is getting dysregulated. This indicates that his amygdala has detected threat and has stimulated his sympathetic nervous system, preparing him for fight or flight. If this is happening, the automatic reaction of the nervous system of the person who feels threatened is to avoid and not approach—the exact opposite of the purpose of communication. Creating a safe space for each other, by noticing such changes and taking care of your partner first, before continuing with the conversation at hand, will allow for information to be shared and for a resolution to be had. You can do this by asking what he is feeling or reacting in a curious manner, not in a judgmental or accusatory way.

Another important aspect of effective communication is starting with a positive. We all like to hear good things about ourselves. Start by saying what you like or appreciate about the other person. This allows him to be receptive to what's being communicated.

A third important factor in communication is to always bring it back to the original point. The other person may become defensive, and that's okay, but don't react to the defensiveness or the conversation will escalate and go nowhere. Validating how the recipient responded, whether with defensiveness or an attempt to put the focus elsewhere, is important, but equally important is bringing the conversation back to what you were trying to communicate in the first place. You might need to do this many times. As long as you don't get derailed and you stay calm, the recipient will eventually have to address what you are trying to communicate.

*Don't make assumptions:* Making assumptions, without checking out if they are accurate, is the single most dangerous thing to do in any communication. How often do we assume what our partners, friends, bosses, coworkers, or even family members are thinking and react as if we know that our assumptions are right on, without a shadow of a doubt, many times causing the other person to feel completely baffled? Assumptions are sometimes based on the other person's past behavior, but they can also be based on our own unresolved past. It is never a good idea to react based on an assumption. Always check out your assumptions first.

In the above scenario between Janet and David, what if Janet had made an assumption and said, "You make plans without checking with me first because I'm not important to you." Chances are she did not feel important to a significant person from her childhood, such as her mother or father, and having been triggered by David's action, projected those feelings onto him. If Janet had assumed that she wasn't important to David, she could have checked it out first by saying, "Is it because I'm not important to you that you went ahead and made plans without checking with me first?" This would have given David the opportunity to say yes or no. If David had said no, Janet could have then explained how his actions made her feel dismissed and share why, provided she was aware of the reason. If David answered yes, then Janet would need to rethink why she was with someone who makes her feel the same way her mother or father had made her feel when she was a child.

There are a number of keys to effective communication. It is quite baffling that we are never taught how to communicate, since we do it consistently throughout the day. Somewhere along the way, however, we do learn to accuse, defend, and assume. It is important to change this way of communicating so we can leave the past behind and enjoy our relationships, seeing them for what they really are.

# Conclusion

Patterns of behavior that are harmful to our relationships and our lives are developed without conscious awareness in childhood and repeated throughout life. The rule of thumb in mental health is that if an area in your life isn't working or not where you want it to be, it is time to take a closer look or, as I like to say, look under the hood. There is truly no reason not to live exactly the life you want or at least to consciously work toward it. Will the journey be easy? Absolutely not. It takes work, determination, and a lot of patience. Will it be worth it? Definitely.

Setting boundaries is an important step in taking care of ourselves. At times we run into people who cross our boundaries without a second thought, even if we have asked them not to. Many times, we think the easier choice is to let them, and certainly sometimes that may be the case. But more often, it makes for clearer communication when we set boundaries and stick to them. People will know where we stand and, if they are respectful, will try not to cross them. Sometimes, the boundary crosser in your life may not change his boundary-crossing behavior, but that should not deter you from taking care of yourself by reinforcing your boundaries. If it is difficult to know where your boundaries are and to stick to them, perhaps you need to dig a little deeper into why. The answer may lie in how you feel about yourself and your worth.

As you work to change old patterns, it is also important to practice feeling empowered and finding your voice—or asking for what you need from yourself as well as others. I have trained myself to see situations as opportunities to practice things that may not be easy for me. When the line at the bank is long and I am in a hurry, I take that opportunity to practice patience. When I make a call and hear a computer-generated voice asking me to push numbers incessantly before I finally get to a human, I take that opportunity to practice regulating my nervous system. Please do not mistakenly believe that I am Buddha-like and live a Zen life. Some days I succeed in my practice, and some days I don't. But knowing what I know now, and that I can rewire my brain, I don't stop trying. I take these opportunities to practice the skills I want to fine-tune.

Communication, as with setting boundaries, is often about taking the opportunity presented to you to practice changing old patterns, especially if you are not comfortable with confrontation. You might think confrontation has to be done in a stern, loud, and abrupt manner. However, we can gently confront someone who is crossing our boundaries or doing something that makes us uneasy. Remember the thirty-minute rule if you find yourself too upset to communicate calmly.

Making changes is not easy. We are all creatures of habit. As illogical as it seems, it is much easier to stay the same, complaining about what isn't working. It is much more difficult to be aware of our actions and behaviors. It requires purposeful thought and focus. The term "ignorance is bliss" is true. You can't do anything about something you're not aware of, and ignorance absolves us from taking any responsibility for our behavior. However, once you are aware of something, it becomes much harder to ignore it, unless rationalization is your defense mechanism of choice! But even if it is, look around you. Your behavior contributes greatly to how your life looks. Is every aspect of your life going the way you want it to? Are you content in all areas of your life? It takes courage to ask for help. Change is not for the weak at heart.

## End-of-Chapter Exercise

Baffle your family and friends and communicate using the techniques on this list.

# 10 Tips for Effective Communication

1. MAKE SURE THE OTHER PERSON FEELS UNDERSTOOD: Always keep this in the forefront of your mind when talking to another person. Ask yourself: *Do I make her feel heard?*
2. LISTEN: When another person is talking, listen and wait until he is finished. Do not talk over him or interrupt.
3. VALIDATE FEELINGS: Start with validating her feelings: "You look sad," "I know you're angry," "Is that scary?" Validating feelings does not mean you agree with her.
4. REPEAT: Repeat what the other person just said and ask him if you got it right to make sure you understand what he is saying.
5. NOTICE CHANGES: If you notice a change in the other person— crying, red face, change in facial expression—stop talking and ask him what just happened. Take care of him first, help him feel safe, and then continue your conversation.
6. DON'T MAKE ASSUMPTIONS: Don't make assumptions and then react based on your assumptions. Check things out: "When you looked away is it because you don't care about what I'm saying?"
7. ASK FOR A TIME OUT: Agree on a time-out signal. If you or the other person is too upset, know that the ability to think rationally is gone. Use your signal, ask for a timeout, and come back in thirty minutes.
8. DON'T MAKE ACCUSATIONS: Use "I feel" statements. Tell her how what she said or did makes you feel. Don't say: "You don't care about me!" Do say: "It makes me feel like you don't care about me, when you don't pick up after yourself."

9. **PREFACE WITH THE POSITIVE:** Preface difficult-to-hear feedback with something positive about the person.
10. **DON'T GET DEFENSIVE:** Listen with curiosity. If someone is accusing you of something, ask clarifying questions. Remember, what they say will upset you *only* if you believe them.

What differences do you notice in the communication with the people in your life?

## Chapter Four Takeaway

Communicating effectively, including setting boundaries and conveying your needs to change patterns developed in childhood, affects every area of life. We all develop patterns of behavior. Discovering your patterns can help you begin to put the pieces of your life together in a conscious way. Changing the way you communicate is a first step to making the more difficult changes in your life. If setting boundaries is challenging for you, ask yourself why. You should be your biggest fan and greatest protector—not in a rigid way but similar to how you would treat a child, friend, or partner. If you treat yourself any differently, ask yourself why and do what it takes to change that.

# 5

# How to Wake Up

*When the pupil is ready,*
*the teacher appears.*
—Anonymous

## Amanda the Adult

When Amanda came to see me for therapy in her late twenties, she complained that every guy she dated couldn't commit. There was the orthopedist, who would end every date crying over his ex-wife; the stock broker she'd seen for six months, who couldn't get "comfortable" sleeping at her apartment or having her sleep at his; the bartender, who really liked her but didn't believe in marriage; and, of course there was Howard, who accused her of smothering him.

With time I helped Amanda see that she had been programmed to believe that she was not worthy of being loved. Due to that programming, she had developed a fear of abandonment. Consequently, a lot of the men she found attractive had a fear of engulfment and would keep her at arm's length, constantly triggering her abandonment fears. The more these men remained distant, the needier she became. Eventually they would end the relationship, thus perpetuating her worst fear—complete abandonment.

We looked at what triggered Amanda's fear of abandonment and found that almost everything her partners did, abandoning or not, triggered it. She was able to see that Howard didn't ignore her when he traveled, but her fear was so great that she reacted to beliefs that were inside her, not based on reality. Amanda also realized that getting what she wanted from men didn't calm her as she thought it would. It actually increased her anxiety, because she would become even more afraid that they would leave her, so she scrutinized everything they did.

She described hanging out with Howard one Sunday afternoon. He told her he was going to the store. Because he didn't invite her to go with him, she felt a sudden surge of anxiety and engaged him in an argument. I explained that the anxiety she felt was a physical response to getting triggered. Howard not asking her to come with him triggered her fear of abandonment. Had she recognized this, she could have talked herself through it or simply asked Howard if she could join him. Their argument could have been avoided.

Instead, the argument caused the rest of their Sunday to be tense. When Howard got up to leave after dinner, Amanda asked why he didn't want to stay the night. This question led to yet another argument, with her accusing him of not loving her enough. The accusation upset him and made his desire to leave even stronger.

Although her relationship with Howard didn't last, we continued working on ways to recognize her triggers and stop reacting to them. She began to understand what her triggers were, the assumptions she made, and the behavior they produced. We were making excellent progress.

Then she met Jack. He was a new broker at her office who had transferred on a temporary basis from Washington, D.C. He swept her off her feet with his good looks and cool demeanor. Amanda told me—after just two dates—that he could be "the one." I reminded her that he had transferred on a temporary basis. Amanda was slipping into her old pattern: falling for someone who was not available.

Amanda told me that she already had strong feelings for Jack. She had begun fantasizing about him moving from Washington,

D.C., to be with her in Los Angeles. (From a psychological perspective, her unconscious belief was that if Jack moved for her, it would heal the deep wound caused by her mother's inconsistent parenting and her father's sporadic visits, which made her feel unloved and disposable. In reality, it would not heal the wound, but her unconscious didn't know that.)

She was clearly setting herself up for another dose of perceived abandonment, which would further reinforce her feelings of being unlovable. We spent a lot of time discussing this issue. A few sessions later, Amanda announced her decision to stop seeing Jack. Having realized her patterns, she decided that by ending the relationship now, she would empower herself and not wait for his inevitable departure, which would surely feel like abandonment. She told me it was difficult, especially because she saw him at work every day. I explained that insight and awareness alone do not stop our old patterns. It is our new behavior that really creates the change, and new behavior isn't always easy.

I felt happy for Amanda. She was on the road to freedom and the kind of love she desired. She eventually began dating a man she said she would never have found attractive before our work together. However, she saw something in him that was different and that she liked. That something different was his ability to commit. Two years later, they got married.

Once you gain insight into your attachment style, your triggers, and your automatic behaviors, they will no longer be able to hide in your unconscious. You will be aware of them, and this awareness will take the power out of them and present a choice. You can either continue to behave in the same manner when triggered—fully conscious of the results your behavior yields—or choose to change your behavior, take back the reins of your life, and start being the person you really want to be. You will be able to *respond*, not *react*. Reacting would have caused Amanda to continue dating Jack. Her *response*, however, was to stop. But insight and awareness alone do not produce long-term change. New experiences do, and these new experiences rewire our brain.

# Recognizing Your Triggers

Now that you have learned to identify your patterns of behavior, and whether or not you are sleepwalking through life, you can begin to sort out your triggers. You are halfway to freeing yourself from old patterns that you may have been locked into repeating since childhood. Everyone's patterns are unique, and so are their triggers. At specific points in this chapter, I have woven in five exercises that will take you step-by-step through the process of recognizing your triggers and regulating your nervous system, so you can learn to respond and not react.

Some triggers get programmed through a process called classical conditioning, discovered by well-known physiologist Ivan Pavlov in the 1890s. In a famous experiment, Pavlov was able to get a dog to salivate at the sound of a bell. He did this by ringing a bell every time he fed the dog. Eventually, when the dog heard a bell, anticipating food, it began to salivate. The experiment demonstrated that two things that have nothing to do with each other can be paired and cause an involuntary physical reaction—one we cannot consciously control. Classical conditioning explains my friend Randy's fearful reaction to rulers (discussed in chapter 2), because when he was a child, his father hit him with one.

Under threat, when our adrenalin (stress hormone) is flowing and we are in heightened awareness, it can take just one experience to cause two unrelated things to get coupled together. Some sleep disorders develop due to this unrelated pairing of events. For example, if you have a near-drowning experience, the sympathetic branch of your nervous system gets activated. Your body goes into fight-or-flight mode, as you try to save yourself from drowning. Once the brain decides there is no way out and death is very near, the parasympathetic branch takes over. It puts on the brakes to shut your body down and protect you from feeling pain. Your nervous system goes into collapse mode, causing you to lose consciousness. Depending on the severity of the situation, you may wake up in the arms of a lifeguard or in a hospital bed with tubes down your throat.

Regardless of the condition you find yourself in when you wake up, an association could have been made—namely, that parasympathetic function, or relaxing and shutting down, is not safe; it means death is near.

Consequently, falling asleep now feels implicitly dangerous because it requires the body to relax and shut down, which is now paired with almost dying. This is a completely unconscious pairing of two unrelated things.

Feeling anxious right before going under anesthesia can also cause sleep disorders, as a similar association may be made. Anxiety is fear, and when the effects of the anesthetic take over, your body shuts down, pairing fear with shutting down. Thus falling asleep can trigger this fear. People who have serious car accidents and wake up in the hospital may have similar difficulties with sleep. Scientists believe that sensations and related emotions get associated or paired with the events that originally evoked them and are stored in the implicit memory bank. This means we are not always aware of what can trigger us and, for the most part, do not have conscious access to this information.

Actions or behaviors that are not directly related to a specific experience but are associated with what our brain has learned to anticipate about others can also trigger us. Such triggers might be subtle. My patient Sally was out at lunch and saw her coworker Kevin, whom she was attracted to, leaving a coffee shop across the street. She thought she had caught his eye. But before she could wave hello, he walked to his car, got in, and took off, in Sally's mind pretending that she didn't exist.

This triggered Sally's fear of abandonment and consequent feelings of rejection. Although she wasn't aware of getting triggered, her heart began to race and her breathing got heavy. She was pissed. By the time she got back to the office, she was fuming. Kevin exiting the coffee shop without waving hello had felt rejecting to her. It confirmed her unconscious belief that she was worthless and not important enough to be acknowledged. The idea that Kevin may not have seen her had not even crossed her mind because of her deep-rooted detrimental beliefs about herself.

The experience caused Sally to interact with Kevin based on an assumption that he did not like her. She became cold, aloof, and even angry toward him at work, making him think that *she* didn't like *him*. She explained that she could tell Kevin was keeping his distance from her. His behavior confirmed her belief that he didn't like her. While Sally was telling me this story, I recall reacting to how angry she got when Kevin didn't say hello. The way she described her anger and how it had grown by the time she got back to the office gave me the clue that she may have been triggered. Her angry feelings seemed a little excessive for what had happened. The fact that it didn't occur to her that he might not have seen her was a second clue. When we have a reaction that is disproportionate to the event or when we don't consider every possible explanation, we have most likely been triggered. The event has touched something in us that has little to do with what just happened. Feeling sad or disappointed when a coworker, especially one we are attracted to, seemingly ignores us is well within the range of expected reactions. However, anger and rage cross over the line of expected reactions and enter into Trigger Land.

I urged Sally to face her fears and check out her assumption by asking Kevin if he had seen her across the street from the coffee shop that day. As it turned out, he had not seen her. He had noticed that she had turned cold toward him at work and just thought she didn't like him. He admitted having been interested in her and wanting to ask her out, but he hadn't because of the way she was acting toward him. The situation was cleared up, and they actually began dating.

I pointed out to Sally how she had not recognized her disproportionate anger, which caused her to make an assumption based on the programming of her past and not necessarily on the present experience. She then reacted in a way that made her fear—Kevin keeping his distance—come true. Someone without a fear of abandonment might have felt disappointed or sad, and simply would have approached Kevin and mentioned that she had seen him leaving the coffee shop, which would have given Kevin a chance to say that he had not seen her. Helping Sally become more aware of her triggers and her reactions based on assumptions and not real facts helped her become less reactive to perceived rejection from others. She began to notice her bodily reactions and started checking to see if her immediate assumptions were accurate before reacting to them.

### Pay Attention to Your Physical Reactions

Noticing your body sensations and reactions is key to noticing your triggers, regardless of what they are. Usually you will find that just one or two things trigger you, but they can get manifested in many different ways and may, cause you to think that many things trigger you. Throughout my own work in this area, I have noticed that my biggest trigger is the feeling of not being heard or understood. My father was an engineer and believed emotions were a waste of time. My mother, on the other hand, minimized emotions but cried during Hallmark commercials. I can now surmise that her emotions were buried so deep that she could not access them, but they spilled out given the opportunity. (Those Hallmark commercials *can* be very touching!) So when I was a child, my emotions were not nurtured or understood and instead were minimized and not taken very seriously.

When I began to do work for my own personal growth and understanding, I took note of every time I got really angry. I attempted to break the situation down to see where the anger stemmed from. How did I break the situation down? By asking why over and over again until a pattern emerged. Taking the time to narrow down what triggers you is important. It allows you to prepare for the trigger before it happens and also to understand what is happening when you have been triggered.

Until the "oozy eggs" experience that I described in chapter 2, I did not realize that my anger was triggered by a feeling of not being heard. As you can imagine, I have had many experiences similar to the "egg oozing"scenario, as I like most of my food very well-done, baffling many a chef in the Los Angeles area, but it doesn't trigger me any longer. I have to admit that the next time it happened after the egg incident I felt pretty angry again, although I noticed the anger was not nearly as strong as the time before. I recall I had not prepared for the possibility of getting my order wrong and was taken aback that I had a similar reaction. Again I noticed what sensations I felt in my body, and I worked through them in a similar fashion. Since then, I now prepare myself for the possibility of a culinary mistake in my order and other than slight annoyance, especially when I'm very hungry, that rage is now gone.

## Understanding Your Triggers

In the first column in the chart below, write down five events or situations (from any time in your life) that have made you extremely angry or very sad. Break down the experience by asking yourself these questions:

- Why did you feel that way?
- Why did you react that way?
- What were your thoughts and why did you think them?
- What assumptions did you make about the others involved?
- What assumptions did you make about yourself?

In the second column, write down the reasons for your angry or sad reactions. Use the strategies and information you have learned so far to figure out the reasons for your reactions.

| Event | Reason |
|-------|--------|
| 1.    |        |
| 2.    |        |
| 3.    |        |
| 4.    |        |
| 5.    |        |

Making sense of what triggers you brings it into awareness. Awareness is the first necessary step in turning an unconscious reaction into a conscious response. Without this understanding we are prisoners of our past, rationalizing our reactions and making excuses for behavior that we may not comprehend. The following section will teach you what to do after you have recognized your triggers.

## How to Regulate Your Nervous System

As we learned in chapter 2, overcoming self-destructive unconscious behaviors that developed primarily as a result of attachment to your primary caregiver in childhood is all about regulating your nervous system.

At the risk of sounding too single-minded, this skill is key to handling anything that comes your way. This does not mean you won't at times have emotions that feel scary, messy, and overwhelming. The huge difference is that you will have the capacity to tolerate them and know that you can and will get through them, that there is a light at the end of the tunnel of emotions. Having the ability to regulate your nervous system will allow you to keep the thinking part of your brain online, or connected with the emotional brain (the amygdala), so you can take a step back, notice what is occurring, calm down, and choose the best response. Noticing when your body gets triggered will help turn implicit unknowing into explicit knowing and you will become much more aware of your true self.

Since the body remembers everything, even when the mind doesn't, the first step in regulating your nervous system is getting acquainted with your body and recognizing the difference between feeling calm and relaxed and feeling fearful, stressed, or anxious. A colleague of mine, Dave Berger, a physical therapist and psychotherapist at the Center for Integrative Medicine in Concord, New Hampshire, explains that when we are in the fear state, our whole body shifts upward. Our pelvic floor moves up, our abdomen moves up, our chest moves up, our neck and shoulders move up, and our mouth and eyes open. From a survival standpoint, this upward movement makes us taller, so we appear bigger and more threatening. It also prepares us to fight or run (flight). As you are sitting there reading this, is your tongue touching the roof of your mouth? Try softening your tongue and notice what happens in your body. What did you notice? Did your body relax? Keep reading, I'll explain why!

Brain research shows that conscious, focused, purposeful attention is essential to change the brain and form new connections, because the brain will form connections around what is being focused on. The following exercises will help you get acquainted with your body. By focusing attention on your body, new connections will be made in your brain that will eventually make it easier to do. You will also learn how to regulate your nervous system when something upsetting occurs. As with breaking any habit, change won't happen overnight; it requires repetition and purposeful attention. The important thing is to just notice and explore with curiosity, and not accusations or judgments. When we judge what we are feeling or thinking, we add to the problem and not the solution. Who cares what you're thinking or feeling? It's there. Best is to just notice what is already there and learn not to react to it.Use the following exercises to help you focus your attention and allow for the response *you* choose.

### Notice Your Body

Most of us take our bodies for granted. If I asked you to notice your butt on the chair or sofa you're sitting in, you'd probably have to concentrate to do so. It is of utmost importance to get acquainted with your body. Research has found that in many situations, the body reacts before the mind is aware of the situation. Certainly we know that the body is connected to the brain, but I don't think many of us are aware of just how connected. There are cranial nerves that travel between the brain and the body, but, as you learned in chapter 2, only 20 percent of those nerves take information from the brain to the body; 80 percent of the nerves bring information from the body to the brain. Consequently, the body tells the brain how we are feeling. If our muscles are tense, the brain will interpret that as danger or threat.

These cranial nerves surround most of our organs. Because of the information they carry to our brain, many of the expressions we use today were created. For example, when we say, "my heart hurts" after a break-up it is because there are literally "brain cells" that surround our heart that take information from our heart to our brain. I have to assume that the person who came up with the expression suffered a break-up, noticed a pain in his chest area and came up with that expression that we consider a metaphor, but in actuality, is a real and literal sensation. When we say, "I have butterflies in my stomach" before speaking in public, it is because that is the actual sensation that is felt. Why? Who knows, but the sensation appears to be universal because most of us who do not like to speak in public have felt butterflies in our stomach. If we put all the "brain cells" dispersed around our organs together, they would amount to the size of a cat's brain.

The language of body sensations is unfamiliar to most of us because we are usually not taught to pay attention to it. If we are taught about emotions at all, we are taught to say things like, "I feel sad." How do you know you feel sad? What sensation do you actually feel in your body? A heaviness or tightness in your chest? Do you feel blocked, stuck, still, numb? A heaviness on your shoulders? See what I mean? Being aware of your body's reactions to sadness—what you are actually *sensing*—is very different from simply saying, "I feel sad." Sadness can feel very different to many people. For some, if sadness was paired with fear, they would feel their heart race or an uncomfortable energy in their chest or stomach. Others might feel heaviness in their chest or a lump in their throat. For those of you who don't know what emotions you're feeling, tuning in to your body sensations will help clue you in.

## The Vocabulary of Sensation

The following is a list of "body sensation words" taken directly from the somatic Experiencing Training Manual. These words will help you recognize and describe how emotions are felt in the body. Identifying your body's reactions to your emotional states is an important step in learning how to regulate your nervous system.

| | | |
|---|---|---|
| achy | cool | frantic |
| airy | cozy | frozen |
| alive | crampy | full |
| bloated | damp | furry |
| blocked | dense | goose bumpy |
| breathless | dizzy | gurgling |
| brittle | dull | hard |
| bubbly | elastic | heavy |
| burning | electric | hot |
| buzzy | empty | icy |
| chilled | energized | intense |
| clammy | expanding | itchy |
| closed | faint | jagged |
| cold | flaccid | jittery |
| congested | fluid | jumbly |
| constricted | flushed | jumpy |
| contracted | fluttery | knotted |

| | | |
|---|---|---|
| light | ragged | strong |
| loose | raw | suffocating |
| moist | rolling | sweaty |
| moving | shaky | tender |
| nauseous | sharp | tense |
| numb | shimmering | thick |
| open | shivery | throbbing |
| paralyzed | shuttery | tickly |
| pounding | silky | tight |
| pressured | smooth | tingling |
| prickly | soft | trembly |
| puffy | spacious | tremulous |
| pulled | spasming | twitchy |
| pulsing | spinning | vibration |
| quaking | sticky | warm |
| quiet | still | wobbly |
| quivering | stretchy | |
| radiating | stringy | |

For me, feeling body sensations was once very foreign. When people talked about them, it was as if they were speaking a language I didn't understand. The following exercise was very helpful to me when I started getting in touch with my body sensations.

## Progressive Relaxation

This exercise will help you get acquainted with different parts of your body. In progressive relaxation, you isolate and then contract and relax specific body parts. Clenching a muscle first and then relaxing it allows you to notice the difference between the two sensations. It helps you get in touch with the difference between being tense and feeling relaxed. Focus all your attention on the sensations you feel when you tense a specific area and then when you allow that area to relax. Don't worry about clenching the "right way." The purpose of this exercise is to notice the release and how it feels.

- Clench your toes, count to three, and release.
- Clench your feet, count to three, and release.
- Take a deep breath.
- Move to your calves, clench them, count to three, and release.
- Move up to your thighs, clench them, count to three, and release.
- Move to your buttocks, clench them, count to three, and release.
- Move to your torso, clench it, count to three, and release.
- Move to your hands, clench them, count to three, and release.
- Move to your arms, clench them, count to three, and release.
- Move to your neck, clench it, count to three, and release.
- Move to your face, clench it, shut your eyes tight, count to three, and release.
- Clench your entire body, count to three, and release.

Now allow your whole body to relax, letting a warm wave of relaxing sensations flow downward from the top of your head, through your body, down your legs, and into your toes. With practice, this technique can help you to regulate your nervous system. It can also help with sleep problems and with general stress or anxiety.

### Find Your Calm Place

We've learned that information coming in from our senses, including our gut (viscera), can trigger us. Our perceptions, real or imagined, can also trigger us. Likewise, our thoughts can guide our emotions. Getting upset and feeling stressed is not good for optimal health. As discussed in chapter 2, when stress hormones flood our brains and bodies, we can't function at our highest potential, and we begin to break down. Our memories aren't as sharp as they used to be, our immune systems are weakened, and we begin to feel run-down. The stress will show up one way or another.

Many people are not used to feeling calm, and it actually scares them. They are so used to feeling anxious and believing that the tiger is around the corner and can pounce at any time that relaxing or calming down can actually trigger more anxiety. Their window of tolerance for a calm state is very small, and their window of tolerance for fear, anxiety, and panic is huge. To expand the window of tolerance for your calm place, find something that makes you feel good the second you think about it, and notice your body sensations. As you focus on it and notice how your body feels, you are anchoring the sensation of calmness in your body. Doing this for a few minutes or even a few seconds every day will help expand your window of tolerance for a calm state and change your brain.

## Discovering Your Calm Place

Think of something that automatically brings a smile to your face. It can be your child, your pet, your room, your backyard, the beach, the mountains, your best friend, your friend's kids, your favorite flower—anything that the second you think about it, you notice an immediate feeling of calm and happiness. Let's say you're thinking about your pet. Notice your face. Is it smiling? Notice your shoulders, chest, and abdomen. How do they feel? What sensation words (calm, relaxed, strong, and so on) would you use to describe how they feel? Your calm place can also be internal. Maybe the manner in which you handled a situation in the past brings a smile to your face. It could be your courage, empathy, kindness, or loyalty.

In the chart that follows, write down five calm places that bring an immediate smile to your face and a relaxing sensation in your body:

### Calm Places

1. _____

2. _____

3. _____

4. _____

5. _____

If on a scale from 1 to 10, 10 is the worst stress you can imagine, think of something that happened to you in the past week that created a level 5 stressor. It could have been getting stuck in traffic, being late to an appointment, or forgetting something at work. Notice your body as you're thinking about this event. Do you feel your heart beating fast, tightness or heaviness in your chest, or knots in your stomach? Notice that. Now bring one of your calm places to mind. If the calm place is a pet, recall a funny moment with it, the first time you brought it home, or your favorite time spent together. As you're thinking about that, notice your body. Is your heart beating slower? Is the tightness or heaviness in your chest gone? Are the knots in your stomach dissipating? Is your body calming down? Spend a few minutes practicing this exercise, especially when you feel stressed. Noticing that moment of calm, even for a split second, will begin to expand your window of tolerance for the calm state. Remember, your brain is plastic. Every time you practice this exercise, you are activating new connections that will eventually become permanent.

### Ground Yourself

As I have mentioned many times, when we overreact, like my rage about eggs not being cooked to my liking, something inside of us is getting triggered. The present experience is tapping into an unresolved implicit memory from our past. That rush of emotions we feel is a reaction to the present experience *and* the past experience. The unresolved emotions piggyback on the current emotions. The problem is that implicit memories don't *feel* like memories, so we can't tell the difference in that moment.

A way to separate past emotions from present emotions is to ground yourself. This simply means noticing where your body is in that exact moment, which brings your awareness into the here and now. This will help you separate the old implicit memory from the experience in the present. The present experience might be anger or anxiety provoking, but by grounding yourself and putting yourself in the here and now, you will be able to respond to the actual event in front of you. This greatly decreases the possibility of reacting in a way that is not the authentic you. Emotions can sweep us into the past, because we are coming from our amygdalae and activating implicit memories. Grounding yourself keeps you in the present, in the here and now.

## Separating the Past from the Present

Use this exercise when you notice your body reacting strongly to something that doesn't warrant a strong reaction or when you feel a sudden surge of anxiety for no apparent reason. As in the previous exercise, think of something that stressed you out to a level 5. As you're thinking about this event, notice the sensations in your body. Is your heart racing? Does your chest feel tight? Does your stomach feel nauseous?

As you are noticing your body sensations, begin by also noticing your feet on the floor. Does the ground feel hard or soft? Do your feet feel warm or cold? Feel the back of your legs on the chair or sofa. Does its surface feel hard or soft? Feel your back on the chair or sofa. Does that surface feel hard or soft? Notice how the chair or sofa supports your body in the sitting position. Notice how the floor supports your feet. Stay with this for a few seconds, noticing your feet on the floor, your butt on the seat, your back on the chair. After a few moments, go back to the part of your body where you felt the uncomfortable sensations and notice if that area is beginning to feel calm. Go back and forth until the sensations in your body that felt like stress have dissipated and your body begins to feel calmer.

Grounding yourself immediately puts you in the present moment. I also ground myself throughout the day, noticing different body parts for a split second, just to stay in close contact with my body and to keep myself in the here and now. Initially, it was difficult to remember to notice my body, as it was not something I was used to doing. To remind myself I put little notes all over with the words feet, butt, hands, arms, and legs on them. Every time I noticed a note I would quickly focus on whatever body part was written on it. This practice has become habitual and keeps me very much in touch with my body. It has been instrumental in helping me keep my cool under stress. Making this practice a habit will allow you to become well connected to the sensations in your body. You will be able to notice the slightest changes, giving you sufficient time to take a step back and keep the thinking part of your brain on line. As much as possible, you want the thinking brain to stay connected with the emotional brain. Those of you who come from a traumatic past may find it very difficult to notice your body, as that alone can trigger a reaction. If this is the case for you, I recommend that you seek professional help, so you can take back your power, reconnect your brain and your body, and break the chains that keep you living in the past. See the Resources page at the end of the book for a link to find therapists trained to work with the body.

### Engage Your Thinking Brain

If anxiety means fear and fear triggers the fight-or-flight response and causes the thinking brain to go offline, the way to reduce anxiety is to keep the thinking brain online and engaged. Seriously, it is that simple. I do not mean to minimize how difficult it can be at times, especially if you suffer from overwhelming anxiety, but I have found that understanding the brain mechanism behind anxiety and breaking it down to its simplest form can help reduce your stress. The goal is to keep the thinking brain connected with the emotional brain.

Remember that once you notice your heart racing, tightness in your chest, or nausea in your stomach, the sympathetic branch of your nervous system has been activated. Your body is preparing for fight or flight. In this moment, you have a split second to keep your thinking brain online. This is why it is so important to get extremely acquainted with your body sensations, so you can always be a step ahead. Remember that going into fight-or-flight mode does not require thought, so you will not always be consciously aware of when something has triggered you and your body is preparing to fight the tiger lurking around the corner. Notice your body, assess the situation, and ask yourself, "Is a tiger coming at me?" If the answer is no, engage your thinking brain.

Here are some tricks for engaging your thinking brain:

*Look around the room, turning your neck to the left and then to the right:* Notice your surroundings, whether you are inside or outside. What color are the walls? How many trees do you see? Moving your neck muscles allows your social engagement system, part of the parasympathetic nervous system, to come online. This will start to calm you down.

*Wherever you are, look for ten pink or purple things (any color will work):* The focused attention in looking for the colored objects engages your thinking brain.

*Count from three hundred backward:* Counting from one to ten is too common and doesn't engage your thinking brain as much as counting numbers that aren't that practiced. Doing multiplication tables in your head also works well, unless you have them memorized. If so, choose something more challenging.

*If you have a fear of flying and are about to get on an airplane, buy the most boring magazine you can possibly find:* Technology or computer magazines usually do the trick for me (no offense to the technology and computer experts who find them fascinating!). As soon as you're sitting on the airplane, start reading. It doesn't matter if you understand the words—just read them. Reading automatically engages the thinking part of your brain because the skill used to read is located in that area of the brain. If you become distracted and find yourself thinking about how scary airplanes are, notice that, but then go back to reading. It doesn't matter if you get distracted and have to do this one hundred times—keep going back to reading. It's important to choose a boring magazine because a topic that is interesting or exciting might trigger your sympathetic nervous system, which is the last thing you want to happen. Threat and excitement cause the same sympathetic activation. The difference is the emotion that is associated with the activation. In other words, feeling excited is fun, but you are still activated and your brain is still sending the signal to release adrenaline, cortisol, and other hormones released by sympathetic activation. Eventually, you calm down, your body metabolizes the chemicals, and there is no trauma, because the activation was not associated with threat or fear. However, in this situation, it is best not to trigger your sympathetic nervous system at all.

### Create a Balance between the Left and Right Brain

Creating a balance between the left and right brain helps to regulate the nervous system. As you now know, different parts of the brain have their own specialized talents. The left side of the brain is more linear and logical. It likes words, explanations, planning, details, and facts. The right side, on the other hand, enjoys creativity and abstract concepts. It is more emotional, is not concerned with details, and looks at the big picture. This is not to say that when you are thinking logically there is no activity in the right side of your brain or that when you're painting, your left brain falls asleep. However, it is true that right-brain-dominant people, due to their creativity, might have a harder time focusing and following a scheduled plan, while their left-brain-dominant counterparts might find it hard to let a detail go. They might delay a project, for instance, even if that detail is irrelevant in the big picture.

As usual, the first order of business is to get to know yourself. Are you prone to see life through a left-brain lens or a right-brain lens, or can you use a skill that best fits the situation in front of you, regardless of what side of the brain that particular skill stems from? Noticing and becoming aware of your own tendencies will help you become more of a balanced-brain thinker.

My patient Rhonda had five projects going at once and couldn't figure out what to do first. She had deadlines to meet, but she felt overwhelmed. She couldn't get organized enough to get anything done. I realized she was one big right brain, with a tiny, nearly nonexistent left brain. Rhonda was highly creative and had made a living in the arts and entertainment world, but it was becoming more difficult for her to get things done, and she had no idea why. While she was telling me about her projects and what stages they were in, I asked her to invite her left brain into the conversation. Her perplexed look told me she had no idea what I was talking about. I explained the differences between the two sides of our brain and how they worked. She understood what I was saying and looked relieved.

I talked to Rhonda about how we can rewire our brains. For the next few months, we worked on inviting her left brain in to help her with focus, planning, and organizing her time, so she could get her projects done and on time. Rhonda was able to complete every one of her projects and said she felt more balanced in how she saw and approached her life. Similarly, if you find that you are too left-brain biased, it is important to invite your right brain in to help you either let your hair down, think outside the box, or take a step back and look at the big picture.

### *Keep Your Social Engagement System On*

In chapter 3, I introduced you to Steve Porges, a scientist who has studied the sympathetic and parasympathetic nervous systems in depth. As you recall, one branch of the parasympathetic nervous system is activated when our amygdala is not detecting threat and we feel safe, thus allowing us to be in a relaxed mood. He called this the *social engagement system* because this relaxed mood causes our ocular (eye) and facial muscles to soften, inviting others toward us because, to their nervous systems, we appear safe. Being in this state also allows our hormones to be in balance and our bodies to work correctly, decreasing the risk of disease and increasing the likelihood of connecting with others, which numerous studies show strengthens the immune system. Given all these wonderful side effects of living within the social engagement system as a baseline, this should be a goal for all of us. Unfortunately, the baseline for many people is more on the vigilant or suspicious side or, conversely, on the down, low-energy, isolation, or frozen side. Such people visit the relaxed state only on occasion and only with the people they trust.

Stimulating the parasympathetic branch of your nervous system helps keep your social engagement system on. You can use tricks to activate the parasympathetic nervous system, for example, relaxing your tongue. Earlier in this chapter, I had you notice your tongue and relax it. Doing so might have caused you to feel a slight calm in your body. Digestion is part of the parasympathetic branch, because we have to be relaxed to digest food. When we get excited or scared, blood flows away from the digestive system and into other parts of the body, to prepare them for the possibility of running or fighting. The tongue is at the beginning of the digestion process, so when the tongue is relaxed, it activates the parasympathetic branch. Pretty interesting, right? Exhaling is a parasympathetic function, while inhaling is a sympathetic function. When you inhale, your heart rate goes up slightly. When you exhale, it calms slightly. If your exhale is *longer* than your inhale, you are stimulating your parasympathetic nervous system.

All the exercises I describe in this chapter will help your social engagement system come online more often. The more you practice bringing your social engagement system online, the more you are stimulating your brain to build new circuits in this area to better tolerate this state. Thus you are rewiring your brain. These exercises will also help you build a resilient mind—a mind that can sustain all emotions and thoughts without resistance; a mind that can just *notice* if sadness arises, if anger comes, if panic takes over, or even if you are feeling calm, happy, or excited, without reacting.

It is the same with thoughts. Just notice your thoughts without reacting or responding to them. Sometimes we can be afraid of our own thoughts, but they are just thoughts, just as emotions are just feelings. We get to decide if we want to respond to our thoughts and emotions. For now, they are just thoughts, just emotions.

Creating an inner calmness, with the knowledge that you can handle whatever comes your way, will give you the skills to handle anything and will allow you to be open to and welcome connection with others. This does not mean you will not have feelings; the goal is not to be emotionless or thoughtless. It is to believe that emotions or thoughts don't control you.

## A Reminder about Your Amygdala

The previous exercises will help you get in touch with your body. Many of us can *see* that our bodies exist, but unless we are in pain, we don't notice or sense their existence. These exercises will also help you learn to regulate your nervous system when things happen and emotions are strong. To move forward at this point, it is necessary to remind you about your amygdala and how it works.

There is one very important thing you need to know about your amygdala; it is not the brightest bulb in the bunch or the sharpest tool in the shed. Remember Francois, the lounge lizard from chapter 2? Like Francois, your amygdala has a one-track mind, and it doesn't diverge from its job. Don't get me wrong—the amygdala does an excellent job at scanning for danger, but it does not have the capacity to think outside the box without the help of the thinking brain.

Flashbacks from PTSD showcase the inefficiency of the amygdala. As I mentioned in chapter 2, flashbacks happen when we have witnessed or experienced an event that felt life threatening. When we think of the event, or something unknowingly triggers a memory of it, we might have a flashback or see the scene as if we were there, in it, and reliving it. PTSD symptoms usually interfere with everyday life; that is what I mean by the ineptitude of the amygdala. The amygdala didn't get the memo that you are safe and the threat is gone. It continues to believe you are in imminent danger and causes your mind and body to believe it as well.

According to scientists who study the brain and nervous system, the symptoms from traumatic events persist because in the face of danger, our brains and bodies go into automatic fight-or-flight mode. If this threat response is not completed, freeze takes over, and the fight-or-flight impulse gets stuck in the nervous system and muscles. The body keeps signaling to the brain that danger is still present, causing the brain to believe that we are still under threat, continuously keeping the body prepared to run, fight, or freeze. If this cycle doesn't get interrupted, we can start to develop physical ailments that can be traced to the hormonal and chemical chaos that being stuck in the fight, flight, or freeze response is creating.

Remember that digestion shuts down when we are preparing to fight or run away. Technically, there is a decrease in secretions of digestive fluids in the stomach and a decrease in the natural contractions of the sphincter muscles in the intestines that move food through. This interferes with the natural flow of our digestive functioning, resulting in constipation, indigestion, and other gastrointestinal problems. Eventually, the stomach and intestines get used to not working correctly and serious issues can arise.

This situation can even affect how we look. I recall working with a man who had come from neglect and a lot of unpredictability in his childhood. He never knew what to expect because his mother was a drug addict. She was sometimes coherent but usually not. He never knew what condition she'd be in when he got home from school. I asked him what that felt like in his body. He immediately said it felt like he was always bracing himself for the worst. One particularly hot day, after I had been seeing him for about six months, he came in wearing flip-flops. I noticed his toes were stuck in a curled, or "bracing for danger," position. It was only then that I realized how much bracing he had done in his childhood. He was still bracing for danger, and all this bracing had actually altered the shape of his toes. In cases like this, it is important to gently interrupt this cycle and allow the blocked defensive impulses to be released and renegotiated.

## Releasing Stuck Impulses

So far, you have learned some exercises that will help you regulate your nervous system when you react in the present based on an unresolved past traumatic experience. It is also important to learn how to release stuck impulses in a more permanent manner, to dissipate and decrease the things that cause you to react. As you know, your amygdala scans for danger and reacts to it, real or perceived, without the benefit of the thinking part of your brain. The perceived threats could be stuck impulses or reactions from long ago.

As discussed in chapter 2, Peter Levine developed a technique called Somatic Experiencing Therapy, which allows the nervous system and body to release stuck impulses, melting them away, restoring the mind and body to their pretrauma states. I use this approach with almost everyone I work with. Getting in touch with the sensations in your body—noticing and allowing the body to do what it needs to do to release the stuck impulses—resembles the unfolding of a beautiful symphony heard for the first time.

If you think about an event from your past and notice strong emotions or sensations in your body, there is a good chance that your body is holding onto something that doesn't need to be there. The key is to *notice with curiosity and not judgment.* Say you remember your first day of school and the excitement you felt while getting ready. Thinking about this day may cause you to notice your heart beating a little faster. You might remember feeling a little scared when you walked into the classroom full of kids you had never met before and a teacher who was a stranger to you. At recalling this memory, you may notice having a slight sensation of butterflies in your stomach in *this* moment. Sometimes, just noticing the sensation will dissipate it. If so, you have just released a stuck impulse in your body from that experience. Release can come in many different forms: yawns, belches, stomach gurgles, laughter, pleasant or neutral electricity or tingling running down your arms and legs or in your body.

Sometimes noticing the sensations in your body when telling a scary or traumatic story from your past may actually make the sensations stronger. You might also notice other sensations that feel unpleasant or uncomfortable. If this is the case, you are tapping into a fight-or-flight response that is stuck in your nervous system and requires more work to be released. For example, the first day of school can be a very scary experience to a little kid—one that would automatically put the body into fight-or-flight mode. For a kid, fighting or running away is usually not an option, so a child will stay in the classroom feeling scared, and the fight-or-flight impulse might turn into a freeze and get stuck in the body.

Focusing on the present body sensation, not the one you may have felt at the time, allows that stuck impulse to wake up and complete what it didn't get a chance to do back then. So if the first day of school was really scary for you, you might notice a fairly strong bodily sensation, such as a racing heart, at recalling it. Maybe focusing on the sensation causes it to get stronger and move to your legs. Maybe you feel an uncomfortable electricity or tingling sensation in your legs. Focusing on this sensation might cause you to think about running. Surprisingly, if you imagine yourself, as a five-year-old, running away from that scary classroom, away from all those new scary kids and teacher, maybe into the arms of someone you feel very safe with, you will notice your body beginning to relax and feel calm again. The skeptics out there may be thinking, "That's stupid! That's not what happened in real life. That wouldn't calm me down. You can't rewrite history." Well hold onto your hats, Don and Debbie Doubter, because you can! That's the beauty of the amygdala's shortcomings. Since the amygdala can't tell the difference between the danger of long ago and the safety of the present moment, it also can't tell the difference between what really happened and a newly imagined outcome. Therefore, tricking the amygdala is not too difficult. All it takes is your imagination. The goal is to complete the threat impulse that got stuck or thwarted and to restabilize the nervous system.

### Changing the Past: Infusing New Memories

Remember my dad, the engineer, who said emotions are a waste of time? Well, he trained me to think very logically. The idea of changing the ending to an event didn't make sense to me, however neither did flashbacks before I had my own professional training and personal therapy. But since I have been working with my patients by using the techniques I learned in my Somatic Experiencing Training, I have come to realize that helping them come up with a different ending and inserting it, if you will, into an already experienced trauma allows the nervous system to correct itself and come out of shock. After working through it in this manner, the old traumatic event is paired with the new outcome, and the two form a new association. When you think of that old memory, the new "inserted" ending automatically also comes to mind, so consequently, recalling the event doesn't trigger you the way it used to. As soon as the upset of the trauma piece comes up, the calm of the "new" resolution gets activated. The traumatic event loses its power or hold on you because the new inserted outcome causes your body to feel safe. Your body stops sending a signal to your brain that you are still in danger, which stops reinforcing the fear circuitry, allowing your brain to be less reactive overall, rewiring your brain, and making room for a calmer state.

Carol, a patient I had for many years, was able to replace an old, debilitating memory with a new one using the techniques I describe. Carol had moved to Los Angeles from England. She often told me about her father and how scary he was. He raged at her often, and she never quite knew what was going to make him angry. It is believed that our auditory sense has the most direct line into the emotional part of the brain, which is why yelling is so unbelievably scary to kids. Carol recalled how paralyzing her father's yelling was and the thought of it still had the same paralyzing effects. As an adult, she was thinking about getting out of her current job, as it was beginning to require her to speak in public, which she couldn't do without an immediate image of her father's face yelling at her, causing her to feel that same frozen state she felt long before.

Carol's fear of her father was still so present that when she talked about him, I noticed her shoulders slump and her posture change—as though she had shrunk an inch. I could see how debilitating the memories still were, but nothing I tried seemed to help much. One day she told me that she had had a dream about her father and couldn't get him out of her head. At that point, I decided to try my newly discovered Somatic Experiencing techniques.

I asked her to tell me about a memory of when her father was yelling at her—the first one that came into her mind. She replied, somewhat sarcastically, "Every day, any day, he would come into my room and start letting me have it." I stopped her there and asked, "As you're telling me this, what do you notice in your body?" She immediately said, "My heart is beating fast." I asked her to notice her heart beating fast and just see what happened next. She mentioned that she felt electricity running through her arms. I asked her if this sensation was pleasant or unpleasant. She said it was very unpleasant. I then asked her to notice the electricity and to see if her arms wanted to do something: slap, hit, or push. She immediately said, "I want to punch the crap out of him!" To this, I said, "Imagine punching the crap out of him." I made it clear that I was not suggesting that she actually hurt her father but that she just imagine doing it, right there in the office with me.

Carol was quiet for about four minutes. I checked in a few times, and she said she was imagining punching, hitting, kicking, and stomping on her father. A lot of pent-up anger and threat responses had been stuck in her for many years. When I asked her what she was noticing, she said, "It's so weird. I feel freezing coldness traveling down my arms and legs. It feels like a huge block of ice is melting in the middle of my body and going out through my arms and legs." I asked her if it was okay to let herself feel that. She said it was, but she added, "But I want to continue punching and kicking my dad." I said, "Okay, keep imagining it and take all the time you need."

This exercise allowed Carol to melt away the freeze that was stuck in her nervous system from all the years of yelling she had endured. What was underneath the freeze was a fight response that had also gotten stuck, because reacting to her father's yelling was not something that had occurred to her as a child and it usually doesn't.

For twenty-five minutes, Carol described everything she wanted to do to her father but couldn't. She hit him, punched him, and kicked him. She also imagined that she was a superhero and had powers to freeze him so he couldn't move. Then she flew in the air like a ninja. She kicked him so hard that he fell over and his frozen body broke into a million pieces. The amygdala doesn't care if the fantasy is real or make believe. It doesn't know the difference. The point is to awaken these threat responses and allow them to complete what they started long ago.

As Carol described to me what she was imagining, I started to notice her body relaxing. I asked her what she was feeling in her body and she said that a calmness was coming over her. She noticed her heart beating slower. A few minutes later she had a smile on her face and said, "That felt so good." I asked her to notice the calmness in her body and to just sit with for a few moments to anchor that new sensation. I then asked her to imagine the same scene she had told me about before we started the exercise. She said, "I'm in my room and I can see his face. His mouth is opening to yell at me, but I can also see me hitting and immobilizing him." As she said this, I noticed her sitting up straight. Her shoulders were no longer slumped. I pointed this out and asked her to notice what this felt like in her body. She said, "Empowered; I feel empowered."

I continued working with Carol for a few more years. Every time I asked about her father, a smile would automatically show up on her face and she would say, "Every time I see his face, I also see me kicking his ass." This "fake" memory that was inserted into her amygdala allowed a new association to be made. Her father yelling, and Carol cowering, morphed into her father yelling and Carol defending and protecting herself.

Carol did not quit her job, and although she still did not enjoy public speaking, and probably never will, she was able to do it. The trauma from her past no longer controlled her present. This may sound too good to be true, but I have seen it happen many times since my work with Carol and the results still amaze me. Peter Levine's Somatic Experiencing Therapy is powerful and is based in brain science.

Corrective experiences, as they are called, are not the same for everyone. My patient Gerard, a mild-mannered food delivery man, had been robbed at gunpoint by the people who opened the door when he made his last delivery of the night. During the robbery, he froze and couldn't move. He could still feel the coldness of the gun on his forehead. He had been having nightmares and flashbacks. He felt so uncomfortable in crowds that he stopped leaving his house and started to isolate. I asked him what he was feeling in his body as he told me he felt electricity running down his legs, and he was feeling very uncomfortable. I knew this was a stuck impulse needing to be released. I assumed it was a fight response, perhaps an urge to kick the robbers to immobilize them.

I asked Gerard if his legs felt like doing something and he said he felt the urge to run away, so I had him imagine that he was running. He explained that his legs felt calmer, but his heart was still racing. When I asked him to focus on his heart, he said the thought of the robbers finding and killing him came to mind. Because the robbers had not been captured, his amygdala continued to send the signal that he was still in danger. I asked him to imagine being at the front door again and making his delivery. I asked what needed to happen—if anything at all were possible—for him to feel safe. I thought he might imagine the Incredible Hulk standing next to him and kicking the robbers' butts the minute they opened the door, or that he grew twenty feet and stepped on them like little ants. Oh yes, I had all of these wonderful fantasies that I thought would be great to help him get through this trauma. Of course, he needed to come up with one of his own, and after a few moments he said that he imagined the police walking by and arresting the robbers and that they stayed in jail forever. He added, "And then I ran away."

As he was imagining this new scenario, I asked him what he was sensing in his body. He noticed his heart calming down and in an incredulous way said that his legs were still. I wasn't sure what to make of the stillness in his legs, so I asked if that sensation felt pleasant or unpleasant. He said that his legs had not felt still since the event. In fact, a doctor had diagnosed him with restless leg syndrome. A smile came over Gerard's face as he said that the stillness felt really good, like a huge relief.

Gerard's freeze response and subsequent inability to protect himself, coupled with the fact that the robbers had not been caught, caused his nervous system to stay in the flight response, sending a message to his amygdala that he was not safe. His legs were still trying to run away. For Gerard, getting physical and attacking the robbers was just not his style. He had to come up with what would allow him to feel safe. For him, imagining the police walking by and arresting the robbers worked. It allowed him to complete the flight response by running away. In this work, there is no right or wrong. Whatever works works. Your body will tell you. Gerard stopped having nightmares and the flashbacks were gone.

## Releasing Your Stuck Impulses and Infusing New Memories

The following exercise takes you step by step through the process of releasing impulses that might be stuck in your nervous system and infusing new memories. The exercise will help rewire your brain because as you release stuck impulses, your brain becomes less reactive and more tolerable of a calm state. Use the exercise for minor events that you notice a charge from, such as an argument with your boss or a disagreement with someone at the grocery store. If you had a highly traumatic childhood in which you suffered abuse or neglect, I strongly suggest you seek professional help instead of trying this on your own. On the resources page, you will find the Somatic Experiencing Therapy Web address, which will lead you to trained therapists in your area. As in any area where you hire someone to provide a service, interview potential therapists to find one you feel comfortable with. Just because someone has a degree and a license doesn't automatically make her competent.

Think of an event that caused you fear or anger. Choose one that's a "5" on a scale of 1–10.

_____

_____

_____

As you are thinking about this event now, notice where you feel the fear or anger in your body, and describe it using sensation words (see "The Vocabulary of Sensation," page 167).

_____

_____

_____

Notice that sensation. You are not trying to make it do anything. There is no right or wrong. Just observe it like you're observing the wind blowing through the trees, and see what happens next: Does it move? Does it get stronger? Does it get weaker? Does it have a color? A shape? Does a thought or image come to mind? _____

_____

   If the sensation gets too strong, ground yourself and stop the exercise here. Feel your feet on the ground, feel the back of your legs on the seat, feel your back on the chair. Notice how the chair supports your body in the sitting position. Notice how the floor supports your feet. Continue feeling your feet on the ground and your body in the chair until you notice the sensation dissipating.

   If the sensation is tolerable, notice if it feels pleasant, unpleasant, or neutral. _____

_____

   If it feels pleasant or neutral (even if it's a "weird" neutral), just notice it and end the exercise here. Your nervous system has released old, stuck threat responses.
   If it feels unpleasant, notice if the sensation wants to do something. If the unpleasant sensation is in your throat, does it want to say anything, yell, scream? If it's in your arms, does it want to hit, punch, slap? If the sensation is in your legs/feet does it want to kick, walk, run, jump? If the sensation had a voice, what would it say? _____

_____

   Maybe the image of someone you trust, a super hero or the police saving you from the situation comes to mind. Maybe simply thinking about how you would have liked to have reacted at that time comes to mind.
   If the sensation wants to do any of the above suggestions (or any you come up with), imagine doing it. Go anywhere your imagination takes you; just notice it and let your imagination go. This is your body completing the fight or flight response. You are not really hurting anyone or wishing ill on anyone. You are simply reacting the way you would have at the time of the event had you been given the chance.

Notice your body, what sensations are you feeling now?

_____

_____

_____

Note: You may feel very tired after this exercise. This is common after releasing stuck impulses. Make sure to take care of yourself by resting and not overexerting yourself afterward.

## Respond, Don't React

Practicing the above techniques will allow you to respond and not react. For people on the ambivalent side of the attachment continuum, emotions can take over and often do. Ambivalents are prone to anxiety and experience many emotions. As we have learned, emotions are part of our humanness. We cannot escape them. A valuable lesson if you have ambivalent attachment is that you don't need to react to every feeling you notice. It is also not about judging your emotions, calling them irrational, or telling yourself that you shouldn't be feeling certain emotions. Feelings don't always make sense, but there's a reason for them. Noticing them and knowing that you don't have to react to them can be a huge relief to someone with an ambivalent attachment style.

While people with ambivalent attachment styles often feel overwhelmed with emotions, people with avoidant attachment styles most often feel underwhelmed. They first need to learn what an emotion feels like. Learning to tune into your body will help you crack the code of your emotions. You will begin to fit the pieces together and understand that that feeling of heaviness in your chest after the guy you like canceled your date could be sadness. Instead of reacting by immediately going out on ten dates to cover up that sadness, you may start by being okay with letting yourself feel the sadness. Then you can decide if a response is warranted or if simply feeling and acknowledging the sadness is enough. The sadness will pass. It is just a feeling.

Now that you know what to look for, pay close attention to your physical reactions to things. Notice physiological changes in your body. Take a step back, do not react, and think about what just happened. What is your body telling you? Talk yourself through it and then *choose* a behavior. Do you need to ask a clarifying question? Do you need to take a thirty-minute breather?

### *Learning Not to React to Triggers*

I had been working with Monica for a few months. One week she told me that she had gone out to lunch with her best friend, Paul. They each ordered soup and a salad. The waiter brought all the food at the same time. Paul began to eat his soup. Monica began to eat her salad. Paul looked at Monica and said, "Don't you want to eat your soup before it gets cold?" All of a sudden, Monica felt hot all over. Her heart started to race and she felt like she was about to lose it. She realized that she wanted to yell at Paul and say, "I'll eat my soup when I damn well please. Don't tell me when to eat my soup. Maybe I want to eat it cold. What the hell do you care? I'm not a little kid. Who the hell do you think you are?" To say the least, Monica was really surprised by her extreme internal reaction to Paul's suggestion.

Because of her work in therapy, she realized that his comment had been a trigger that related to her engulfment issues. Her mother was so overprotective and infantilizing that at times Monica felt she couldn't breathe without her mother wanting to make sure she was breathing correctly. In fact, her mother was still reminding forty-year-old Monica to wear a jacket on cold days and to take an umbrella when it rained.

Because Monica had learned to recognize when she was being triggered, she was able to choose *not* to react to Paul, although it took all her willpower not to. Because Paul was a good friend, she felt safe telling him how it made her feel when he made the comment about the soup. Paul appreciated that she confided in him. Of course, he never meant to tell her what to do nor to treat her like a child. He said he would try to be more mindful about making comments or asking questions that might sound infantilizing.

Monica shared with me that changing her behavior by *not reacting* and instead, working through being triggered and choosing a response, was one of the most difficult things she had ever done. She was thrilled that the incident hadn't hurt her relationship with Paul, as it might have in the past.

This experience was instrumental for Monica to realize how her new behaviors could bring about change. What could have ended up as an awkward and uncomfortable lunch continued to be an enjoyable visit with her friend that actually brought them closer. Her new behaviors and experiences began to create new neural pathways in her brain, taking the power out of her triggers.

## Know Your Audience and Speak Their Language

In chapter 4 we learned basic communication skills. Now I'll teach you to take your communication a step further. You'll learn to get to know your audience from many different perspectives, which will help you communicate more effectively.

Many times, what starts out as a benign conversation turns into an argument, leaving both parties feeling unheard and misunderstood. Paying attention to *what* is being said is very important, as we learned in the previous chapter. But paying attention to *how* it's being said takes communication to the next level. For example, what part of the brain is he using while talking to you? Is he coming at you from his right brain or his left brain? His thinking brain or his emotional brain? What might his attachment style be? Having this information and paying attention to these nuances will change the way you communicate, often resolving in minutes what could potentially turn into hours of back-and-forth negotiations.

### *Right-Brain and Left-Brain Communication*
As you recall from chapter 2, right-brain and left-brain functions have different characteristics. The right brain is more creative and emotional, and the left is more logical and linear. Suppose your partner, friend, or coworker comes to you and says, "I'm so frustrated! The deadline for this new project is around the corner. I can't do anything until the design department finishes its part, but the designers don't seem to know what day it is or even care. It's my butt on the line!" Your first response might be

_ jump into fix-it mode (left-brain activity) and say, "Did you talk to your boss about that?" To which the person might respond, *"Of course I did!"* Her tone tells you that your suggestion was not helpful and that she is coming from her right brain—in other words, just venting her emotions.

Switching to your right brain and speaking *her* language would sound something like, "It's so frustrating when you have to wait on someone else to finish before you can continue." This statement allows her to feel heard and understood. She is communicating an emotion, and you are responding in kind—right brain to right brain communication. On the other hand, if someone says to you, "My car broke down on my way to work today. Do know a good mechanic?" and you respond, "Wow, that's so frustrating. I bet that pissed you off!" he might respond, "Yeah, whatever. Who's your mechanic?" He is communicating with his left brain and looking for a left-brain response. This is not to say that your comment wasn't well intentioned. However, he is in left-brain mode, and a right-brain response will not make him feel heard by you. Recognizing which side of the brain someone is coming from and matching it can be a helpful tool when communicating. It will make the other person feel heard and understood. Certainly, as with most things, situations are not always black and white. If you're not sure where the other person is coming from, ask her. You can say something like, "I see you're very upset, and I'd like to help you out. What do you need from me right now? Do you want my suggestions, or do you just need me to be one big ear and just listen?" Then you don't have to guess and if you're prone to go into fix-it mode, you can relax, listen, and know that you are giving her what she needs at that moment. People who automatically jump into fix-it mode usually feel they are not being helpful by just listening, however, by asking, you can be sure that you are being helpful, even if it is out of your comfort zone.

### Keeping the Thinking Brain Connected to the Emotional Brain

When what starts as communication turns into an argument and things get heated, we need to stop ourselves in that split second before we enter Never Never Land, where amygdalae run wild and free. Otherwise, as you already know, we will stop communicating and begin reacting, our emotions will overpower our ability to think and consider the consequences of our behavior (a thinking brain function). This may cause us to say things we may mean in the moment due to anger but not really believe in general, like "I hate you" to spouses we actually love or, "I quit" to bosses when we had no intention of leaving our jobs —things we will be sure to regret saying and doing later.

This is not an easy task, but when you notice your partner, boss, friend, or child, start to get agitated, and you can tell that at any moment the emotional brain will take over, it is imperative that you ground yourself and help him stay calm and connected to his thinking brain. There are many ways to do this:

*Lower your voice or make it more monotone:* It is a psychological phenomenon that we mimic each other and will cause the other person to "simmer down" and mimic your volume and tone.

*Excuse yourself and come back when emotions have calmed and a conversation can be had:* Remember, it takes about twenty or thirty minutes for the nervous system to calm down.

*Speak at a slower rate, pacing yourself:* This will help slow down and pace the other person.

*Simply reflect how upset the other person is, attuning to his feelings:* Saying how you feel or providing an explanation at this moment will only add fuel to the fire. For instance, when your five-year-old is having a tantrum because you won't buy him the toy helicopter he wants, giving him the reasons why will not help calm him down. Saying something like, "I know it makes you mad at Mommy when you can't get what you want. Sometimes it's hard being a kid" validates how he might be feeling and makes him feel understood by you. The same applies to anyone who is agitated and about to go into the Twilight Zone. Taking care of his feelings first, before trying to resolve the argument, will allow you to reach a quicker resolution because he will feel safe again, which will dampen his defenses, and you can get back to the original point of the conversation.

*Engage the person's thinking brain:* When communicating say things like, "What do you think about this?" "How can we come up with a compromise?" or "How do you think we can resolve this?" Make sure you are not engaging her emotional brain by making statements that can agitate her further, such as, "I can't believe how emotional you're getting. It's really no big deal." She's already emotional, and saying that won't help and will fuel the fire.

### Understanding Others' Attachment Styles

Understanding your own attachment style is critical to understanding your behavior as an adult—your overreactions, your triggers, and your seemingly unexplainable feelings. Recognizing the attachment style of the people around you can also prove to be very helpful as you get to know and understand them. This process is not meant to label or pigeonhole people but simply to allow you to better understand them. Keep in mind that causing a person to feel deeply understood and accepted by you creates a very strong bond. In chapter 1, I described the different attachment styles and how they generally manifest in adulthood. Even if someone doesn't fall neatly into one style, trying to get to know her at this level is still extremely helpful.

Unless it's very obvious, you may not be able to recognize the attachment style of people you have limited interaction with or do not spend a lot of time around—for example, a boss, coworker, or acquaintance. However, a boss who is more on the avoidant side may show up as quiet and reserved. Learn to speak her language and don't send e-mails that are too wordy or overwhelming. With someone like this, report the facts—just the facts. Conversely, speaking the language of a boss who is more on the ambivalent side may involve more detailed communication.

As we learned in chapter 1 your partner is your next primary attachment figure, so it can prove extremely helpful to learn her language from an attachment perspective. More often than not, people with opposite attachment styles get together and form relationships. Familiarize yourself with your partner's attachment style. Learn to speak her language. Know that if she is on the ambivalent side of the attachment continuum, she needs to feel connected to feel safe—plain and simple. And what is the goal of all human beings? To feel safe in the world. So why not connect with her throughout the day? The more connected she feels, the safer she'll feel in the relationship and the calmer she'll be. When going out doesn't include her, remind her that you will be back. You may be wondering if this approach is enabling, in other words, perpetuating a problem.

What happens if your efforts are still not enough? All excellent concerns. If connecting with your partner causes her to calm and feel safe in the relationship, then it's not enabling. It's you learning to speak your partner's language and taking good care of her. If, on the other hand, you can't do enough to calm your partner down, then a compromise has to be agreed upon. For example, you can agree to connect with her five times a day. A compromise takes both people out of their comfort zones, as they do things they ordinarily wouldn't do, but the change is not overly disruptive. If reaching a compromise does not reduce your partner's anxiety, then professional help may be warranted.

If your partner's on the avoidant side, he needs his space. Alone time is very important to him. Give it to him. He will feel safe in the relationship and will want to come toward you. Remember, it is not you specifically that he is avoiding. But if giving him his space causes him to want more alone time, then, again, a compromise needs to be agreed upon. For example, a compromise in this situation might be to choose certain days of the week that he gets alone time and other days that are spent together. Getting to know your partner at this level is truly a win-win for both.

Couples inadvertently develop a "dance" as they get to know each other and spend time together. This dance can either be beautiful and symmetrical or jagged and invasive. It takes two people to work at a relationship. However, change in one person will automatically bring about change in the other. Initially people may resist change, but if you stay consistent, they will either join you or let you know that they won't, in which case you get to choose whether you want to be in the relationship or not. Since knowing your partner from an attachment perspective allows you to anticipate what she needs, by putting this into practice, you may find that your partner will automatically begin to feel safer with you. The process will calm her defense mechanisms, stimulate her social engagement systems, and allow her to join you in changing the dance.

As I mentioned earlier, many times you will get together with partners who have traits that are similar to those of your parents such as making you feel scared or unloved. Without this awareness, the person you fall in love with may be the very person you will feel the need to protect yourself from. You might start to feel as though you are living with the enemy or that you have invited the tiger to live in your home. Your partner should be your go-to person, the person you can depend on and trust above anyone else. He should be the first person you want to call and celebrate with when you find out about a promotion and the first person you want a comforting hug from when you learn about the death of a loved one. This is not to say that couples should isolate and not have other friends. As always, a balance is the healthiest way to go. However, to develop a secure attachment in your relationship, even if individually both of you are of insecure attachment, whether avoidant or ambivalent, you need to believe that your partner has your back and you have his. A lot of people ask me, "Why should I have to do all the work? Why can't he change?" To which I ask, "Will doing this work lessen the stress between the two of you? If the answer is yes, then why not do it? It takes one person to take the chance and change the dance!

# Conclusion

Waking up from sleepwalking means becoming aware of your physical and emotional reactions and developing the skills and insight needed to discover what is causing these reactions. Childhood attachment experiences almost always hold the key to this awareness. Getting to know your body is possibly one of the most important things you can do in your quest to decrease your reactivity and to become more thoughtful in your responses. The exercises in this chapter will help you get acquainted with your body and also learn to calm your nervous system down, giving you greater control over your emotions.

Beneath emotions are body sensations. It is essential to work at the sensation level, because sensations hold the key to unlocking trauma. Remember, trauma can result from any experience that overwhelms your capacity to cope. By noticing the sensations in your body, you are metaphorically inviting your body to do what it needs to do to allow your nervous system to reset. Melting stuck threat responses will allow you to be more authentic, autonomous, and empowered. Your body won't be constantly telling your brain that you are in danger, causing you to walk around ready to fight or run, or conversely, walk around frozen and detached. You will feel safe in the world and will walk around in a calm state, knowing that if your environment becomes dangerous, you will react accordingly.

Science has shown that purposeful, conscious, focused behavior will change your brain. The catalyst to change is the focus of attention, which is why it is so important to notice what your body is telling you and to understand what emotion corresponds to that body sensation. If your emotions are running high, ground yourself, so you can regulate your nervous system. Take a survey of the situation at hand and then decide the best way to handle it. This sequence of focused attention stimulates a set of neurons that begin to form a pattern in your brain—one that is very different from the reactive, no-thought-involved pattern of survival and attack.

After many years of working with me, a patient who had endured an enormous amount of trauma in childhood described the change she experienced by saying she was no longer looking for what was "behind the noise" or who was "lurking in the shadows." Instead, she could now hear the birds singing, notice the colors of flowers, and smell the earth under her feet. Her social engagement system was waking up and coming online. She was no longer living in fight-or-flight mode and was able to notice her surroundings. She had released herself from her past trauma and the triggers that resulted and was able to live her life fully and in the present.

## End-of-Chapter Exercise

Practice grounding yourself often throughout the day. Notice your feet on the floor, your butt in a chair, the sheets on your skin if you're lying in bed, your hands on the steering wheel in the car. One second of awareness, several times throughout the day, will train your brain to be in touch with your body sensations and have an open line of communication and awareness. Set a gentle alarm on your phone or put a note on your desk.

Every time you hear the sound or see the note, take a second to feel your body in whatever position it is in at that moment. With practice, this will become a habit that will serve you very well.

## Chapter Five Takeaway

Knowing your body so well that you can pick up on even the slightest change or shift is an essential first step in becoming "awake." Just notice with curiosity what comes up inside you. Have no judgments, just curiosity, as though you are observing yourself like a character in a movie. Notice your thoughts, feelings, and sensations as just that: thoughts, feelings, and sensations. They can't hurt us unless we react to them. If we believe a negative thought about ourselves, it will feel painful and stop us from doing things. If we react to anger, we may behave in a way that we regret. If we try to ignore a tightness or heavy sensation in our chest, we may take a pill or overeat in an attempt to mask it. Just notice without judgment. Use the sensations as cues to what is going on inside. They will eventually help you change unconscious behavior rooted in your childhood attachments, and you will no longer *sleepwalk* through life.

# 6

# Now That You're Awake

*Love and compassion are necessities, not luxuries.*
*Without them, humanity cannot survive.*
—the Dalai Lama

## The Real Amanda

Amanda's ambivalent attachment showed up at work in the form of a fear of failure. Living with this pervasive fear of abandonment led to a level of anxiety that compelled her to question herself often and made it very difficult to make decisions. Her fear of making the wrong decision and not doing well or failing was too much for her to bear, so she kept herself safe and stunted. Amanda's belief that she was unloved permeated all areas of her life and caused her to be very careful. If she messed up at work, she did not even consider that she was liked and would most likely be given the chance to rectify her mistakes. She assumed that one mistake would cause her to get fired, and the anxiety about not having a job and not being able to support herself was terrifying. The fact that she had worked at this office for eight years, had wonderful reviews, and had been offered a promotion did not reduce her anxieties. Of course, she knew on an intellectual level that she could handle more responsibility, but at an emotional level she did not believe it. She had learned to rationalize away why she couldn't take the promotion: she was either too busy or had time conflicts. She was actually beginning to believe her own excuses.

Our core beliefs, planted when forming our first attachments, are often expressed in our behaviors. I helped Amanda redefine herself and begin to change her core beliefs. Amanda eventually learned to nurture and love herself. However, for change to occur, she had to face her fears. I urged her to take the promotion for a six-month trial period—she didn't have to commit forever. She agreed, and as I suspected, she excelled in the new position. Her confidence began to grow, and her fear of failure took a backseat.

Before Amanda came to me for therapy, she was sleepwalking through life. Amanda knew what she wanted out of life, but unconsciously she didn't feel she deserved it, so her own behavior sabotaged her every time. Through therapy and a growing awareness of her patterns of behavior, Amanda learned to make different choices that finally put her on the road to living the life she wanted, as well as feeling deserving of it. These new choices slowly rewired her brain, making the new behaviors familiar and the old ones a thing of the past.

## Compassion and Self-Esteem

I wish I could say that learning new things about myself through my own therapy and training immediately increased my self-esteem and enabled me to become patient and compassionate with myself, but it didn't. Awareness is certainly a start, but beliefs and behaviors that result from our programming and have become habits are not easy to change. Change doesn't happen overnight. Often we are pretty good at loving others, but it's the being loved or letting others love us part that is an issue. Additionally, learning to love ourselves can be a tremendous challenge after a lifetime of self-loathing. It's much easier to encourage a friend to face their fears, ask for a promotion, or walk away from an abusive relationship than to encourage ourselves to do the same. We hardly ever show ourselves the same kindness and respect we show our friends. This is truly a double standard.

How easy is it to get mad at yourself when you forget your keys, take the wrong exit, or miss a deadline? Immediately we might say something like, "How stupid can I be?" or "I'm such an idiot!" and so on. Conversely, do we ever praise ourselves for doing something right? More often than not, we don't even notice and just move on to the next thing.

Barbara came to see me because she was unhappy and couldn't figure out why. I started to notice a pattern: she began every session by telling me the "stupid" things she did during the week and the "dumb" decisions she had made. I asked her to name three things she thought she did well, and she couldn't even come up with one. The more I asked about what worked in her life, the more she insisted on telling me what didn't.

One day I asked her if she loved herself. She immediately responded, "Of course I do." Then I asked her if she loved her daughter, who was five. Again, she emphatically said, "Of course!" I then asked her if she pointed out every little thing her daughter did wrong. For example, did she point out when her daughter colored outside the lines or call her clumsy if she fell off a swing? Barbara, now thinking that I had gone mad, said, "Of course not. I tell her she colors beautifully and comfort her when she falls." I pointed out how differently she treated herself compared to her daughter, even though she claimed to love both her daughter and herself. Barbara began to cry. She realized what I was getting at and said, "I guess I don't treat myself well at all." The antidote to shame is self-compassion.

## Why We Focus on the Negative

The first step to changing anything is to notice it. I asked Barbara to just notice when she had a self-deprecating thought, or, as I like to call them, Debbie Downer moments (Debbie is a character on the TV show *Saturday Night Live*). This was difficult at first, because self-deprecation had become a habit for Barbara. Changing negative thoughts is also challenging because our brain has a negativity bias. In other words, we are innately programmed to go toward the Debbie Downer side of things. As you know from chapter 2, this is because our brains evolved to ensure that we do not make mistakes that would have eliminated the human race, so everything that is possibly dangerous sticks like Velcro, and other more pleasant things get easily forgotten. In caveman days, forgetting that the medium-size red berries were poisonous cost us our lives—no second chances.

Rick Hanson, a psychologist who has written on this phenomenon, explains, "There are two kinds of mistakes a person can make in life. They can either think there is a tiger in the bushes when there really isn't one, or they can think there is no tiger in the bushes, but there actually is one about to pounce. Mother Nature wants us to make the first mistake a thousand times over to avoid making that second mistake even once." If our childhoods were lacking, this innate capacity to hold onto negative experiences, coupled with an anticipatory belief that people are not trustworthy and the world is unsafe, is a recipe for disaster. It causes us to overfocus on things that can be threatening and to underfocus on things that are not (such as a having a good day at work, acing a test, or getting flowers from your partner).

It is important to purposely and consciously focus on positive events by spending time noticing how a positive experience feels and what sensations it causes. Does your chest feel light and more expansive? Is your breathing easier? Does your body feel calm and relaxed or excited and energized? Noticing your body sensations when you experience something positive anchors that feeling in the body and begins to stimulate different parts of your brain, making new connections that help you tolerate and retain good feelings. Purposefully spending time focusing and anchoring positive experiences will increase your ability to feel good, creating a nice balance with your innate negativity bias. Incidentally, although focusing and anchoring a positive experience right after it happens is good, you can do it any time. Just think of an experience that made you feel good and notice your body sensations. That's it. Really, it's that simple!

When we were children, depending on how dangerous our environment was, being aware of the threat was necessary for protection and a feeling of safety. By being focused on the threat, we were better able to avoid danger and survive. However, as adults, we have a greater ability to protect ourselves (and we no longer live on the savanna), so it's not usually necessary to be ever-vigilant and focused on potential threats in our environment. Rest assured that your fight or flight will take over should a real threat arise. Focusing on the negative interferes with our ability to be happy. Ironically, our natural capacity to focus on and remember the negative in order to stay alive also makes us miserable.

You might be asking: "How do we go from being Debbie and Donald Downer to being Susie and Sandro Sunshine?" Once again, brilliant question! To help answer this question, we need to learn different techniques to increase awareness of our reactions.

## "Just Notice"

I asked you in previous chapters to "just notice" your thoughts and feelings with curiosity and without judgment, without trying to make things happen or make them go away. Many times we believe that if we pay attention to a feeling such as sadness or anger, we will make it worse. The exact opposite is true. A saying among brain scientists goes, "Name it to tame it." Naming the feeling causes it to lose its hold on you. The simple act of labeling whatever you are experiencing activates the thinking brain, stimulating new connections between the emotional brain and the thinking brain. And as you'll recall, keeping your thinking brain online won't allow your old pal amygdala to take over, causing you to react. So to tame the feelings behind our thoughts, it is important to name them. For example, the feeling behind "I'm going to flunk the exam" may be anxiety; the feeling behind "I forgot my doctor's appointment" may be anger; the feeling behind "I might get fired" may be fear, panic, or worry. Also, just notice when thoughts emerge, without reacting or responding to them. Sometimes we can become afraid of our own thoughts, but they're just thoughts. We get to decide if we want to respond to our thoughts or not.

This practice might seem a little awkward, and because it's so simple, you may feel you are doing it wrong. But the beauty of this practice is that there is no right or wrong, because you're just noticing what is already there. It could be anything. On the other hand, if you are judging what's going on in your mind, just notice that too. A sportscaster announces a running description of what is going on in a game without changing what he sees. You are the sportscaster of your own mind, announcing your experiences, not trying to change them.

An experience I had illustrates this idea of just noticing. I awoke one morning, and my heart was pounding as if it were going to jump out of my chest. I noticed that and thought, "Wow, it's like the tiger is coming right at me at this very moment! I am in total panic mode!" I was most definitely in fight-or-flight mode, but I had no idea why. I continued my morning routine of brushing my teeth, all the while noticing my heart racing. I didn't react, panic, or get anxious, which I would have done in the past as it was not a comfortable feeling, but this time I just noticed. Eventually, as I was leaving my house to go to work, my heart slowed down and I began to feel calm. I still don't know what triggered me that day. It could have been a dream, the way I moved my body while getting out of bed, or a noise from the outside, any of which could have triggered an implicit memory. I will never know. What I do know is that my newly found ability to "just notice" and to be curious about it, allowed me to keep my thinking brain online and to not react.

## Achieving Equanimity

Equanimity results from just noticing. It is defined as the ability to be aware of and to accept the present moment, whatever it may be. Equanimity takes *just noticing* and adds *acceptance* to it—noticing what is there and remaining balanced, not reacting to our reactions, not *becoming* our reactions. Equanimity is about being present with a painful memory or feeling and not getting sucked in. It empowers you to respond rationally to emotionally stressful situations. It is like sitting at home and noticing the weather outside through a window. Sometimes it is sunny and not much is happening. At times you notice wind blowing through the trees. Sometimes the wind is strong and sometimes it's not. Sometimes it is raining or snowing, and at times there is a powerful storm with thunder and lightning. All the while, you are sitting inside your home calm, safe, and sound, deciding whether you're going to wear shorts, put on a sweater, or grab an umbrella should you decide to go out.

To achieve equanimity—that is, the ability to notice negative thoughts and emotions and not get swept up in them—we need to make our thinking brain (the neocortex) stronger. Given the harsh conditions that were present in caveman days, our brains evolved to react and remember danger. They did *not* evolve for equanimity. We need to change that manually, so to speak. Studies show that people who have meditated for years have thicker neocortexes. As you may recall from chapter 2, the neocortex helps put the brakes on Francois (the amygdala). It is also involved in self-awareness, empathy, and compassion. So having more connections in that area of the brain is definitely a good thing. I would love to say that I meditate regularly. I certainly try to do it often. But the truth is, I don't meditate on a regular basis or often enough. If you're like me, don't fret. The exercises in chapter 5 and on the pages that follow will help you engage your thinking brain and will stimulate that area, making connections stronger.

When you stimulate any part of the brain, connections in that area get stronger, which is why just rehashing a traumatic experience if there is nothing to be gained and without any type of therapeutic intervention causes that "'traumatic experience circuitry'" in your brain to become stronger, making you more vulnerable to triggers. We used to think that talking about a traumatic experience was necessary to working through it. However, talking can actually re-traumatize a person if the right intervention is not employed. Of all of the interventions I have studied, Somatic Experiencing Therapy has proven to yield the best results.

## Refocusing Your Attention

Refocusing your attention requires a little more energy than having equanimity or just noticing. Research shows that focused attention stimulates brain cells, causing changes in brain circuitry, which is exactly how the placebo effect works. In placebo effect studies, people with chronic pain are given a pill and told it will reduce their pain. A percentage of participatants almost always report that their pain is significantly reduced, although they have been given only a sugar pill. Dr. Donald Price has done research in this area and has found that it is people's *expectation* of pain reduction that causes the actual reduction in pain. It turns out that expecting something to happen causes us to think about it, and thinking about it causes us to focus attention on it, stimulating a specific set of brain cells. In the placebo effect studies, expecting pain relief caused the participants to think about pain relief, stimulating the "pain relief circuitry" in their brains, causing *actual* relief of pain and altering their reality. As you learned in chapter 2, our early experiences cause connections to be formed in our brains. These connections influence how we see the world and how we make sense of it. In other words, our early experiences cause us to form *expectations* about others and about our world. Consequently, our personal mental maps influence our reality, so that what we see may not always be what is really there. We may expect certain results in our encounters with others and in our relationships that don't necessarily reflect reality.

Focusing attention on new beliefs, thoughts, and outcomes can change our reality because we are stimulating new connections and creating physical changes in the brain. However, focusing on something that is not within our repertoire of experiences and expectations, such as positive thoughts, is not easy to do. The connections that were made long ago given our experiences are well-traveled paths that are familiar and most often do not require conscious thought. If your brain is prone to expect danger and feel fear, you will have an overactive threat detector (amygdala) and live in an anxiety-ridden world. You may be tormented with thoughts of the past that show up as things you should have or could have done to change your present reality. Or you may be frozen by an inability to make decisions, too frightened to make the wrong decision, and repeatedly go over every possible scenario in your mind until you feel exhausted. There may be so many thoughts going through your mind at any given time that you may not know what it is to have a quiet mind. Either way, these are well-established circuitries in your brain that are not easy to alter.

The first step in learning how to refocus your attention is simply *noticing* what is going on in your mind. Next is *focusing* your attention on something you *choose* to pay attention to as opposed to what your mind is automatically paying attention to. If you want to move away from thinking about what you could have or should have done, notice when your mind is there and purposefully, consciously focus your attention elsewhere. When you notice your attention going back to the "shoulda-coulda dance," purposefully take your attention back to where you want it to be. This back and forth might happen every second at first, then every minute, then every five minutes, and so on. Remember, you are trying to break a well-entrenched habit, and that is not easy. If you stay determined and with a lot of practice, you will notice that it will become easier to focus your attention where *you* want it to be.

## Dual Awareness

Just noticing and becoming an observer of your own mind and body will come in handy when you get triggered. Keeping yourself in the here and now when you're triggered by past trauma is another key component to changing self-destructive behaviors. Having the ability to recall something from your past while staying in the present is called dual awareness. It is another important skill to learn.

Leo had been sexually molested as a child. When he first came to see me, he did not want to talk about the molestation at all. He mentioned it in passing during one of our first sessions but also made it clear that he was not ready to talk about it. It took years of working together for Leo to trust me enough to explore those memories. He eventually wanted to explore them because he began to have issues with his partner regarding the lack of sexual intimacy in their relationship. One day, after we had been working through some of his memories using Somatic Experiencing techniques, he told me this story. He had gone to the dentist, which was always a very uncomfortable experience for him given that his sexual abuse included oral copulation. On this particular day, Leo's regular dentist (he had chosen a female dentist to lessen the trigger, because his molester had been male) was not in. Her colleague, a male dentist, was going to clean his teeth.

As the male dentist entered the room, Leo noticed his heart begin to race. When the male dentist began to work on Leo's mouth, Leo had a flashback of the abuse. But he also *knew* he was in a dental chair getting his teeth cleaned. Leo was able to notice the traumatic memory being triggered by the dentist and also know he was at a dentist's office and safe. This is an example of dual awareness. It is when we are able to stay in the here and now but also remember, *not relive,* a traumatic memory from the past. Leo thought he was having a flashback, but as I explored the situation further, I determined that what he thought was a flashback was actually a memory. With a flashback, we can dissociate and actually relive a traumatic experience as if we were back there again, something he had experienced many times. A memory, on the contrary, may have strong emotions attached to it, but we are aware of our present surroundings, aware of being in the here and now, and recognize that it is an experience from our past.

The ability to have dual awareness when we get triggered is very important in the healing process. Grounding yourself by feeling your feet on the ground or your body in the chair, while recalling a traumatic event from your past, will help keep you in the present. Looking around and noticing your surroundings; feeling someone's touch on your skin; or petting your dog or cat and noticing how its fur feels against your fingers and if its body feels warm, hot, or cold are all ways to keep you in the here and now. We can't change what happened to us, but we can certainly change how we are affected by our past in the present.

## Be the Change

So far there is enough evidence to confirm that in order to keep our species safe, our brains evolved to pay attention and hold onto negative experiences, so we would not make the same mistakes, be prepared for danger, and stay alive. Meanwhile, our positive experiences slide off into no-man's-land. This process worked for us in caveman days, but in this day and age, it may actually be our downfall. We need to change the way our brains evolve in the generations to come because it is imperative to keep positive experiences within our awareness. This will require us to rewire our brains to hold onto positive experiences and to learn to live in a calm, socially engaged state. Changing our brains to retain positive experiences will not alter our ability to react when something dangerous comes our way. Our brains are built to do this; it's innate. However, the survival of our species now depends on a balance between these two states. The exercises in this book will help you reach that balance.

## Coming Full Circle

My purpose in writing this book is to share with you the information that changed my life and the way I practice my craft. My world shifted when I became aware of the "why" of me on that fateful trip to Tahiti. When I came home, I attended every single conference on attachment theory and the brain that I could find, and with every conference, I learned more and I made more sense.

You see, I felt bad for taking up space in the world. Many times I would drive on a crowded freeway and think, "The person behind me would reach their destination that much quicker if I didn't exist and take up this space." The belief that I didn't have a valid reason for feeling the way I did just added to how awful I already felt about myself. A diagnosis of depression could have been slapped on me. I could have taken medication and possibly done fairly well, but why put a bandage on something that can be healed from the inside out. I am not against medication and believe it can be very helpful in some cases. However, I also believe it is important to rule out other possibilities, given that medication can have side effects and other complications.

Understanding that my parents, although unintentionally, were unable to be sensitive to my needs and did not engage or play with me often, causing me to develop an avoidant attachment, was crucial information. The feeling that I was defective and not worthy of their time became a deep-rooted belief that I didn't even know existed inside of me. Eventually, I transferred this belief onto others. I walked around the world with the assumption that they saw the same defective human being that I felt myself to be. I recall walking into restaurants, and if men turned to look at me, I filled with rage, "'knowing" they were mocking my repulsion.

My parents' lack of attunement or sensitivity to my needs caused me to bury my feelings and needs so deep inside that I didn't realize I had any. At the same time, I developed a template that people were not dependable. Back then, I did not realize why I just couldn't ask for help. I now understand that in my mind, asking for help would have felt like a spotlight was being put on my perceived shortcomings. Additionally, I did not feel deserving of someone else's time. Consequently, asking for help felt very shameful, relationships felt suffocating, and only being alone felt safe. I rationalized everything away and was in deep denial, although at some level I knew there must be a "why" to my feelings and beliefs. I suppose this might have been the unconscious reason that human behavior always fascinated me and why I chose a profession in mental health.

It is also not a coincidence that I investigated child abuse for ten years, which I always attributed to my love for children. However, in taking a closer look, I'm certain it had to do with my feeling neglected and not being heard, so I became an advocate for children whose voices were ignored or who were too scared to speak. How's that for sublimation!

Because of the core belief of being defective, given a parent's lack of interaction, kryptonite for the avoidant is shame. Because of the core belief of being unloved, given a parent's sometimes-there, sometimes-not involvement, the ambivalent's kryptonite is abandonment. It doesn't matter how many people say you're not defective or unloved or how much evidence you have to the contrary. That core belief needs to change from the inside out.

The exercises I have shared with you helped me become aware of my triggers and reactions and only then was I able to alter them. Initially, I did not know how I was feeling. However, by noticing my spontaneous reaction to things, I started to become aware of my likes and dislikes, what brought up an emotion versus what was really no big deal. These practices, which I do on a daily basis, have rewired my brain. I am now much less reactive to things that would have triggered me in the past. This kind of work takes time, patience, and perseverance. Some days are easier than others, but isn't that how life is? It is with humility and gratitude that I share this information with you. I sincerely hope it provides the information necessary to put you on your journey to heal from past wounds, wake up, and start living.

# Conclusion

I designed this book to build on itself. Once you get an idea of your attachment style and how your brain developed given that attachment style, you can better understand your behavior. The defense mechanisms we use, our reactions, and our ability or inability to regulate our nervous system—in other words, to navigate through our emotions—came about for a reason. We survive our childhoods the best way we can, and as adults we are left with the emotional scars to prove it. Some scars are barely visible; some are deep and pronounced. But the story shouldn't end there. Our past does not have to define our present. We can rise above mistakes that caused us to develop core beliefs that just aren't true. How do I know they're not true? Because if we had been nurtured, "felt," and loved, and had a sense of belonging in this world, we would have developed very different core beliefs.

We all deserve to feel lovable and worthy of being on this planet, with a healthy sense of self that allows us to own when we mess up and not take personally something that isn't ours to take on. Achieving this involves waking up and recognizing that we are free to live exactly the way we want to live.

Sometimes we expect change to come in earth-shattering ways. But it often comes like rain, one little drop at a time. It doesn't matter where you begin. You may decide to simply notice your feet on the ground for a day, a week, or even a month, until noticing your feet, whether they are walking, standing, leaning, or resting on your bed, becomes something you do automatically throughout the day. You may then decide to notice your butt as it sits in a chair, in your car, on a sofa, or on a bed, until noticing your butt becomes something you do automatically throughout the day, and so on with the rest of your body. You may decide to simply find your calm place, something that brings about an automatic sense of peace, and practice bringing this place into your mind and noticing your body as it relaxes and calms, even for just a second. These little add-ons to everyday life may not seem like much, because unfortunately we cannot actually see the changes they produce in our brains. But rest assured, the long-term effects will be profound.

When I suggest that people take the time to nurture themselves, they usually say that's not realistic. They say they have a certain routine that cannot change. All the minutes of their day are accounted for, and they can't fit in any time for themselves. It's sad that some people feel so trapped in their routines that they don't feel they have a say over their own lives.

Give some thought to what makes you feel nurtured and pampered. You can start very slowly. Light a candle or play soft music in your home or work space. Take a bubble bath with candles or drink your favorite beverage while listening to your favorite music. When was the last time you did something nice for yourself? When you truly love and nurture yourself, you can begin to allow others to treat you in a loving and nurturing way. In fact, anything less will become unacceptable.

When we are able to love and nurture ourselves, we realize that everyone else's opinions are secondary. We may have feelings about others' opinions of us—no one likes to be criticized, judged, or told they are wrong—but their opinions shouldn't shatter our sense of self; that should remain intact. When we are able to love and nurture ourselves, we also come to understand the difference between wanting and needing. We may *want* our parents to be loving and nurturing, but we no longer *need* them to be. In other words, the fact that our parents cannot be who we want them to be will no longer affect our lives. This is not to say it won't sadden us or make us angry at times, but it won't have the power to influence our lives like it used to. Once you have learned to love yourself and feel worthy of love, your old programming will no longer influence you.

Best-selling author Eckhart Tolle said, "Your task is not to seek for love, but to find the barriers in yourself that you have built against it." Tolle's books *The Power of Now* and *A New Earth* emphasize the importance of being aware of the present moment as a way of not being caught up in thoughts of the past and the future. He believes that present awareness is the gateway to a heightened sense of peace. Now we have the brain science to back up that idea. Tolle stated, "Being in the now brings about an awareness that is beyond the mind, and which helps transcend the ego." In Tolle's view, all *wanting* implies is that the future is more desirable than the present. By constantly seeking to reach some point in the future, you are using the present as a means to an end instead of living every moment for itself. He believes that you don't need the future or the past to find yourself—who you are is sufficient. However, *believing* that is the struggle.

I cannot control how the information in this book will be used. My hope is that it will increase your awareness of who you are and what makes you tick and will expand your empathy for the behavior of others. It would be a shame if the information were misused to label or reduce others into just attachment styles, faulty brain functions, or defense mechanisms. Information is power, but when our nervous systems are dysregulated, we are prone to react. We might be tempted to use information as a weapon to hurt or to punish.

"If you weren't such an avoidant, we could ... "
"If your amygdala wasn't so crazy you wouldn't ..."
"You rationalize everything!"

These are all accusations that will help no one. Truly understanding others and learning how to ask for what we need takes purposeful communication that can only happen with a regulated nervous system. I urge you to use this information to better understand yourself and others, to depersonalize what isn't yours to take on, and to learn to respond without reacting.

We can all live the lives we truly want, feeling deserving and empowered. The information and exercises throughout this book will help you regulate your nervous system, increase your tolerance for positive feelings, and let go of old beliefs and behaviors, becoming free of the past and making new, conscious choices for your future.

## End-of-Chapter Exercise

In the left column below, write down one mistake you made in each of the four categories. In the right column, write down three things you did well in each category. For example, your mistake was forgetting about a staff meeting. Your achievements could include how you brought in two new clients, worked late to meet a deadline, or learned the new computer program on your own time.

| Mistakes | Achievements |
|---|---|
| 1. Career | 1._____ <br><br> _____ <br><br> _____ |
| 2. Relationships | 2._____ <br><br> _____ <br><br> _____ |
| 3. Friends | 3._____ <br><br> _____ <br><br> _____ |
| 4. Family Life | 4._____ <br><br> _____ <br><br> _____ |

## Chapter Six Takeaway

Change is not easy, but where there's a will, there's a way. You don't have to do it alone. Invite your family and friends to take the challenge with you. First, start noticing—nothing more, nothing less. Then decide what your next step needs to be. Is it learning how to regulate your nervous system? Is it turning your social engagement system on more often? Is it expanding your ability to focus more on the positive in your life? Is it taking a step back and responding instead of reacting? You now know the "why" of you. Now it's time to become the *real* you.

# Resources

### Adult Attachment Specialists

To find a specialist trained in giving and scoring the Adult Attachment Interview, contact Naomi Gribneau Bahm: NGBReliability@gmail.com.

### Attachment Parenting International

To learn more about parenting based on attachment styles, visit www.attachmentparenting.org. The site includes articles on creating secure attachment during childhood.

### Blue School

This school, located in New York City, is based in brain science. Visit www.blueschool.com.

### Center for Reflective Parenting

Located in Los Angeles, this center offers an attachment-based reflective approach to parenting for parents, caregivers, and professionals from a wide range of cultural and socioeconomic backgrounds. Visit http://reflectiveparenting.org.

### Mind to Mind Parenting

Located in New York, Mind to Mind Parenting teaches you how to develop a bond with your child by practicing reflective parenting. An innovative approach, reflective parenting draws from state-of-the-art research to help you understand yourself as a parent and to build a deep, intimate, and enduring connection with your child. Visit www.mindtomindparenting.com.

### Somatic Experiencing

To find a professional trained in Somatic Experience Therapy, visit www.traumahealing.com/somatic-experiencing.

# References

Allen, Jon G., Peter Fonagy, and Anthony W. Bateman. *Mentalizing in Clinical Practice*. Washington, DC: American Psychiatric Publishing, 2008. Print.

Arden, John Boghosian. *Rewire Your Brain: Think Your Way to a Better Life*. Hoboken, NJ: Wiley, 2010. Print.

Begley, Sharon. *Train Your Mind, Change Your Brain: How a New Science Reveals Our Extraordinary Potential to Transform Ourselves*. New York: Ballantine, 2007. Print.

Blakeslee, Sandra, and Matthew Blakeslee. *The Body Has a Mind of Its Own*. New York: Random House, 2008. Print.

Cassidy, Jude, and Phillip R. Shaver. *Handbook of Attachment: Theory, Research, and Clinical Applications*. New York: Guilford, 1999. Print.

Cozolino, Louis J. *The Neuroscience of Human Relationships: Attachment and the Developing Social Brain*. New York: W. W. Norton, 2006. Print.

Doidge, Norman. *The Brain That Changes Itself: Stories of Personal Triumph from the Frontiers of Brain Science*. New York: Viking, 2007. Print.

Fogel, Alan. *The Psychophysiology of Self-Awareness: Rediscovering the Lost Art of Body Sense*. New York: W. W. Norton, 2009. Print.

Fonagy, Peter, Gyorgy Gergely, Elliot L. Jurist, and Mary Target. *Affect Regulation, Mentalization, and the Development of the Self*. New York: Other Press, 2002. Print.

Fosha, Diana, Daniel J. Siegel, and Marion Fried Solomon, eds. *The Healing Power of Emotion: Affective Neuroscience, Development, and Clinical Practice*. New York: W. W. Norton, 2009. Print.

Grossmann, Klaus E., Karin Grossmann, and Everett Waters, eds. *Attachment from Infancy to Adulthood: The Major Longitudinal Studies*. New York: Guilford, 2005. Print.

Hannah, Mo Therese, and Wade Luquet, eds. *Imago Relationship Therapy: Perspectives on Theory*. San Francisco: Jossey-Bass, 2005. Print.

Hayes, Steven C., Victoria M. Follette, and Marsha Linehan, eds. *Mindfulness and Acceptance: Expanding the Cognitive-Behavioral Tradition*. New York: Guilford, 2004. Print.

Hendrix, Harville. *Getting the Love You Want: A Guide for Couples*. New York: Holt, 2008. Print.

Iacoboni, Marco. *Mirroring People: The New Science of How We Connect with Others.* New York: Farrar, Straus and Giroux, 2008. Print.

Kabat-Zinn, Jon. *Wherever You Go, There You Are: Mindfulness Meditation in Everyday Life.* New York: Hyperion, 1994. Print.

Karen, Robert. *Becoming Attached: First Relationships and How They Shape Our Capacity to Love.* New York: Oxford University Press, 1998. Print.

Levine, Peter A. *In an Unspoken Voice: How the Body Releases Trauma and Restores Goodness.* Berkeley, CA: North Atlantic Books, 2010. Print.

———. *Waking the Tiger: Healing Trauma.* Berkeley, CA: North Atlantic Books, 1997. Print.

McGilchrist, Iain. *The Master and His Emissary: The Divided Brain and the Making of the Western World.* New Haven, CT: Yale University Press, 2009. Print.

Mikulincer, Mario, and Phillip R. Shaver. *Attachment in Adulthood: Structure, Dynamics, and Change.* New York: Guilford, 2007. Print.

Ogden, Pat, Kekuni Minton, and Clare Pain. *Trauma and the Body: A Sensorimotor Approach to Psychotherapy.* New York: W. W. Norton, 2006. Print.

Panksepp, Jaak. *Affective Neuroscience: The Foundations of Human and Animal Emotions.* New York: Oxford University Press, 1998. Print.

Porges, Stephen W. *The Polyvagal Theory: Neurophysiological Foundations of Emotions, Attachment, Communication, and Self-Regulation.* New York: W. W. Norton, 2011. Print.

Rholes, W. Steven, and Jeffry A. Simpson. *Adult Attachment: Theory, Research, and Clinical Implications.* New York: Guilford, 2004. Print.

Rothschild, Babette. *The Body Remembers: The Psychophysiology of Trauma and Trauma Treatment.* New York: Norton, 2000. Print.

Sapolsky, Robert M. *Why Zebras Don't Get Ulcers.* New York: Owl Books, 2004. Print.

Scaer, Robert C. *The Body Bears the Burden: Trauma, Dissociation, and Disease.* New York: Haworth Medical, 2001. Print.

———. *The Trauma Spectrum: Hidden Wounds and Human Resiliency.* New York: W. W. Norton, 2005. Print.

Schore, Allan N. *Affect Dysregulation and Disorders of the Self.* New York: W. W. Norton, 2003. Print.

————. *Affect Regulation and the Repair of the Self.* New York: W. W. Norton, 2003. Print.

Schwartz, Jeffrey M., and David Rock. "A Brain-Based Approach to Coaching." *International Journal of Coaching in Organizations* 4.2 (2006):32–43. Print.

Siegel, Daniel J. *The Developing Mind: Toward a Neurobiology of Interpersonal Experience.* New York: Guilford, 1999. Print.

————. *The Mindful Brain: Reflection and Attunement in the Cultivation of Well-Being.* New York: W. W. Norton, 2007. Print.

————. *Mindsight: The New Science of Personal Transformation.* New York: Bantam, 2010. Print.

Siegel, Daniel J., and Tina Payne Bryson. *The Whole-Brain Child: Twelve Revolutionary Strategies to Nurture Your Child's Developing Mind, Survive Everyday Parenting Struggles, and Help Your Family Thrive.* New York: Delacorte, 2011. Print.

Solomon, Marion Fried, and Daniel J. Siegel, eds. *Healing Trauma: Attachment, Mind, Body, and Brain.* New York: W. W. Norton, 2003. Print.

Solomon, Marion Fried, and Stan Tatkin. *Love and War in Intimate Relationships: Connection, Disconnection, and Mutual Regulation in Couple Therapy.* New York: W. W. Norton, 2011. Print.

Somatic Experiencing Trauma Institute. *Somatic Experiencing Professional Training Manual.* Beginning: Module 1. Boulder, CO: Somatic Experiencing Trauma Institute, 2007. Print.

Tolle, Eckhart. *The Power of Now: A Guide to Spiritual Enlightenment.* Novata, CA: New World Library, 1999. Print.

————. *A New Earth: Awakening to Your Life's Purpose.* New York: Plume, 2006. Print.

Van der Kolk, Bessel A., Alexander C. McFarlane, and Lars Weisaeth, eds. *Traumatic Stress: The Effects of Overwhelming Experience on Mind, Body, and Society.* New York: Guilford, 2007. Print.

# Index

# About the Author

Dr. Shirley Impellizzeri received her doctorate in psychology from the University of California, Los Angeles, and has a successful practice in Beverly Hills, California. Her work focuses on individuals, families, couples, and group therapy. She has been featured on *Celebrity Rehab with Dr. Drew*, Bravo's *Workout* and *Tabitha's Salon Takeover*, and HGTV's *Smart Solutions*. She was also a recurring guest expert on *Celebrity Justice* and the Spanish television program *Mujer Today* and appeared on the cover of *Woman's World* magazine. Dr. Shirley served on the Board of Trustees for Olive Crest, an advocacy agency working with abused and neglected children. She is currently on the Associates' Board of Directors for the Inter-Agency Council for Child Abuse and Neglect (ICAN), a Los Angeles-based organization dedicated to coordinating services for preventing, identifying, and treating child abuse and neglect. In addition, she is a member of the American Psychological Association. Dr. Shirley's fluency in Spanish has enabled her to work effectively with Southern California's diverse Latino community.

Born in Los Angeles, Dr. Shirley moved to her family's native Argentina when she was a teenager and was inspired by a high school psychology class to pursue a career in psychology. Dr. Shirley began her career in the area of child development where she first learned about attachment theory. Working in group homes and investigating child abuse for more than ten years for the County of Los Angeles, Department of Children and Family Services, she saw firsthand how early attachment affects a person's development and behavior.

Because of her intense personal interest in this area, Dr. Shirley went on to study how the brain is affected by one's attachment style. Her vast knowledge, in addition to her many years of experience, compelled her to write a book to help readers understand the *why* of their behavior and with this information, empower them to change.

# Also Available from Sunrise River Press

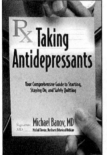